Sea Monsters And The Sun God
Salman Rashid

3000.00 PKR

SAEED BOOK BANK
Leading Importers, Exporters, Distributors,
Booksellers & Publishers of Pakistan
F-7 Jinnah Super Market, Islamabad-Pakistan.
Tel: 92-51-2651656-9, Fax: 92-51-2651660
E-mail : info@saeedbookbank.com
Web : www.saeedbookbank.com

Sea Monsters and the Sun God

Travels in Pakistan

SANG-E-MEEL PUBLICATIONS
25-SHAHRAH-E-PAKISTAN (LOWER MALL) LAHORE (PAKISTAN)

954.9143	Salman Rashid Sea Monsters and the Sun God / Salman Rashid.-Lahore: Sang-e-Meel Publications, 2006. 240pp. : Photos I. History - Pakistan. I.Title.

2006
Published by:
Niaz Ahmad
Sang-e-Meel Publications,
Lahore.

Designed & Printed by:
Topical Printers

ISBN 969-35-1901-9

SANG-E-MEEL PUBLICATIONS
Chowk Urdu Bazar Lahore. Pakistan. Phone 7667970
Phones: 7220100 - 7228143 - 7667970 Fax: 7245101
http://www. sang-e-meel.com e-mail: smp@sang-e-meel.com

25-Shahrah-e-Pakistan (Lower Mall), P.O. Box 997 Lahore-54000 Pakistan

Contents

The Invisible Saint	11
Palace of Fairies	19
Last train to Thal	23
Who remembers Karam Hussain Shah	30
Dust unto Dust	37
Canal Journey	42
Fort with a view	53
Greeks in Pukhtunkhwa	59
Chinar City	67
Mystery on an ancient Highway	77
Seat of the Gods	81
The enigmatic George Tyrwhitt	90
'No one believes the Professor'	95
'Chup Shah! Hari Singh raghle!'	100
'Not a soul was left living!'	103
The unsung Hero	110
Stranger in Alai	117
Encounter with a lovelorn Poet	131
Sakhia Revisited	134
History's forgotten Page	140
Return to Ari Pir	146
Sea Monsters and the Sun God	154
Lore of the Mansion	165
Into the heart of the Suleman Mountains	170
Menhirs, Stone Circles and Graves	184
Philosopher Poet of Vehowa	190
The Saint who lives	193
A rest house and a memory	196
The 'Bumba Mail' called here	200
History's uncharted Backwater	205
Date City	209
A Town called 'Tomb'	219
Riddle in the Kech Hills	224
Gateway of the Breeze	229
Upon the 20,000-Foot Mountain	236

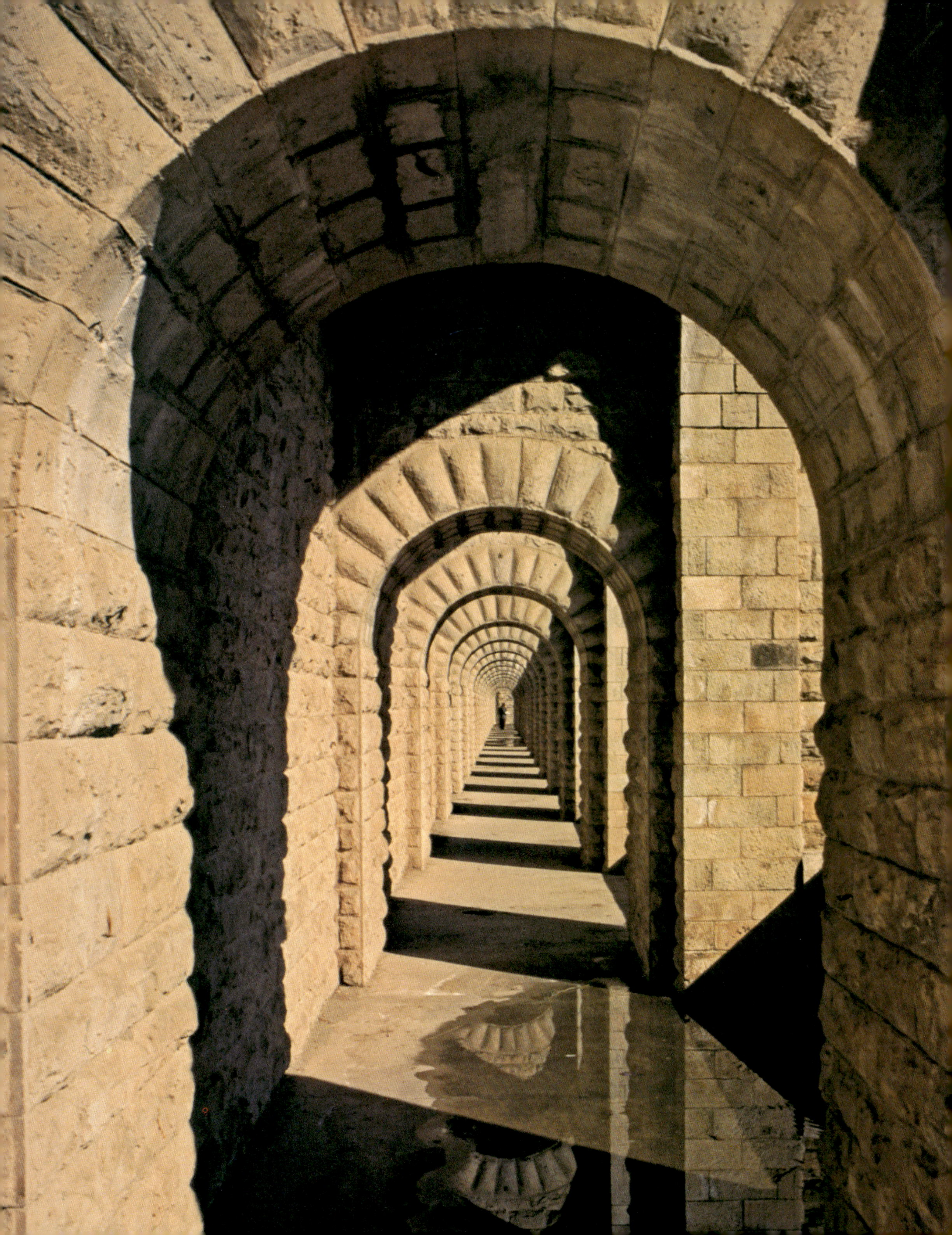

for

Saneeya Hussain

1954 – 2005

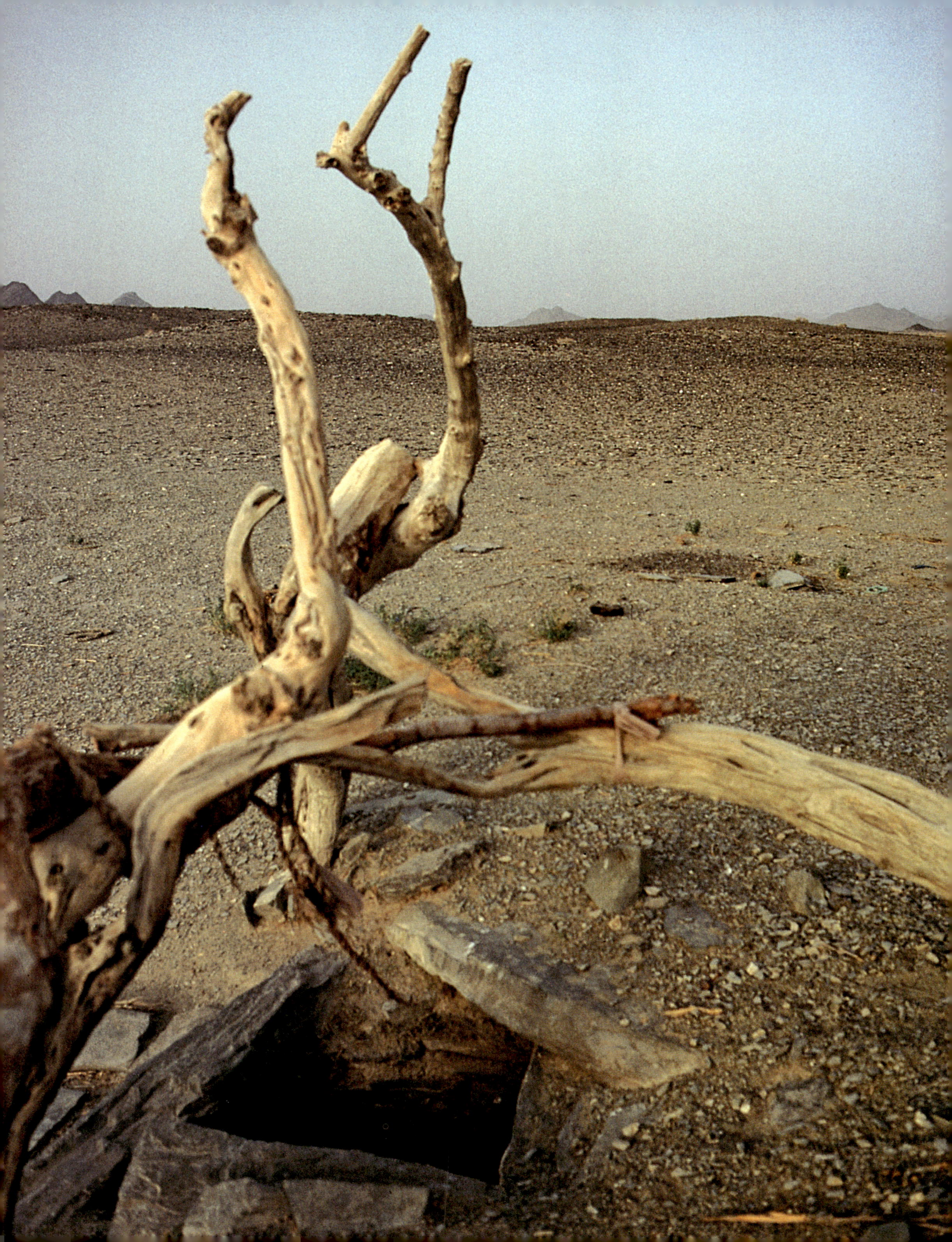

Preface and Acknowledgements

For my previous anthology (*Prisoner on a Bus*) I likened the publication of one's newspaper articles in book form to an ego trip. And so this book sets me off on my second such journey. But if truth be told, not only are we fast losing our built heritage and forgetting old stories, but we are changing culturally as well. Things that I saw and wisdom I heard over my quarter century as a vagabond have been lost to 'modernism'. Therefore I think it is essential to preserve whatever still remains – even if it has to be in the pages of a book.

In another few years, another traveller following up in the footsteps of Baron Karl von Hugel may not be able to locate the *haveli* in Gujranwala where the Austrian was entertained by General Hari Singh Nalwa back in the 1830s. In fact, when they pull down this ancient building (protected by law that is never enforced) and replace it with another 'plaza', the plaque (pg 101) that commemorates the name of the great Sikh general will forever be lost. Certainly lost will be the story of George Tyrwhitt as told by that remarkable raconteur Nawaz Ali Khosa of Nagarparkar for he has, sadly, departed from this world. I have tried to preserve these and other stories and pictures for anyone who will ever care to know something about Pakistan.

This book is a celebration of the wonderful people that live across this country, the real people of Pakistan: honest, hard-working, hospitable, persevering and full of life and humour. These are the people who open their homes and their hearts for hobos like me and who make a journey memorable. They must never be forgotten. Not long in the future when we will have irrevocably changed our ways, these pages will still tell the chance reader the way we once were.

These articles were published in *The News on Sunday* and *Herald* between 1998 and 2000. Most of them appear as they were first published, but some have been added to for now there is no restriction on space. Though I have tried to keep them in order of original publication, they might be a little out of kilter. But that is of little consequence.

Lest I be faulted for the use of certain words, I must clarify. I use Pukhtunkhwa for NWFP for I say this is the land of the Pukhtuns and it ought to be called after them. I may also appear to be indiscreet in my use of 'Pushtun' and 'Pukhtun'. But I use Pukhtun for the northerners and Pushtun for the southerners in deference to the way they themselves would pronounce the word. As for the Sindhu River, I call it by this name instead of the Hellenised Indus for that is how my ancestors would have known the river for at least four thousand years.

This book owes the most to all those people who I met on the road; people who made my journeys worthwhile. For them my greatest gratitude is reserved. I owe a great deal to friends in the bureaucracy and a few of my army friends who made things easy for me in such remote places as Parachinar or Bahawalnagar or Alai.

To Messer Niaz and Afzaal Ahmad of Sang-e-Meel I am particularly grateful for having faith in my work. I appreciate their undefeatable optimism and courage: to publish books in English when Pakistani readers of the English language are fast on their way to extinction requires these sterling qualities.

And last of all I am grateful to Naseer Baluch of Topical and his team of young designers. Among this good lot I am particularly thankful to Aamir Ali for speed and expertise. For use of maps I am grateful to Yasmeen Lari for permission to reproduce the map of old Lahore (pg 19) from Lahore Heritage Guide. All other maps are reproduced from *The Atlas of Pakistan* with the kind permission of the Surveyor General of Pakistan.

Salman Rashid
Lahore, July 2006
odysseus@beaconet.net

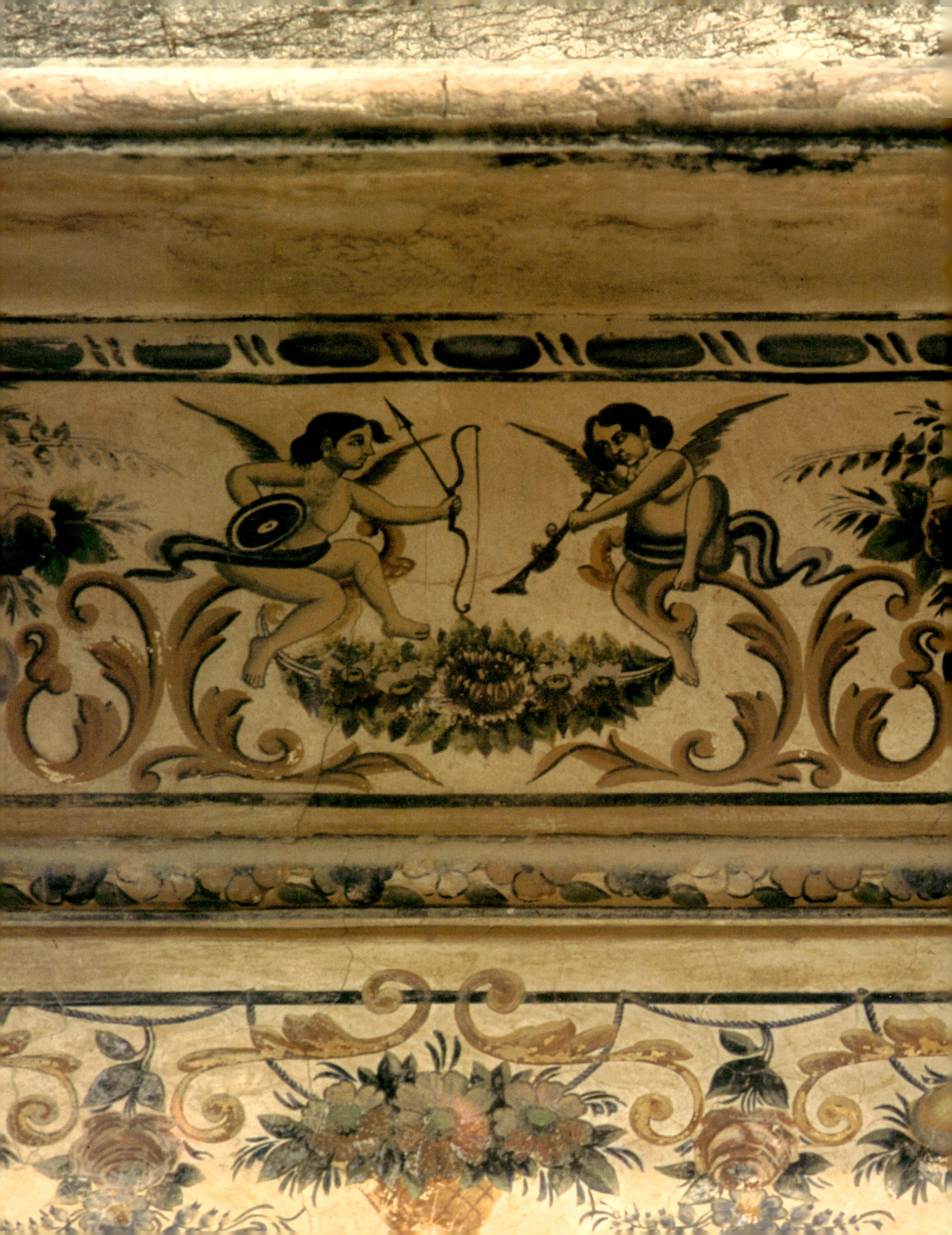

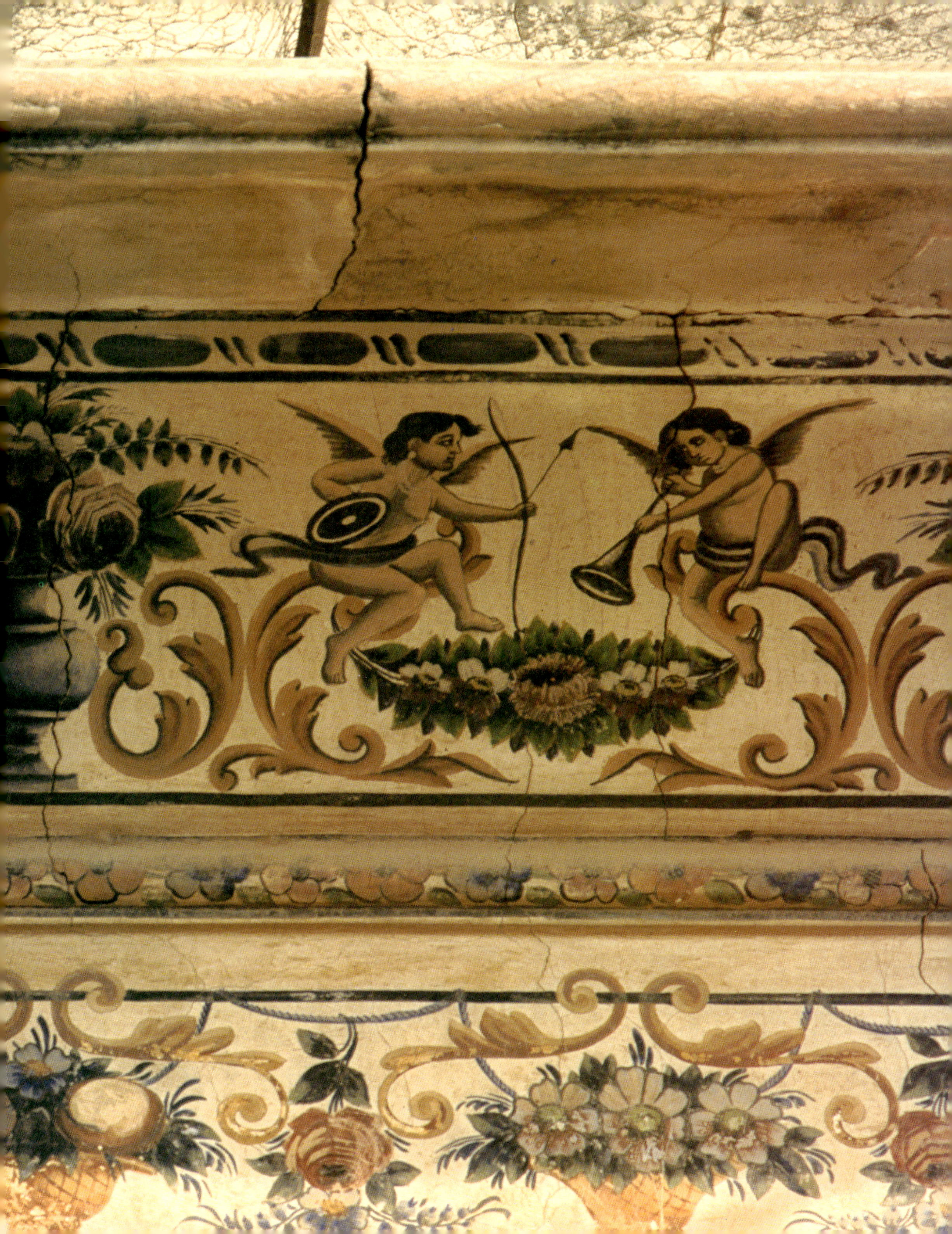

نقش ہیں سب ناتمام خونِ جگر کے بغیر
نغمہ ہے سودائے خام خونِ جگر کے بغیر

اقبالؔ

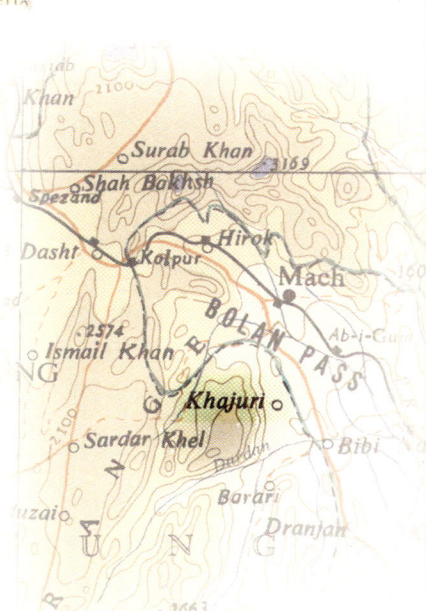

The holy tree with the cradles and the tomb enclosure.

The Invisible Saint

The hills – as gold-brown as sun-dried chaff, or dark grey like fire-scoured lead, rise sharply on either side of the narrow gorge. Rarely is their burnished starkness broken by vegetation; rarely, save during a downpour, does one see a trickle of water on these slopes. Desiccated, harsh and barren, the slopes run down to the pebbly bed of the Bolan River where the water flows in a narrow channel. Rarely does the entire riverbed know the feel of water sluicing over it – and that again only during a downpour.

Long, long before Alexander the Macedonian

The bubbling spring that marks the spot where the holy man supposedly entered the rock wall.

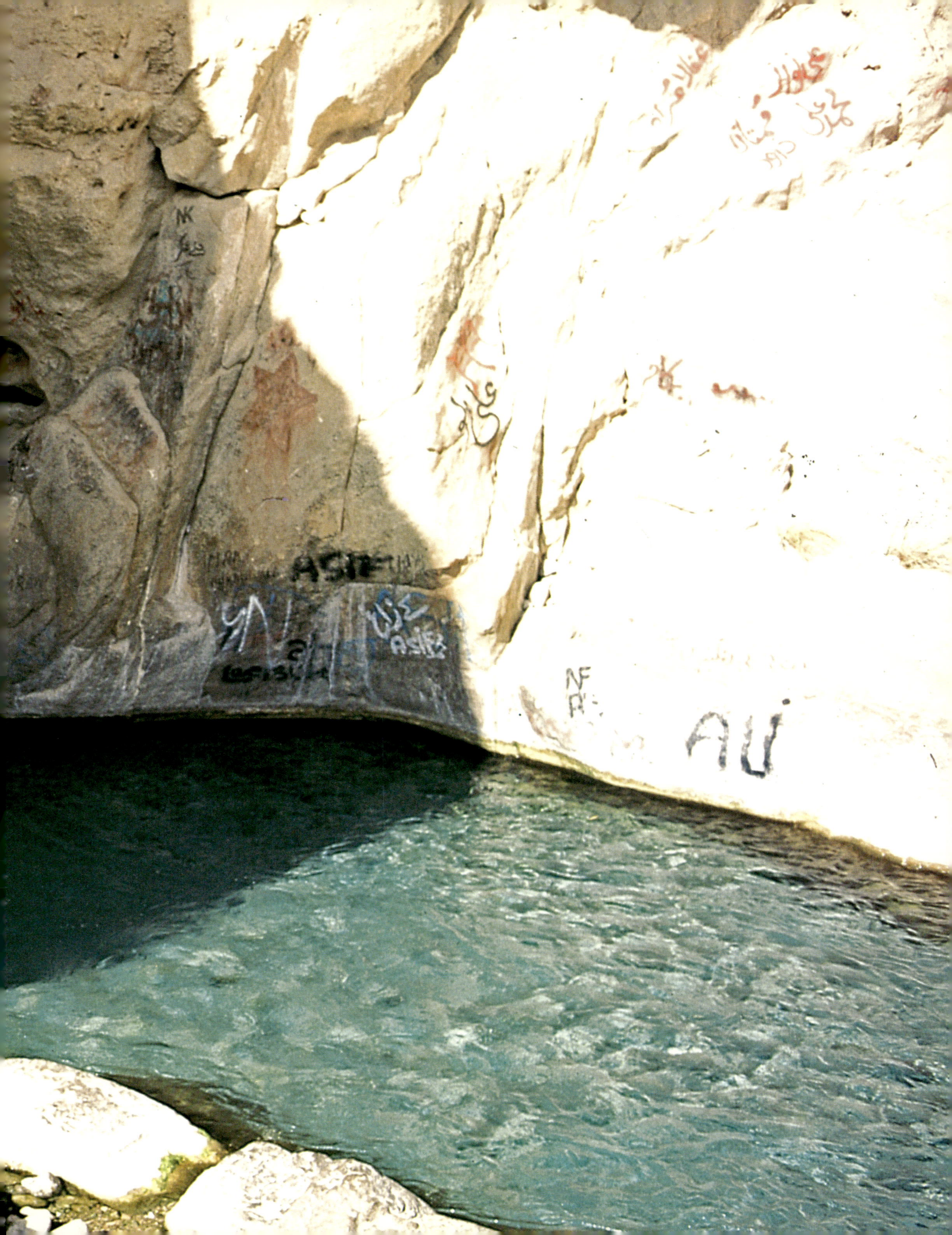

was born; long before the Aryan hordes swept into the plains of the Sindhu-Ganga river system to give rise to a new religion and a new culture; even before the great tragic hero Gilgamesh, the king of Uruk (lower Mesopotamia), disturbed by the demise of his dearest friend, undertook his epic quest for immortality; the Bolan Gorge had resounded to the tramp of marching feet, to the clink of armoury and the jangle of camels' bells. For this was the highroad leading west from the plains of Sindh where one of the great civilisations of prehistory flourished. The discovery of the ruins at Mehrgarh near Sibi at the lower end of the Pass and the verification that this ancient city had flourished as far back as the eighth millennium BCE testifies that the Bolan route has certainly been used as long as that.

Through this extended passage of time, surely a great two-way exchange of ideas would have taken place between the Sindhu Valley and Mesopotamia. And it was this prodigious exchange; the exact details of which we may perhaps learn in due course, that occupied my mind as we drove out of Quetta early one morning on the way to the shrine of Pir Ghaib – the Invisible Saint. Once again, I had left home without reading up and so my mind was not encumbered by the theories and beliefs of those who had gone before me. I was open to every bit of information, to every stimulus, that would come my way.

Seventeen kilometres south of Mach a freshly painted roadside sign, saying Pir Ghaib was ten kilometres away, pointed us off the road to the right. The rough, stony trail crossed a dry watercourse and wound around small hillocks that had, even at eight in the morning, started to magnify the heat of the sun blazing out of a cloudless sky. In that great lunar jumble of barren, brown hills the sprawling green splash of the village of Khajuri appeared bizarre and alien. Suddenly there were channels running with clear water, blocks of ploughed land with young wheat, date trees with cooing doves, two neurotic dogs taking vociferous exception to our fleeting presence and a couple of waving children. And then as suddenly, we were on the moon once again.

Khajuri and Mach mean the same: the former in Sindhi, Punjabi and Urdu signifies the connection with date (*khajur*). The latter is the name for the date palm in Balochi. I could not help but remark on the fact that separated by only a few kilometres; the two places had the same name in different languages.

The trail seemed to be headed straight for a large cleft within the rock wall that loomed in the distance. We took a curve and another blotch of green greeted us. The jeep climbed up the last bit to the solitary house with a sign outside proclaiming that it cost ten rupees to have one's car minded. We called for the car-minder; and though we could hear people inside the house, no one answered. We decided it was free for we had arrived when the blistering heat had put an end to the tourist season. It was another thing, however, that the boy appeared to relieve us of the money when, we were reversing to leave a couple of hours later.

Below, at the bottom of the gorge, the trees

grew thickly. A winding path led down to the clump of *shisham* and date palms narcissus-like encircling a beautiful emerald pond where the clear water rippled over limestone and in its shallow depth fish shimmered. Two twines of water, frayed by the wind, fell into this pond from a height of about twelve metres. Centuries of pouring water had enriched the rock with a thick coating of lichens in the most dazzling shades of green and brown. The latter signifying that the flow contained sulphur. If anything, the stark aridity of the surrounding hills accentuated the verdant beauty of the spot. In all my years of wandering about the country, I had never seen anything quite as remarkable as the pond at Pir Ghaib. It was something straight out of a film.

We climbed back up again and followed the water channel past the grave of the Invisible Saint to the spring. It was a round hole in the grey-white limestone rock wall some thirty centimetres across from which the water spouted abundantly. Though it was warm, it was without the stink of sulphur and pleasant to the palate. Back at the tomb, a family had arrived. Rahim, leading this group, said they were from neighbouring Khajuri and visited the saint's tomb whenever they were faced with difficulties. This day, however, he had no supplication to make. He and his four children (the youngest about six) had walked these five kilometres in the blazing heat only to visit with the keeper of the shrine.

The shrine had 'always been here,' said Rahim. As far back as he could remember the little swings, too, hung on the tree shading the grave. The saint miraculously cured sick children placed in these swings, said the man. The shrine was unchanged since his father's childhood. Therefore, said our man, it must be from the time of the 'Gohars' – Fire Worshippers. The man's concept of time and space was fantastic: from his father's youth just fifty years before, he had jumped straight across fifteen hundred intervening years and connected the shrine with the Zoroastrians. Though it was not said explicitly, the saint seemed to have been a Muslim who was tormented by the local population on account of his faith.

This saint, whose real name was not known, arrived in the area with his sister the venerable Bibi Nani who is buried under a bridge in the Bolan Pass. But the Gohars intent upon chasing them away came for them with soldiers. The story does not disclose where the Fire Worshippers came from, though. The sister and brother fled, but unable to shake off the soldiers, decided to split up at some point. The one going lower down the Bolan and the other coming this way. Their pursuers, however, did not relent and when the holy man saw no hope of escape, he simply disappeared into the rock wall. From that exact spot where the saint entered the rock, so the story goes, sprang a clear and copious spring that flows to this day. So much for the saint, but Rahim did not know how the sister died and came to be buried in the Pass not many miles away.* He did say, however, that Pir Ghaib was also revered by local Hindus, a fact that was later validated by the *Bolan Gazetteer* of 1906. For them, says the *Gazetteer*, the saint is Mahadev which, incidentally, is another name for Shiva.

---

* The shrine of Bibi Nani is some ten kilometres south of this spot.

The waterfall and the pool, gift of the saint who disappeared.

There are several shrines in Pakistan now revered by Muslims but that come from a distant pagan past when our ancestors yet worshipped more temporal gods and goddesses than saints who disappeared into rocks. We do not know how long this spring has poured forth its blessing of water, but if it ran in the remote past, surely trading caravans originating in cities of the Sindhu Valley would have detoured from the grim walls of the Bolan Gorge to propitiate whatever gods they attributed this blessing to. Here they would have sought the sanction of their gods to preserve them in the long and arduous journey to the marts of Mesopotamia. In about 1800 BCE came the singers of Vedic hymns and they would have assigned their own gods to the spring. In the first century CE, when this part of Balochistan came under the fire-worshipping Sassanians, the fount would yet again have gained a new and appropriate legend. Finally, at some unknown time, the story took its Islamic guise.

Though we may never know which gods the Sassanians or their predecessors worshipped at Pir Ghaib, there can be no doubt that these gods would all have had an ancient, timeless core with layers of change and accretion. As for Bibi Nani, her identity is no puzzle. She is simply Nana or Nania; the goddess revered in ancient Mesopotamia and Persia in the very remote past. It was in the year 2280 BCE that Kudur-Nankhundi, king of Elam (southwest Persia), sacked the city of Erech in the kingdom of Ur (Mesopotamia). Among other treasures, the victor carried away from Erech to his capital city of Susa, the highly revered idol of the goddess Nania. Such was the reverence for Nania among the people of Mesopotamia that for a no less than one thousand six hundred and thirty-five years successive Mesopotamian kings smarted under the humiliation of that defeat and theft of their idol.

It was only in the year 645 BCE that king Assurbanipal taking advantage of the weakness of the Elamite kingdom set out to right that ancient wrong. A bitter contest followed and after fourteen Elamite cities had been sacked, Susa fell to the Mesopotamians. The city was pillaged and trashed, but before that came to pass, the idol of Nania was secured and restored to the temple of Erech. The cult of Nania, or Bibi Nani as we know her, is thus one of the oldest in the world: it has survived for more than four thousand years. Over these millenniums, caravans carrying trade and philosophy back and forth between Mesopotamia and the cities of the Sindhu Valley would have dispersed the name of this goddess across the countries.

When 19th century archaeologists translated the cuneiform inscriptions of Western Asia, we learnt the names of the western gods. At home in the valley of the Sindhu, however, translation of the ancient script has been a baffling impossibility. Despite the best efforts of the greatest minds in the field today, the script of Moen jo Daro remains tantalisingly unread. And so we do not know the names of the deities worshipped in the Sindhu Valley, or of the kings and queens who ruled over it or even of the poets and philosophers who would have compiled its religious and literary lore.

As likely as it is that the name Nania or Nana travelled from the west to the east, it could just as well have originated in the Sindhu Valley and dispersed across ancient Persia and Mesopotamia. Who knows how the goddess would have metamorphosed as she was escorted across the ancient civilised world by generation after generation of Sindhu Valley traders and philosophers? Who knows which of the many goddesses – big bosomed with heavy buttocks and fabulous headdresses, recovered from the ruins of Moen jo Daro, Harappa and Mehrgarh, was called Nania? It is a teasing, somewhat self-involved, thought, but it is certainly not without logic for recent discoveries show the transfer of superior crafts and knowledge from the Sindhu Valley to Mesopotamia rather than the other way round.* It should be of no surprise then if the most powerful goddess of ancient Sindh, Punjab and Balochistan also made her way westward to a new home in Mesopotamia.

Experts now believe that after taking the Sindhu Valley the Aryan speaking peoples adopted some of the gods already in vogue in this country. As Shiva was modelled on a Sindhu Valley god, surely the god of the bubbling spring too would have been suitably adapted to Vedic belief on the first leg of its long journey of metamorphosis. More than three millenniums later the Muslims made him the Invisible Saint just as they turned Nania into their Bibi Nani – the Venerated Lady. At some stage the believers thought it handy to turn these two into siblings, perhaps for added colour to the legend.

Someday the script of the Sindhu Valley will cease to frustrate and vex; someday it will have been read as thoroughly as Egyptian and Western Asian scripts. Then perhaps we will learn that Nania did indeed travel west from the east. Then we shall also know the name of her brother, the god of bubbling springs and flowing water. Meanwhile, even as scholars ponder over ancient texts, Hindus and Muslims, each according to their own faith, can together seek the benediction of the Invisible Saint – as ancient as Nania but one whose name is yet unknowable.

---

* Jonathan Mark Kenoyer has shown in *Cities of the Indus Valley* that some techniques, notable among them the crafting of beads, were highly developed in the Sindhu valley and travelled from here to Mesopotamia.

PALACE OF FAIRIES

Palace of Fairies

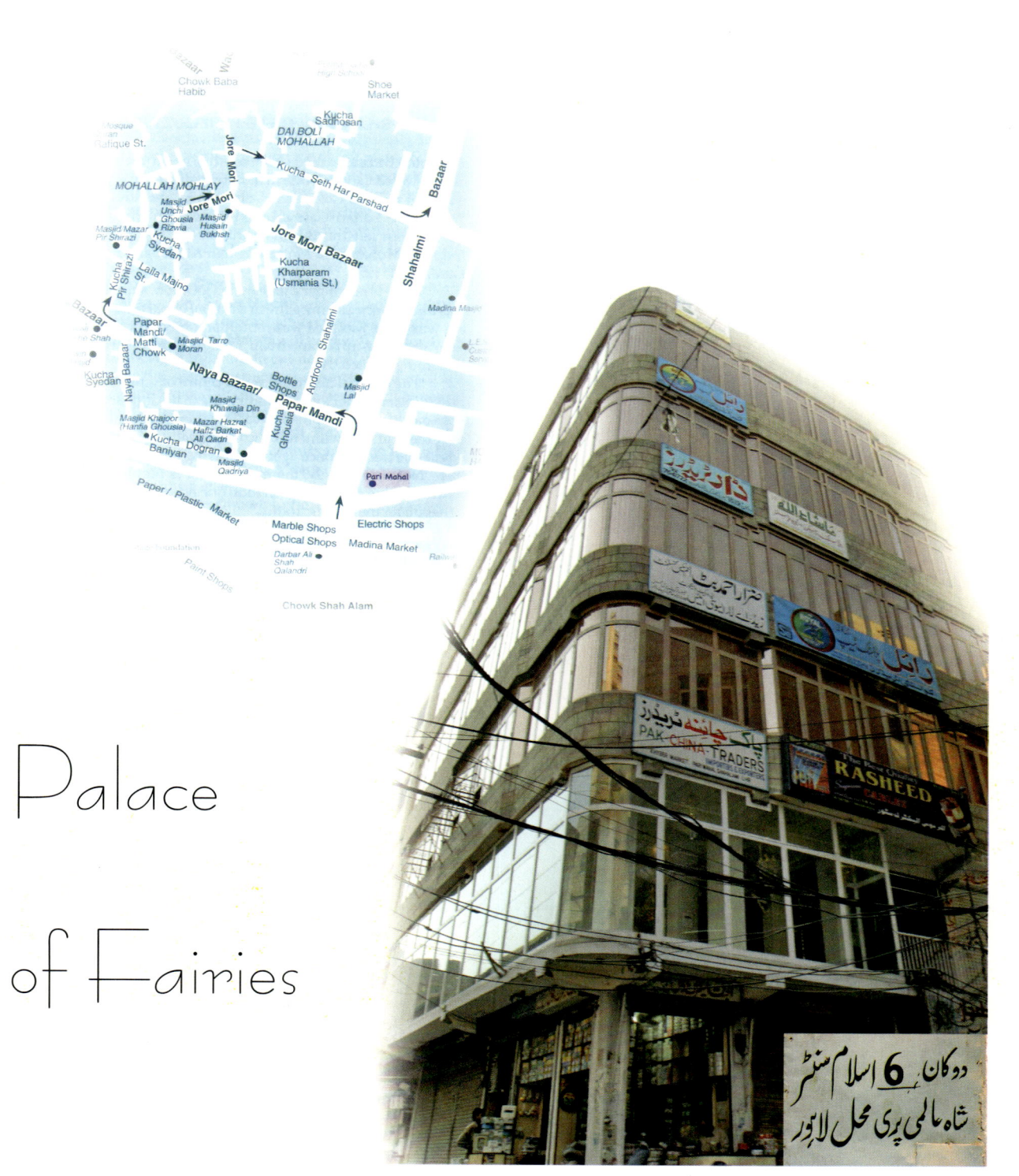

This monstrosity now sullies the site of Wazir Khan's Palace of Fairies. (Inset) Pari Mahal continues to live on in local collective memory, however.

19

Among other Mughal buildings mentioned by S. M. Latif in his book on Lahore written a hundred years ago, there is one called Pari Mahal: 'The Pari Mahal, or the "palace of fairies" is situated in the Shah Almi Gate quarters. It was founded by Nawab Ilmud Din, surnamed Wazir Khan, Minister of Shah Jehan, and was his private residence. He also held court here. It was furnished with magnificent halls, gardens, baths and other elegant buildings; but the three governors of Lahore, and, after them, Ranjit Singh, stripped it of its costly materials. The shops attached to the *haveli*, together with certain other buildings, still exist and are substantial works of architectural beauty.'

Latif does not say anymore and the 'three governors,' one can assume, were those who ruled over the city immediately following Wazir Khan. But the fact that the building was called Pari Mahal and that it was his 'private residence' implies explicitly enough that Wazir Khan housed his wife (or wives and concubines – the last if he kept them) in it. So when friend and fellow writer Sarwat Ali read out this passage to me, I resolved to see this 17th century building that had missed my notice thus far. Even before I set out for Shah Almi, I harboured little hope of re-discovering a grand Mughal relic. I knew there would be no more than a crumbling ruin rendered ungainly, almost ugly, by the growth upon it of cement concrete excrescences – as is the wont in our country.

Sarwat remembered seeing the address 'Pari Mahal' on certain businesses in Shah Almi, and so, we concluded, there must be something left of Wazir Khan's seraglio. But he also reminded me of stories of the great fires that had raged through this quarter of the old city in August 1947. Indeed, Bapsi Sidhwa in her *Ice-Candy Man* mentions how the sky-scraping flames of Shah Almi could be seen from afar. There was thus also the possibility of this grand building having been burnt down during the partition riots.

As one enters Shah Almi, the large shopping centre set some thirty metres in the alley to the right is known as Pari Mahal. The modern tradition of building in Pakistan lays down the unwritten law that all shopping malls must be as hideous as they can get, consequently Pari Mahal is an eyesore too. The unsightly building with cubicles on the ground floor serving as shops rises five floors above the narrow alley in a grey block of concrete, steel and glass. It has every look of impermanence, of having been hurriedly constructed to last only thirty odd years before it is pulled down to be replaced by an even uglier monster. Where beauty was once as essential to a building as functionability and durability, the only consideration now is monetary profit.

The signs above the shops all marked the place as Pari Mahal. Yes, said the man who claimed to have done business in the area since the early 1950s, there used to be a *haveli* at the site of the ugly building. It was called Pari Mahal because the arch above the main entrance featured a stucco fairy with spreading wings. Others said there was no fairy; only the building was so called because of the 'fairies that lived within.'

Some remembered the protracted litigation that began as early as 1952 and only came to an end forty years later. Until then, said my informant, Pari Mahal was still standing. Then, with the case settled, the 'rightful' owners (read: 1947 refugees) quickly tore down the old edifice and raised the concrete eyesore. The man only remembered the exterior of boarded up windows and padlocked main entrance, for no one had entered the *haveli* since the commencement of court proceedings. He seemed surprised that anyone should have considered saving a 'worthless old building' that was anyway on the verge of collapse. It was news for him that a law deemed all buildings whether public or private older than seventy years protected. He was surprised that even the owner of such a property could not alter it, much less tear it down.

According to the account of local shopkeepers, Pari Mahal had stood until less than ten years ago.* Strangely, however, not one person could describe the building – save for the boarded-up windows. Some said it had a rich reddish-brown wash, others said it was washed yellow. No one was certain how many floors it had and its attached gardens as mentioned by Latif were completely forgotten.

Elderly men remembered the conflagration of 1947 when a 'Syed of Bhati Gate' led a mob of arsonists to this largely upper class Hindu and Sikh precinct. When they were finished, innumerable buildings had been burnt down, untold wealth plundered, even more destroyed and hundreds of lives lost. But nobody remembered if Pari Mahal had suffered from arson as well. Nobody remembered, too, who lived in it before and if it was ever inhabited after Independence. The only memory was of the boarded up exterior and the plaster fairy that may or may not have adorned the entrance.

The status of this once impressive building became more and more intriguing and so the quest for the answers led to the works of early travellers and writers. If anything, it was by a singular fluke of good fortune that I chanced upon a paper written by J. P. Vogel, an early 20th century historian. This paper deals with the deputation in the early years of the 18th century of a Dutch ambassador to the court of Shah Alam, the able king of the moribund Mughal Empire.

Jan Joshua Ketelaar, a businessman of good standing from Surat (Gujarat, India), was appointed ambassador to the Mughal court and arrived in Lahore in December 1711. Eager to impress the freshly arrived diplomat, the king inquired if the ambassador would be 'inclined to see the Imperial pleasure-garden, situated outside the town of Lahore and named Salamar (*sic*), likewise the Palace Paerimahal standing inside the town.' That the king placed Pari Mahal in the same class as the Shalimar Gardens to be showed off to visiting dignitaries implies that it must indeed have been an edifice of remarkable beauty and grandeur. The envoy visited both sites and having waxed eloquent on the Shalimar left a brief description of the *haveli* as well.

---

* This would be 1989.

In Ketelaar's account Pari Mahal was, 'a fair edifice wherein in a large gallery the image of our Saviour surrounded by the Angels is carved very skilfully in alabaster.' The rendering of Christ on the walls of the private residence of a devout Muslim is somewhat hard to understand, it is likely, therefore, that Ketelaar simply misunderstood the sculpture. Of course the possibility cannot be ruled out that Wazir Khan, connoisseur of the arts that he was, might have hired the services of a wandering European maestro to adorn his palace. In which case the artist would have created what was right and proper according to his own religious sensibilities. But one thing is certain: that there were in Pari Mahal paintings of fairies or angels that could have been the reason for the name, a name that persisted long after the building had crumbled.

Not finding anymore material, I returned to Latif. It then occurred to me that even a hundred years ago he spoke of the *haveli* in the past tense and that only the attached 'shops together with certain other buildings' still existed and were 'substantial works of architectural beauty.' Could it mean then that the main edifice of Pari Mahal had not weathered the treatment meted out by the three governors who succeeded Wazir Khan and by Ranjit Singh?

It seems, therefore, that Wazir Khan's mansion was no longer extant from sometimes in the latter part of the 19th century. The shops and the outhouses were probably what the mob might have tried to set alight in 1947. These same buildings became the subject of the lengthy litigation that lasted until the early 1990s. Surely these last surviving structures would not have been decorated with angels or fairies. The fairy that the men told me about was merely what is a part of the collective memory of the residents, something they had heard mentioned by elders who in turn had heard of it from their elders. This was something they had never actually seen, something that only their minds had conjured up.

As so it is that years after the original disappeared, the ugly block raised in place of the seraglio of Wazir Khan is still called Pari Mahal. Only because the exquisite beauty of the paintings in the interior of the long gone palace have been a part of the collective memory of the Shah Almi quarter of Lahore.

LAST TRAIN TO THAL

Narrow gauge rolling stock at the siding in Kohat.

Last train to Thal

The last train from Kohat to Thal ran sometime in June 1991, so the Station Master at Kohat informed me. Then the section was closed. For a while afterwards, the staff remained at their stations; slowly they were re-assigned. The first to go were the Station Masters from the several stations strung out between the two termini. Gradually went the others, until only a very small nucleus of gang men remained – ostensibly to look after the abandoned one hundred-kilometre Narrow Gauge line. And ostensible was all the looking after there ever was.

Even before 1991 the Kohat-Thal line had shown every sign of impending demise. Back in early 1987 when I was doing my series called The Little Railway Bazaar pompously named

23

Hangu railway station.

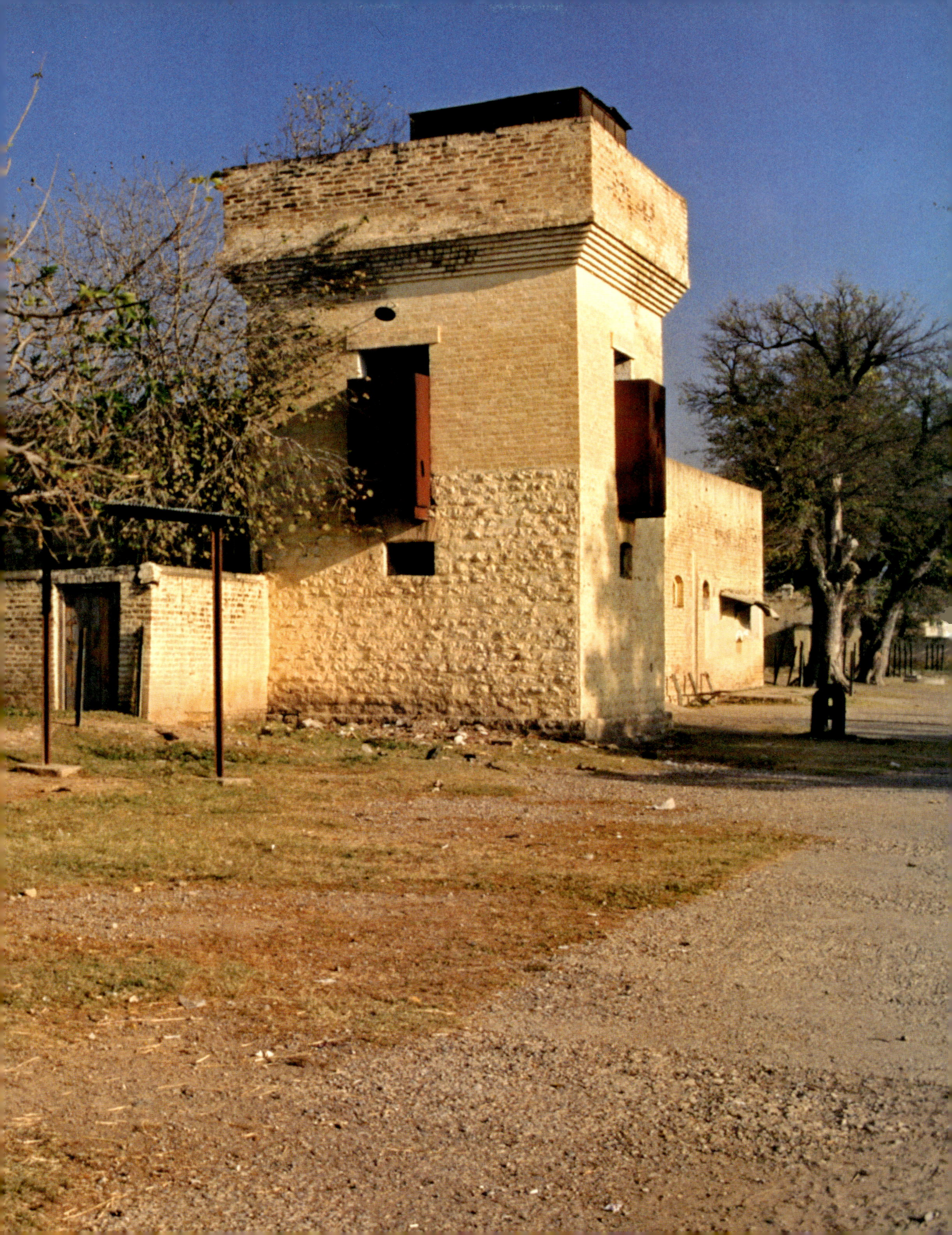

after one of the good travel books of the 20th century, I had arrived in Kohat to ride the once-a-week train. The coolies around the station said that the Thal line being closed I would be better advised to ride the bus which was not only a sight more comfortable but faster too. My Pakistan Railways timetable said the service was still in operation, so not trusting the red-shirted coolies I sought the Station Master.

The man, perhaps one of the old guard who hate to concede inefficiency, said the service was indeed running, but it being the wrong day of the week, I could not avail of it. I asked what day it ran, he said Tuesday. I held up my watch close to his face for him to read it was Tuesday and the man said my watch was wrong. I argued and he eventually agreed that it was indeed Tuesday but since the last adjustment in timings, it now ran on Thursday. Foolishly I showed him my copy of the current timetable that said it was still Tuesday. He didn't like it one bit, but he offered to let me ride the scheduled freight train to Thal. For that, he said triumphantly, I will have to wait a whole day. I gave up on the Kohat-Thal Narrow Gauge section.

Looking back now, I realise that the service may not have been closed as early as 1987. It may have become increasingly irregular, or may have closed for a short while before resuming. At that time the railways would have been concentrating more on freight transportation than passenger service. Freight on this line, incidentally, was largely mats made from dwarf palm fronds – the ones that one sees in mosques all over the country. In those days of slower road traffic freight was the big revenue on this line.

It was only recently that I heard Pakistan Railways had auctioned the entire line and that contractors were busy uprooting it. It was time to re-visit Kohat to see for myself the demise of a railway line. Friend Mian Mumtaz Ahmed at Railway Headquarters had arranged with Abdur Rehman, a young official from Kohat, to show me around. And when I arrived at the railway station Rehman was waiting with tea and biscuits.

At Kohat the last vestiges of the Narrow Gauge are some forlorn looking passenger and freight cars that have not moved from their roosting place for the past seven years. The last of the locomotives, said Rehman, was shipped to Mughalpura shortly after the line was closed in 1991. There was nothing to see in Kohat and so in a borrowed car we set off for Thal through a wintry landscape with poplars turning gold.

Ustarzai, the second railway station out of Kohat but the first we stopped at was a sorry piece. The good people of the village had stripped it of everything of value. Here timber seemed to the only thing of value so all the doors, windows, ventilators and signboards were gone. Rehman was surprised that they hadn't removed the rails as well. The arms factories at not so distant Darra Adam Khel could benefit from all this high quality steel, I observed. But then again, perhaps they had not yet exhausted all those busted T-Series Soviet tanks from the Afghan War.

At Raisan we paused in the bazaar to ask directions. The elderly Pukhtun gentleman nearly fell out of his shoes when we asked for the railway station, 'It's been *years* since a train went past here!' he said. 'What in God's name do you want at the station?'

We persisted and he kindly directed, bewilderment refusing to leave his face. The station was a veritable fortress with a high loopholed wall and a corner turret. Entrance was via a heavy timber and steel door and the King of this Castle was Habibullah the gang man with his extended family in retinue. The handsome building was kept so well that I did not have the heart to ask if he was living in it by leave of the authorities or had simply taken over.

Within the high walls was a crowded enceinte: living apartments on three sides and a well in the middle. Behind a wall to afford privacy to the inmates, the apartments were two or three rooms each. Just the basics for small families of officials who were obviously new to the service (and therefore young with small families) to be posted to the backwoods. Once, when the line was running, the station master lived within the safety of this fortress together with his Pointsman, Waterman and a couple of policemen. Now Habibullah presided over it.

Hangu station had a corner turret even more impressive than the one at Raisan: higher and like a proper castle turret. The interior, too, was grander. The apartments were only marginally bigger than the ones at Raisan, but there were no partition walls between the various houses. It seemed as if the staff at Hangu were ordained to live like one big happy family. That was the past, today Hangu railway station serves as barracks for a detachment of policemen. They were a jovial lot, happy for this break in their tedium. Hearing that I was from Lahore, they took me for a foundry owner looking for quality scrap steel. A journalist with an academic interest in old railway lines was sort of hard to figure.

We drove on to Kahi, a chunk of a square building with a formidable steel door blocking entry. As we pottered about outside, half a dozen young women who had been filling at a nearby water tap came ambling back, each balancing a pot on her head and cradling another in the crook of her arm against her waist. They sauntered past and disappeared into the station building. Presently, the master of the house emerged to tell us that he and his family had taken over the decaying building several years ago. Emphatically he added that we were not permitted to enter. Even at the time of his taking over there were no railway relics. No, he said, there had been no clocks, Morse keys or furniture in the Station Master's office. Everything had been removed, but he did not by whom.

Stopping briefly at Doaba, we eventually made Thal, the end of the line. The station lies within the militia cantonment, and if we had thought Raisan and Hangu were impressive, this was all the more so. Here was a real castle that was clearly much bigger than the ones we had already seen. The walls and the turret were higher than the ones we had already seen. Atop the turret sat a steel water tank with a pitched steel roof, all painted the regulation deep red that defies rust.

From within rose the cacophony of life: cocks crowed, children screamed, laughed and cried, women chattered. I tried to stick my head into the oblong opening in the heavy steel door and a dark unshaven man with thick moustaches asked what I wanted.

'I'm from a newspaper and just want to look around,' said I.

'There's nothing to look around here because this is a private residential area and it isn't nice to look around other people's houses,' he returned rather rudely.

We were joined by a younger more garrulous man and he called for the women to hide themselves as he led me in. His call was in vain for they all remained at their various stations some brushing their children's hair, others washing up or doing the laundry, and yet others sunning themselves and gossiping. It was like entering a Punjabi *mohalla*, where everybody spoke the dialect of Sialkot. These were indeed men and women of Sialkot, Christians all of them who looked after cleanliness in the cantonment of Thal. The railway station of Thal had been their home for the past six years or so. I sent up a silent prayer for the poorer Christian families of Punjab for without them this country would long ago have turned into a putrefying rubbish dump.

Abdur Rehman had earlier told me that he had joined the service just when this line was dying. He remembered that passenger traffic was hardly ever substantial and that the railways only revenue was from hauling goods. Unfortunately for the Kohat-Thal section the Russians invaded Afghanistan and American money paid for the roads to be improved in this area in the early 1980s. This made for faster and more efficient freight transportation by road. Consequently, clients who earlier had no choice but to avail Pakistan Railway facilities now turned to private truckers. This service covered the distance between Kohat and Thal in about two hours' time, while the train took five when it was not running late. And it always, without fail, ran late.

Revenue fell drastically. The Army, according to Abdur Rehman, was the only client that abided faithfully by the railways. For one, rules required that wherever possible revenue should go to the government. Secondly, the greatest excitement that the sleepy militia garrison at Thal ever knew since the end of the Afghan War was perhaps morning P.T. Other than that there was never any hurry to get the practice ammo over from the ordnance factory at Wah. Time came that even the Thal Scouts sought alternatives. The railway's losses mounted and soon the only way to handle this line was to axe it.

Casually Abdur Rehman mentioned that Pakistan Railways owned great tracts of property at Parachinar town where they had once maintained an 'Out Agency' and where they still had a beautiful rest house. He insisted we should drive the extra seventy odd kilometres to check out those establishments as well. I declined because the car had to be back in Kohat before nightfall. But I had established that the section had not yet been auctioned to be uprooted and carted off to some foundry or other. That incidentally has been the fate of the Bannu-Mari Indus Narrow Gauge section as

Abdur Rehman informed me.

One thing I know, however: the British railway authorities had not laid the line to Thal for nothing. They may not have known how to surmount the vast mountains ahead, but surely there would have been plans to extend the line to Kabul. I have not been able to find anything to this effect in the skimpy histories that I have access to, but I am sure that there are in railway headquarters somewhere in the subcontinent forgotten files that evoke the railway enthusiasm of that day, files that evoke the excitement of building the first railway over the high passes into Paktiya province of Afghanistan.

Sadly, even before we might find those files, this section too will be auctioned. The railway stations will remain with whoever might hold them at the final hour. The bridges, the line and other civil works will be dismantled for the steel to be removed to be turned into iron grills and steel plates. If anything will remain it will very likely be the rest house at Parachinar. I wonder, however, if Pakistan Railways will be able to maintain that one isolated building.

SEA MONSTERS AND THE SUN GOD

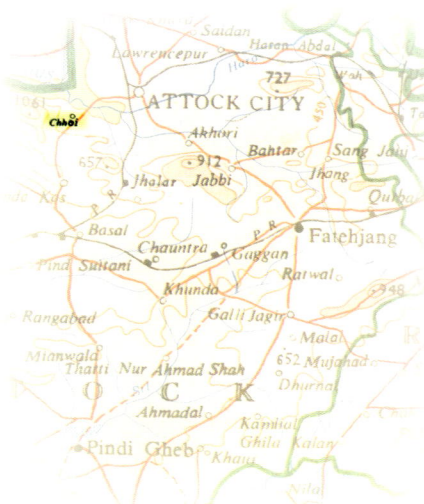

Mustard blossom near Chhoi.

Who remembers Karam Hussain Shah?

My friend Brigadier Humayun Malik has a canny eye for detail that makes him a storyteller par excellence – a storyteller of the old school. And this is the true story of a man called Karam Hussain Shah as told by my friend the brigadier. Karam Hussain Shah of the village of Chhoi lying some twenty or so kilometres southwest of the town of Attock on the highroad to Basal. Though I tell the story in the third person, there isn't a grain of addition or subtraction. It is told in the exact words of Brigadier Malik.

The year was 1959 when Malik, as a young captain in the Special Service Group (SSG) was posted at Attock Fort. Among those of his commando battalion was a soldier called Nazar Hussain Shah. A stout, handsome specimen he was of the trans-Sindhu country of Attock then called Campbellpur. Yet shy of his twenty-second birthday, he was as fine a soldier as they made them in bygone days.

Now, in the SSG of those days, in order to promote initiative and independence, one was not required to get sanction from superiors to leave the station for the weekend. All one did, and this included NCOs and enlisted men as well, was sign a register and put down the time one was expected to return at the end of the furlough. What was taken for granted was that no good man will ever overstay his leave by so much as a minute. No matter howsoever he may, he will make it back to base at the appointed hour. Those were the rules of business at SSG and they were strictly adhered to.

And so it was that one day Nazar Hussain went away to visit an uncle at Nowshera for the weekend. On the Sunday evening Captain Humayun Malik received a telephone call from the Station Master at Attock Khurd (the station nearest to Attock Fort) that the body of a beheaded soldier in uniform had been found on the tracks and that SSG being the nearest army he was being informed to take appropriate action. What the captain and his two men saw at the station was this: the body of Sepoy Nazar Hussain Shah lay between the concrete of the end of the platform and the track while his head lay upright in the middle of the two tracks. The eyes were open, the face calm, hair scarcely ruffled and the maroon beret was only slightly askew. There was no other sign of injury on the face. Nearby lay his overnight bag with its change of clothing inside.

Inquiry revealed that Nazar Hussain, seen off at Nowshera by his uncle, planned to disembark at Attock Khurd. Only he had not realised that he had boarded an express train that did not stop at his station. As the train clattered over the sidings and began to sweep past the station buildings without reducing speed, Nazar Hussain would have felt a pang of panic: the train would stop at Campbellpur seventeen kilometres away, and even if he were to jog back along the tracks there would not be time enough for him to reach base on schedule. And in those days buses were not as common as they are now.

To be late was to lose face. And so, impetuous as his youth made him, Nazar Hussain attempted to get off the speeding train. Even in those pre-diesel steam locomotive days trains did a good eighty odd kilometres on level stretches. The platform had very nearly ended when Nazar Hussain hit it. He tried to run along, but that is no speed for a man's legs to work at. He had no control; he stumbled and fell. The train sped on; the driver staring hard into the night ahead was oblivious of the loss of a young and priceless life. Only those who shared his compartment and perhaps saw him disappear into that narrow slit between the speeding train and the concrete platform knew of the fate that befell young Nazar Hussain. Even they would only have sent up a prayer for the Lord to preserve him.

Captain Malik found Nazar Hussain's body where it had fallen between the track and the concrete of the platform, his uniform stained but slightly from the final gush of blood. In his attempt to get back on time, young Nazar Hussain had delivered himself into the hands of death. Now it devolved on the captain to take the body home. The dossier said that he came from Chhoi. The severed head was sewn back on and with the enshrouded body in a coffin following in a truck the captain rode ahead in a jeep. Past Campbellpur they took the road to Basal. At the Chhoi rest house that overlooks a bend in the highroad, the convoy paused to ask for Karam Hussain Shah, the dead man's father. He lived a little distance outside the village, they told the captain.

Leaving the highroad the captain led his brief and sombre convoy down a side road. Past a small graveyard, across a pebbly stream and up an incline where there were a few scattered farmsteads. Near one house he paused, got off the jeep and called out aloud, 'Karam Hussain Shah?'

It was a simple mud-plastered house with two rooms, a veranda and a courtyard in front. A flock of chickens and a few goats browsed around the yard. A man that Captain Malik hadn't noticed working in a plot of land stood up. Tall and slim with a grey beard and a kindly countenance Karam Hussain Shah, a retired corporal of the First World War, marched up and saluted smartly.

'Captain sahib! Welcome. You come in peace? What brings you to my humble home?' he asked. He wore a coarse homespun cotton *shalwar-kurta*. The *kurta* was the old-fashioned kind that did not come with buttons down the front, but with one shoulder open that was tied together with a simple tassel. In Malik's estimation Karam Hussain at that time was about sixty years old.

'Nazar Hussain, the one who is in the army. I have come about him,' said the captain.

'Yes, that's my son, captain sahib. What of him?'

Whatever plans the young Captain Malik had in his mind of gently breaking the news of the horrible death, dispersed of a moment, 'I am
sorry to tell you, sir, that your son is dead.'

'What do you say?' said the man, 'What is that again, captain sahib?'

The captain repeated his grim words and half expecting the man to fall down in a swoon prepared himself to steady him. At best, he thought, there would be a beating of the old chest and a wailing litany of the injustice of Providence. But Karam Hussain Shah, tall and erect, appeared taller still to the bringer of the tragic news as he looked skyward and raised up his hands in orison.

'He was Yours, Lord. You gave him to us and You took him away. You are the Almighty. Your will is done, all praise to You.' The voice, clear and loud, did not waver. No tear rolled down the wrinkled cheeks. And then, 'Come, captain sahib, let us bring him home.'

But then realising his own lack of decorum, he hurried to lay out the charpoy that was propped up against a wall of the house.

'Sit yourself down and rest. You have already gone through a lot of trouble to bring my son home. I'll take care of everything now.' Karam Hussain said making himself busy.

The mother of the dead man who was inside the house called to ask what was going on.

'It is Nazar Hussain. He has come home,' said the old man, and then turning to the captain, 'You know, these mothers are mad. They cannot keep control over their emotions.'

Perhaps it was the way Karam Hussain Shah had announced the return of their son, perhaps it was the perspicacity that only mothers possess, that the old woman recognised something was drastically amiss and started to weep.

'Nazar's mother, you silly woman, why do you cry? Our son has come home to us.' Karam Hussain tried to comfort his distraught wife who knew no comforting. 'It is the evening of our time, blessed woman, and soon we shall be reunited with our son. What if he had gone earlier leaving us a long and empty life to live?'

Meanwhile, people having seen the sad convoy and having sensed something amiss were streaming in from nearby habitations. The coffin was unloaded and brought into the courtyard. After some time Karam Hussain asked if he could see his son's face. He took a long look, and kissed the cold young forehead before replacing the lid of the coffin. Still no tear flowed. Still there was no dent in the serenity.

At that time the SSG commandant was a certain Colonel A. O. Mitha who later won acclaim as one of the finest generals of the Pakistan Army. And Colonel Mitha had sent three thousand rupees and some rations for the family of the deceased. But in the short while that he had spent with Karam Hussain, the captain knew that the man would never accept any gifts. He thought it wise to discuss the matter with one of the relatives who had meanwhile arrived. No, it was said, the man was too dignified and self-respecting to accept anything. Nevertheless, since the gifts came from the commandant, the captain decided to talk to the old man himself.

'You are very kind, captain sahib,' said Karam Hussain. 'But we have no need for what you bring. If we needed anything we would take it.
Trust me, our needs are all fulfilled.'

The funeral rites took place and before that day in late March ended forty years ago, young Nazar Hussain Shah was buried in the graveyard that lies athwart of the road leading to the village.

Thereafter every weekend Captain Humayun Malik visited the aged couple bearing whatever gifts he thought prudent. He brought them multi-vitamin pills telling them it was not medicine but a pill to give strength and good health. Many weeks later he discovered that they had not been touched. The couple said they had plenty of strength and good health and did not need the pills. Another time he brought a shawl for the woman and found that she would not use it but had kept it away carefully in a trunk. If he brought fruit they shared it with him and saved the remainder for his visit the following weekend. Time and again he asked them if he could bring something they actually needed. Always the answer was the same: they were content, there was no want. The only offering that was ever used was a cardigan that the captain took for the old man.

And so the year 1959 wore on. With each visit Captain Malik came to know them better and only came away with greater and greater respect for these two people of peerless dignity and character that no lust for any worldly possession could sway. Here were two people who had suffered the loss of their only child born after seventeen years of wedlock with remarkable perseverance – perseverance that is the mark of an unblemished spirit. Here were two people at peace with themselves and with their Maker. Here were two people who were religious in the true sense of the word, but who did not make a show of their religiosity.

Over the year Captain Malik learned that the upright and honourable Karam Hussain had left the family home in the village to his half-brother because the sister in law had once voiced the concern that being the elder, Karam Hussain might deprive the younger of his rightful share in the family's meagre holdings. Such was the man's character that just one word had caused him to give up the house and move out to his own share of agricultural land. And this holding too was no more than a couple of acres. There he built his home and in peace worked his land, sending his son to the army in the tradition of that part of the country.

Some months later Malik moved to Cherat. Two months later, on the first weekend after returning to Attock Fort, he visited Chhoi again. The house of Karam Hussain was locked and deserted. Neighbours said the man was dead and his wife had moved back to the village. Malik tracked her down.

'Remember he had said it was the evening of our time?' she said. 'Simple man. It was the evening of his time only. He has left me to bear the burden alone.'

That was the last he saw of her. He was transferred to Nowshera and when he visited early in 1961, even Karam Hussain's widow, whose name Captain Humayun Malik had never learned, was dead. She was buried next to the two men who had left her earlier.

In Attock recently I took time off to visit Chhoi that has expanded into a conglomerate of three little villages. The only Syeds lived in the hamlet to the west, said the man. The winding road dipped and passed through a graveyard. Then it crossed a small stream. At least this much hasn't changed, I thought. A group of men waited by a pick-up truck to get a ride into Attock. The oldest was no more than forty, and none of them had ever heard of Karam Hussain Shah whose son had died in an accident forty years ago. There were only two Syed households in the village and their oldest men were but boys, one of whom rode as helper on the pick-up truck. Neither had ever heard of Karam Hussain.

Someone said something about Daud Shah. Yes, he was almost fifty and he would remember, said another. But Daud Shah was away and would not return for many days. Another man came around to ask questions and vehemently deny the existence ever of a man Karam Hussain Shah in Chhoi. And he knew, he said, because
he had spent all his life in the village.

'Why are you interested in this dead man that no one seems to know? Are you a relative?' he asked somewhat aggressively.

I had nothing to do with Karam Hussain, I said. I had only come to talk to his kin and learn something more of a man whose soul remained intact until the last day of his life. A soul that was not riddled by lust, mendacity or baseness. I had only come to talk about a man who was a giant among men, and the good woman, his partner for life. I did not tell them for fear of sounding corny that I had imagined the village would be proud of having had children of that stature. But I did say to them that Karam Hussain Shah was the kind of man that Jinnah had made this country for. Not for the pygmies into whose paws it has now fallen and who are bleeding it to death. I told them too that I was sorry they did not remember Karam Hussain and how they stood to lose for this lapse of memory. The loss was not his, entirely their own.

The only likely explanation for this collective amnesia is that perhaps Karam Hussain's half-brother who in 1959 was about fifty or something, had no male children and the daughters, if there were any, moved away after marriage. If there was a male child, though I find that unlikely, he too might have moved away so long ago that even the memory faded. And young Nazar, Karam Hussain's only offspring, had died a bachelor. Surely his childhood mates would remember him. But where were they?

For the past many years piety and godliness in our part of the world have never been seen to lie within. They rest on the tips of forked tongues and are exhibited by false and pompous shows of verbose hypocrisy and hands raised in faithless orison for cameras to see. So long have deceitful men with rotten souls brayed words devoid of substance and spirit into our ears that we take such braying to be religiosity. So long have utterly impeachable men with practiced countenances of piety made shows of donating from ill-begotten wealth to this mosque or that shrine for all to see that this deception has come to pass for godliness. So long have professional mullahs paraded their several versions of Islam that it has lost its essence.

Karam Hussain Shah did none of that. His dignity would never have allowed him to stoop so low. There isn't a mosque in Chhoi that carries a plaque with his name, nor a shrine – even his grave is unmarked and thus unidentifiable. Consequently, so far as the pygmies of today are concerned, he wasn't a good enough man. He is forgotten because in this spiritually impoverished society of paraplegic souls there is no need to emulate a man like him. We have forgotten Karam Hussain Shah and his good wife whose every need was fulfilled by a richness of the spirit that we are not acquainted with today. This act of forgetfulness has taken nothing away from those two good people. Only we have rendered ourselves the poorer.

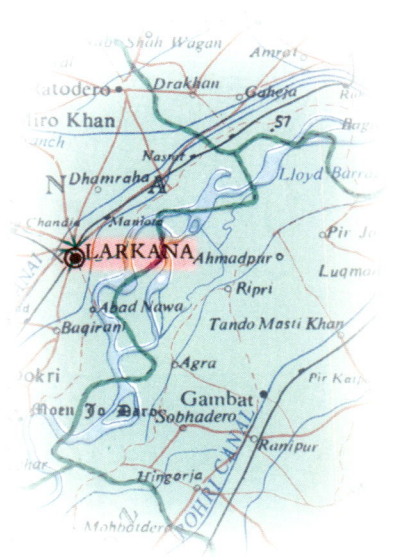

Encroached upon and fading, the collectorate Building at Larkana. The square minarets on the outside corners are remarkable for their very European bartizans complete with loopholes and topped by merlons and crenels. Above them the minaret takes the octagonal shape and rises to the dome which is a smaller replica of the main cupola.

'Dust unto Dust'

In the year 1902 parts of the Shikarpur and Karachi districts of the province of Sindh were carved away to establish the new district of Larkana. Long before that this area was known as Chandka after the well-established Chandio tribe that still lives in great numbers in the western hills of the district. Now the newly established district was to get its new name from the Rajput clan of Larik.

In a paper submitted to the Government of India on 31 December 1847 Hugh James, the Deputy Collector (equivalent to the modern Assistant Commissioner) of Shikarpur, did not hesitate to call Chandka the 'Garden of Upper Sindh.' His reason for this appellation was the number of waterways, both natural and man-made, that meandered across the district bringing it great fertility.

And so when it was established, her British masters thought of bequeathing the new district a monument that would be commensurate with the revenue it was expected to generate. The Collectorate Building was to be the one. From behind its thick walls under high bulbous domes, the Collector (now the Deputy Commissioner) was to bring the European notion of law and order to the unruly Baloch, Brahui, Rajput and Jat peoples of the old land of Chandka.

Completed in 1902, the same year as Larkana district was established, the Collectorate Building is the only one of its kind in the whole of Upper Sindh. In fact, it will not be wrong to say that it is the only such building in the entire province with the exception of the city of Karachi. The building is unique for it is a splendid example of the architectural style so favoured by the British where the local architectural vocabulary was wedded to the European. It is therefore in the same class as, for example, the KMC building in Karachi or the High Court at Lahore. In the words of Kamil Khan Mumtaz, the noted architect, 'It is a superb

Detail of pure Muslim above pure European. Notice the bartizans with mock loopholes and crenels.

example of vernacular architecture with a graft of European veneer.'

The stone and kiln-fired brick building extends in an east-west direction and can be divided into three distinct segments. At either extremity are two identical buildings with

Detail of corbelled tear drop and another form of European bartizan. This device tops the corners of the central part of the building.

mock windows. The domes of these minarets are replicas of the main dome.

The four corners of the structure again have domed minarets. Here the mock balcony below the dome has miniature corner turrets that would be as much at home on an English castle as they are here. It is interesting to note that while the main structure is of kiln-fired bricks, the domes, the octagonal drums below them and the square bases of the drums are all constructed from finely dressed limestone blocks. Similarly, the turrets and drums of the corner minarets too are constructed from dressed limestone.

These domed structures make up the east and west extremities of the Collectorate Building. Each is connected to the central two-storeyed office block by a simple single-storeyed wing. The double-storeyed main office block was certainly designed as a strong statement of 'Europeanism' in Larkana. The balustrades on the first floor veranda and the pediments cause no mistake to be made in this regard. Most interesting in the central block is the curious octagonal turret at each corner with the flat roof and stepped teardrop structure below. This ornament is clearly drawn from

bulbous domes of the kind one sees quite frequently at Makli (near Thatta), especially recalling the dome of Diwan Shurfa Khan, a Mughal nobleman of the 17th century. Each corner of the square base of the dome is adorned with short stubby minarets with two rows of

SEA MONSTERS AND THE SUN GOD

main dome with one on the corner. Notice the beehive ornamentation and the miniature merlons along the parapet.

English castle architecture of the Middle Ages.

For the Hellenistic touch there are wreaths circling the ventilating holes and Corinthian columns where the foliate capitals just about transform into the hooded serpent heads of Indian architecture. Of course there are the Greek pediments already mentioned above.

While the domed structure on the east end houses a branch of the National Bank of Pakistan, the one at the other end is still the office of the Deputy Commissioner. According to Iqbal Bablani, the incumbent DC, the Durbar Hall of the Raj was housed under the main dome. He says, however, that the days of royalty and Durbars being behind us, the hall is now used as a conference room.

Otherwise the story of the Larkana Collectorate Building is a sad one. The rising water table has attacked this priceless piece. Even a casual visitor will not fail to notice the disintegrating salt-caked bricks on the floors. In days gone by there being no damp proof course that we now have in walls at plinth level, the salt-laden moisture has risen to a height of two metres up the walls. In the process, bricks and limestone blocks that make up the plinth have partially been eaten away. Larkana's most impressive building is slowly being undermined by the city's high water table.

Iqbal Bablani is genuinely interested in the district he administers and I find his concern for the decaying Collectorate Building admirable. As a young Assistant Commissioner at Larkana in 1989, he had included this building's conservation in the development plan of the district. Consequently a sum of five million rupees was sanctioned, half of which was released in 1994. Some work was carried out on the west, or the Deputy Commissioner's end, of the building. This included replacement of salt and moisture damaged bricks and limestone blocks from the plinth. For this Bablani had acquired the best stonemasons of Makli. Some minor plastering and whitewashing was also done in the interior.

When this half of the fund dried up, the remainder was not released – a fine example of the ad hocism that plagues government functioning: since the fund was initially sanctioned by a PPP government, the PML regime only saw it appropriate to not release the remainder. Today one can see piles of dressed and undressed limestone blocks lying behind the building, reminding one of the day work was abandoned almost three years ago.

And so while the powers that be find it hard to rise above pettiness, the finest example of Raj architecture in perhaps all Sindh slowly crumbles to dust.

SEA MONSTERS AND THE SUN GOD

The old headworks just below Mangla reservoir.

Canal Journey

Talking of the Upper Jhelum Canal (UJC) friend Suleman Ghani who is currently Secretary Irrigation, Punjab said that that the taking off of the canal at Mangla from the Jhelum River was a truly masterful feat on the part of some *angrez* engineer. Since the canal branches off at Mangla I had always imagined it was built after the damming of the river at that point and had everything to do with Pakistani engineers not with pre-independence *angrez* engineers. What a misimpression that was!

Long before Mangla Dam was conceived in the 1950s, indeed even before the very idea of Pakistan was born, great engineering minds were at work to devise an irrigation system for the vast plains of the rivers Sindhu and Ganga. One

42

such scheme formulated as early as 1902 was called the Triple Canal System, Punjab. It was in May that year that a certain Colonel S. L. Jacob of the corps of Royal Engineers conjured up this plan. One wonders if this man was from the family of that illustrious John Jacob of Jacobabad in Sindh. The earlier Jacob, a great soldier-administrator-engineer, died a bachelor incidentally. But he had not been without brothers who carried the line on. Having retired shortly before from the Punjab Public Works Department, the latter Colonel Jacob wrote a memorandum to suggest the pooling of the waters of the rivers Jhelum, Chenab and Ravi by means of what came to be called link canals. By this system the waters of the Jhelum would have reached as far south and east as the districts of Sahiwal and Multan. Jacob surely was a visionary for, according to a very interesting document, entitled *Punjab Canal Gazetteers Volume II. The Triple Canals (1922)*, he came up with this idea when there were 'no maps, levels or statistics of volume flow' to help him.

The Indian Irrigation Commission initiated a thorough investigation and it was seen that the Upper Jhelum Canal (UJC) taking off from the Jhelum could be aligned to skirt the western fringe of the low, ragged range of hills known as Pabbi between the towns of Jhelum and Kharian. Following a south-westerly alignment to the village of Rasul (now famous for its barrage) it was then to swing east to irrigate the flatlands of the Chaj Doab – the belt of land between the Chenab and Jhelum Rivers. This alignment was to take the unutilised water to the Chenab at Khanki. This inflow of waters from the Jhelum into the Chenab would irrigate the northern part of the Rachna Doab (belt between Ravi and Chenab) through the Lower Chenab Canal (LCC) taking off at Khanki.

The LCC was to dump its unutilised waters into the Ravi at Balloki and another waterway, the Lower Bari Doab Canal (LBDC) was to slake the Bari Doab (taking its name from the rivers Beas and Ravi) south of Lahore. It was a colossal plan involving immense expenditure and the digging of three canals hence The Triple Canals. Of these the UJC is the most interesting. Not only for the way it takes off from the Jhelum and the territory it flows through, but also for the most number (eighty-two) of cross-drainage structures straddling it in its 142 km length. Had the minds of its founding father worked only slightly differently, it would have been just any old canal.

The original reconnaissance threw up three different suggestions for alignment of the UJC. One was for the canal to offtake from the right bank of the Jhelum, cross the river near Jhelum city by an aqueduct and fall into the alignment it now follows. This initial alignment would have avoided Kashmir territory that, it must be remembered, was then the domain of an independent Maharaja who the British did not entirely trust. The second was to offtake just south of Kashmir territory and cross the several Pabbi hill torrents not by level crossings, but by means of tunnels. The third, of course, was the one eventually approved. Along this alignment the canal was to be dug seventy metres wide and three metres deep to convey a peak flow of eight thousand five hundred cubic feet per seconds (cusecs).

Patterns in stone in the old headworks.

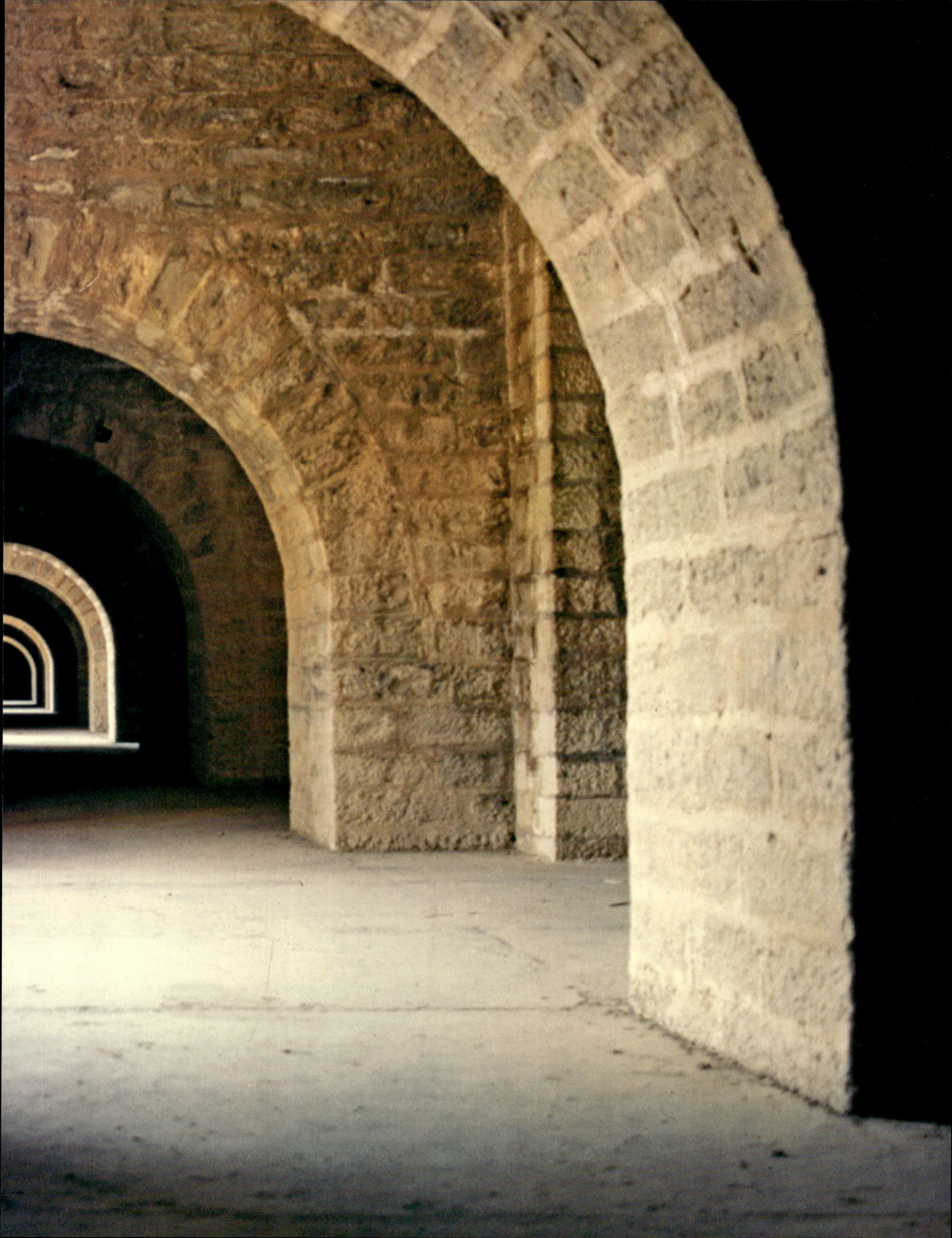

Patterns in stone in the old headworks.

My journey along the Upper Jhelum Canal began at Mangla in the graceful old stone rest house of the Irrigation Department with its crest reading 'Mangla 1912 UJC.' Mahmood ul Hassan Shah, the Executive Engineer, said no journey along the UJC would be complete without first checking out the old headworks. The abandoned headworks stood under the shadow of the towering wall of the dam right next to the power station, serving now only as a bridge across the ditch, once the head of the UJC, but now choked with underbrush. Here the Jhelum River, having skirted the low hill crowned by Mangla Fort, made a loop to the east. At the very apex of this loop, as it again swung to the south, the river had gouged out its deep channel that was never free of water – not even during the dry season when the river ran at its lowest.

Here, as the river swept past the rocky left bank, some surveyor of vision had noted that it was possible to take off a canal without the building of the necessary weir across the river. In this bend of the Jhelum a cross-river headworks to raise the level of water in order to take off the canal was simply not necessary. All that was needed was a cutting in the rocky river bank and an arrangement to control the outflow into the canal. And this was what my friend Suleman had said was the truly masterful feat of canal engineering. The man of vision behind this feat was John Benton, the Chief Engineer of Irrigation Works, Punjab. Actual excavation began in 1905 and on the ninth day of December 1915 the Viceroy of India formally opened the Upper Jhelum Canal. When the Capital Account was closed in 1917, it showed that the canal had cost a whopping Rs 43,849,947.

From the day the gates of the headworks were raised to pass a supply of water into the UJC, nothing changed for the canal for the next fifty-two years. But with the Jhelum dammed at Mangla, there was no longer water sluicing down the river at speed to feed the canal by the old headworks. The canal, however, could not be allowed to die and with it tens of thousands of acres of prime agricultural land in Gujrat district. Consequently water having turned the generators in the powerhouse flows into the new Bong Canal to meet with and fill up the old UJC some eight kilometres downstream from its original take off.

That, said Mahmood ul Hassan with a laugh, was the *phoka* (empty) water of post-storage-dam Punjab. For years I had heard it said in villages across the province how water with all its electricity extracted from it was no longer what it used to be and had laughed at the imbecility of the notion. Mahmood now pointed out the sense in the wisdom of agrarian Punjabis: damming allowed the fertilising silt to settle thus reducing in downstream areas productiveness that was taken for granted since ages. So far as the average village farmer was concerned the dams had deprived the water of its *bijli* (electricity) leaving nothing in it to grow the crops. Small wonder then, I had heard old-timers complain, the younger generation was what it was!

For a better view of the old headworks we climbed up to the fort of Mangla: to the right was the pebbly sweep of the Jhelum – hardly a river after the damming and in the middle the original cutting in the rocky spur to draw the Jhelum waters into the canal. Beyond the cutting, the headworks could be seen with the dark ribbon

The abandoned rest house at Juggu. (Inset) The chunky lettering below the year of construction of the rest house reads 'UJC' for Upper Jhelum Canal.

of the road over it. To the left of the weir was the abandoned reach of the UJC with a dribble of water and just below us the blue arc of the Bong Canal, which now takes water from the river to the UJC. I couldn't help wondering if old Benton had conceived his brilliant scheme standing in a turret of this fort.

Among the many features that make the UJC unique certainly in Punjab and perhaps even in the entire country are its four level crossings. These structures enable hill torrents crossing the canal's alignment to carry their water across the canal. Unlike an aqueduct where the cross-stream passes above in a duct or a siphon where it crosses under, a level crossing, as the name suggests, passes the cross-current *through* the canal. Mahmood had explained how it worked, but I had been at a total loss to grasp the mechanics of level crossings.

Stopping briefly at the junction of the Bong canal and the UJC proper, we reached the Bong level crossing. Here the canal widens slightly as the reedy bed of the Chungar Nalla joins from the northeast. Now, if the Nalla were to be simply dumped into the canal, a flash flood in it could raise the level of the canal dangerously above the designed capacity of 8500 cusecs. Just below the junction were gated regulators both across the canal and the Nalla. In a flash everything was clear. Under normal conditions the Nalla regulator remains closed or only partially open depending upon the flow in it, while the canal gates maintain the standard flow of 8500 cusecs. But as the flood in the Nalla enters the canal from one side, the Nalla regulator on the far side is thrown open to let water out that way. As water follows the easiest path, it simply washes down the Nalla without building pressure on the canal regulator.

Days have passed since I stood at the reedy junction of the Chungar and the UJC and conjured up in my mind the excitement of a flood in the Nalla, and I still believe that the level crossing is the most extraordinary structure a civil engineer could have thought of. The feeling of gratitude for the man who would have first designed this remarkable yet at the same time simple method of regulating flow has not left me. In Lahore some days later I was to learn that level crossings were first used in the British designed Ganga canal system of Central India. I, however, failed to discover the name of the ingenious designer of this system.

Not far below the Bong level crossing was a major canal civil works in progress: a fall being built under the auspices of the Punjab Irrigation Department. Work that began in May 1998 was nearing completion and it was proudly pointed out that it had been executed in record time. This project was warranted by the reduction of silt in the water which, having a certain silt-carrying capacity, will begin scouring out the bed of the waterway to maintain its quantum of silt. This quantum in the UJC fell after the damming of the Jhelum at Mangla with the consequent scouring action leading to an undermining of the various civil works on the canal. The fall, after it is commissioned in February 1999, will flatten the slope and reduce the speed of flow to cut down on scouring.

Such a major project would have warranted closure that would mean depriving the canal-commanded area of irrigation. So they dug a diversion to allow the canal to roll on uninterrupted. Next came the tedious task of pumping the bed clear of water to a depth of almost fifty metres before the foundations could be put in. And now, barely eight months after having begun, the department can compliment itself on a task well done.

If the Bong level crossing was impressive, the one at Jatlan with the bigger Suketar Nalla is even more so. Designed to pass a maximum of 133,000 cusecs the regulator across the Suketar is imposing with its thirty-three gates. And if I had conjured up images of excitement at the Bong crossing, this one had seen near calamity at the peak of the monsoon season in July 1920 when the Suketar swelled up with 211,042 cusecs. Again during the floods of 1976 it once peaked at 160,000 cusecs – both times thankfully without mishap.

There are procedures to follow in an emergency. These had been meticulously formulated by the British designers of these fascinating contraptions and were displayed at all sites along the canal. Not many years after independence, benighted as we are, we lost sight of reality and condemned knowledge of English as anti-ideology. With superannuation replacing the old guard literate in English with the new English-illiterate staff, the displayed instructions became redundant. And since floods did not occur every day, the procedures were slowly permitted to recede into forgetfulness.

One day Mahmood ul Hassan rang the bell to see if his staff knew what each man was supposed to do in the event of a flood crisis. Only vague memory of actual procedures remained and the men tripped over each other. The good man ordered an Urdu translation of the Standing Operating Procedures to be displayed thence onward. Given the national aversion to the printed word, I wonder how many of the staff care to read that page or so of instructions. Perhaps the next major flood in any one of the cross-torrents will rouse the sleeping giant of the irrigation bureaucracy to the need of training in procedures for the staff.

At the village of Rehmanpur the second and lesser Suketar crosses the UJC and we left the territory of Azad Kashmir to enter Punjab. I was reminded yet again that we were travelling down the only Punjab canal that flowed part of the way through Kashmir.

In Lahore Suleman had instructed me to ride the pontoon ferries that have been operating since the canal was first built in the second decade of the 20th century. The first of the three was on the bank opposite to us with no one about to bring it over. This one, Mahmood pointed out, had been established on public demand after independence. Now, when the British established a facility, they provided staff with it. But the Pakistan government, forever starving for cash, had been kind enough only to provide the ferry for people to operate themselves. We waited for thirty minutes with no one turning up on the far bank to bring the pontoon around to our side before eventually giving up.

The second ferry operates below Rehmanpur. But when we arrived there we learnt that reduced flow in the canal (because of falling reservoir level at Mangla it was flowing at 5300 cusecs) had beached the raft so fast that even four men could not lift it free. The third, some kilometres further downstream, had developed a leak in one of the pontoons and had been unserviceable for some months. The raft was to be repaired during the annual three-week closure (due three days after my journey). Until then, the women of a nearby village were using it as an oversized washboard.

We did not pause at the Rehmanpur level crossing but made straight for Juggu, which is also the site of the now crumbling rest house abandoned after the establishment of the canal housing colony in nearby Serai Alamgir. Surrounded by tall trees its isolation must have once

Laundry time as women use one of the pontoon ferries as an oversized washboard.

made it a right romantic place. But now hay was stacked in the verandas whose arches were cracked and sagging. In the backyard guinea fowls, turkeys and chickens scratched about in the soggy earth and from somewhere a concealed peacock called. A short distance away, in the outhouse that was once the stable, a nice looking grey was tethered. The irrigation department had leased out the establishment to a gentleman who introduced himself as Taqui. He apologised for being unable to offer us hospitality on account of the fast and we politely made some noises about there being another time to avail of his kindness.

Juggu being the fourth and last level crossing on the UJC was also the last place where flow could be regulated. If ever a flood at Juggu caught the crew napping, the flood would pass down the UJC as a possible and serious peril. And that is what happened one day in July 1967. Mahmood ul Hassan Siddiqui, an officer of the old school (now retired) who served in the Jhelum irrigation division over the years in various positions remembers the telephone call in his office at Jhelum. The gauge at the Serai Alamgir bridge was reading eleven feet of water as against the stipulated ten, the alarmed caller said.

'As if I had received an electric shock, I jumped out of my seat, got into my car and sped off even forgetting to take my driver along,' recalls

Siddiqui.

By the time he arrived, the UJC was washing over the rails of the railway bridge. He was downstream of the last level crossing; the only way to reduce flow was to let the canal drain into any of the fifteen minor channels that take off direct from the UJC between Serai Alamgir and its outfall into the Chenab at Khanki. He opened the gates of the nearer ones and telephoned his sub-divisional officer at Rasul to drive up the canal undoing the ones on his way. Next Siddiqui drove upstream to the Juggu level crossing only to discover that all was in order. The crew was all present, the gauge was steady at just below the designated level, and everything looked fine.

Cloudbursts and flash floods in the Pabbi hills are not an unknown phenomenon. Siddiqui concluded that a sudden and massive fall of rain somewhere in the hills had brought down a swift flood that had passed into the level crossing and finding the gates of the Nalla side closed, drained down the canal. So rapid and short-lived was this passage of the flood that the gauge, which is simply a stepped masonry well with a foot ruler painted on one wall, simply could not register the rise. However, swift action on the part of Mahmood ul Hassan Siddiqui had saved the day.

Within sight of Serai Alamgir we paused at the Aurangabad siphon. This one was completely washed out in a violent flood in August 1960 and had to be re-built. Seeing the slimy trickle passing through it, it was difficult to imagine that there could be so great a flood in this rivulet that it could wash out a structure as sturdy as the siphon. But it has happened and had the department not undertaken the building of the fall between Bong and Jatlan, the reconstruction of this siphon would have been the greatest civil work undertaken on the UJC since commissioning.

The exciting part of the canal was behind us. All that remained to be seen was the power station at Rasul that is run by water from the UJC. Sunday is a quiet day for such places, but it was quieter yet for it was not generating because of reduced flow. I was reminded that it being a 'secret installation' I should keep my camera away. The man in charge was hyperactive and garrulous. He wanted me to descend into the cavern below to see the turbines. I was interested in the generation machinery, the gauges and the two huge black chutes down which 3600 cusecs of water wash to drive the two generators to produce twenty-two megawatts. A display showed several things about the power station. Among others, it said it had cost just over two million rupees to build.

We were offered overnight accommodation at the lovely Rasul rest house so that on the morrow we may follow the canal to its tail at Khanki. But I had expended all my film and it was dull and looked like rain. Moreover, from Rasul onwards there were no exciting structures to see, no emergencies to imagine and feel the surge of adrenaline. We declined. It was time to go home.

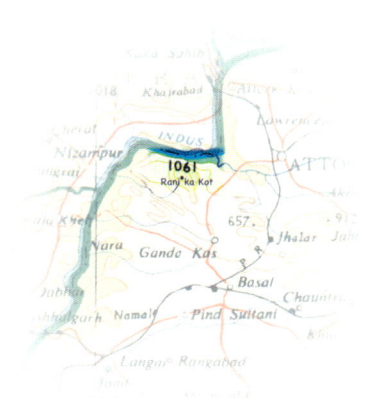

Gariala nestling in the folds of the Kala Chitta hills.

Fort with a view

For a sleepy little village with a population no more than four hundred – and that also tucked away in a remote corner of Punjab, Sojhanda – 'Hundred Flags,' is an evocative name. Lying in a bowl smack on the Sindhu River about twenty-five kilometres due west of the town of Attock, the village is surrounded by the dark *sanatha* (*Dodonea viscosa*) covered slopes of the Kala Chitta hills on three sides. To the west flows the mighty Sindhu. Though locals have no tradition regarding the name, I imagine it was here in some forgotten age that a renegade chieftain or a freebooter on the run might have staked out a claim, very likely for a brief while. In my imagination I see him marking out his claim with a profusion of flags on the surrounding slopes and giving rise to the name.

SEA MONSTERS AND THE SUN GOD

What we know for a certainty is that the year 1221 saw a great flurry of activity as Jalal ud Din Khwarazm found refuge in these hills. The epic battle, in which Chengez Khan the Mongol defeated the Khwarazmian, was fought near the village of Nizampur across the river in Nowshera district. There the defeated Muslim king shamefully abandoned his family to the savagery of the Mongols and fled across the river to hide in the gorges of the Kala Chitta waiting for stragglers from the battlefield to join him. Thereafter he took another ancient road that follows the river southward. But that's another tale.

The one hundred and forty kilometre stretch of river in Attock district has at least ten ferries that have been in use from times immemorial. Being in the vicinity of the wild and broken Kala Chitta hills that have long been a favourite haunt of fugitive outlaws, these ferries have recently been closed in order to prevent free passage between Punjab and the Frontier Province. While these ferries are barely known outside the district, that of Bagh Nilab features repeatedly in history from the 11th century onwards as an alternate to the crossing at Hund that operates to this day some forty kilometres north of Nilab. From each one of these ferries, there ran a connecting road to the major highways in the Salt Range to the east.

One of the now disused ferries was that of Sojhanda. From remote antiquity trade, culture and religion crossing the river at this point meandered through the narrow gorges of the Kala Chitta to the village of Chhoi (on the Attock-Basal highroad) whence a traveller could head either southeast for Kallar Kahar, the great junction of ancient highways, or east for Taxila. On this little explored ancient route from Sojhanda to Chhoi, I was repeatedly told on two previous visits, lay Rani ka Kot – the Fort of the Rani. And so my ever-smiling and talkative friend Rehmat Khan Khattak of Sojhanda having placed me in the care of the guide Amir Mohammed walked us to the edge of the village to bid us Godspeed as we set out on the long walk to Rani ka Kot.

Past the village of Ghora Mar (another evocative name) we left the tarmac road and struck out in a south-easterly direction. At the hamlet of Gariala we stopped to talk to two elderly men. Yes, this village did indeed lie on an ancient and busy highroad, said one. Beyond the village in the area called Bazaar Kandao there were, until not many years ago, ruins of an ancient bazaar and some houses. That, he said, was where the caravans tarried. We hurried through the village with the grizzled pair in tow but I was warned of disappointment. Recently the ruined foundations, said the man, had all been levelled and building material removed to make room for agriculture.

Stories of buried treasures abounded. One of the patriarchs said he had spent all his life digging because he believed some of the passing caravans would surely have interred their valuables during an attack by roving bandits that infested these hills. All he could show for his labours were some badly worn copper coins, three inexpensive earrings and a few beads. He had found an anvil once. A real hefty piece, he said, somewhat bigger than all modern anvils that he now saw. This he had sold to an ironmonger in Attock. Arrow and spearheads turned up every now and then, all of which were discarded as useless.

The legend I had heard two years ago was related afresh: the ranis of the fort, whose raja's name is not given, and who seem to come from an unusual ancient feminist world, sent out a plundering expedition against the township of Gariala. The expedition had the express orders of keeping the flag aloft. Any lowering of it would be taken as a sign of defeat by the ranis watching from their hilltop fortress who, rather than face a life of defeat and ignominy, would then fling themselves to their deaths below.

Though the expedition from Rani ka Kot was successful, the commander, merely in order to test if the ranis would actually carry out their suicidal pledge, lowered the flag. And sure enough the ranis one after the other started to jump off the sheerest part of the fortress. A relay set across the intervening gorges screamed out the beginning of the catastrophe and the prank-pulling commander hastily raised the flag just in time to prevent the remainder from leaping to their deaths as well. Amir Mohammed did not know how the prankster general was punished after his return to base.

Like all such legends this too was made out as the good fight between the Hindu ranis and the Muslim folk of Gariala. Another version, however, talks of just one rani, Kokla by name, who was contemporaneous with Raja Rasalu, the great demon-slaying hero of Punjabi legends known to have lived in the 1st century BCE. In this one, the queen did not jump to her death but had a passionate affair with Rasalu.

Beyond Gariala Amir Mohammed pointed out the 'five-foot road' with its berms clearly marked out by dressed stones. That, he said, had been built by the *angrez*. I knew otherwise. But the collective memory of this area extends only as far as British Raj and everything is attributed to the *angrez*. He could not imagine that this road had been in use perhaps a millennium before the Vikings first contemplated sailing across the North Sea to the land of the Angles who painted themselves blue to go to war. He said his grandfather had spoken of having worked on the building of this road. This time-frame and the name five-foot road probably mean that some zealous Deputy Commissioner of the Raj ordered improvement of the path.

Through thickly growing *sanatha*, we marched on going gradually higher and higher. At one point the five-foot road bore off to the left while we took the narrow path to the right. The *sanatha* was now so thick that it all but obliterated the path and brushed against our faces. About an hour and a half out of Gariala, we made it to the top of a narrow pass and Amir pointed out the hill of the fortress rising sharply in front. If anything, Rani ka Kot perched on the crest of the hill was an eagle's eyrie of a castle. The final two hundred metres of the slope facing us rose to the crest in a straight wall devoid of vegetation and I could almost see the disconsolate ranis leaping off to their deaths.

The five-foot road passes under the northern

Looking northeast from what remains of the bastion of Rani ka Kot.

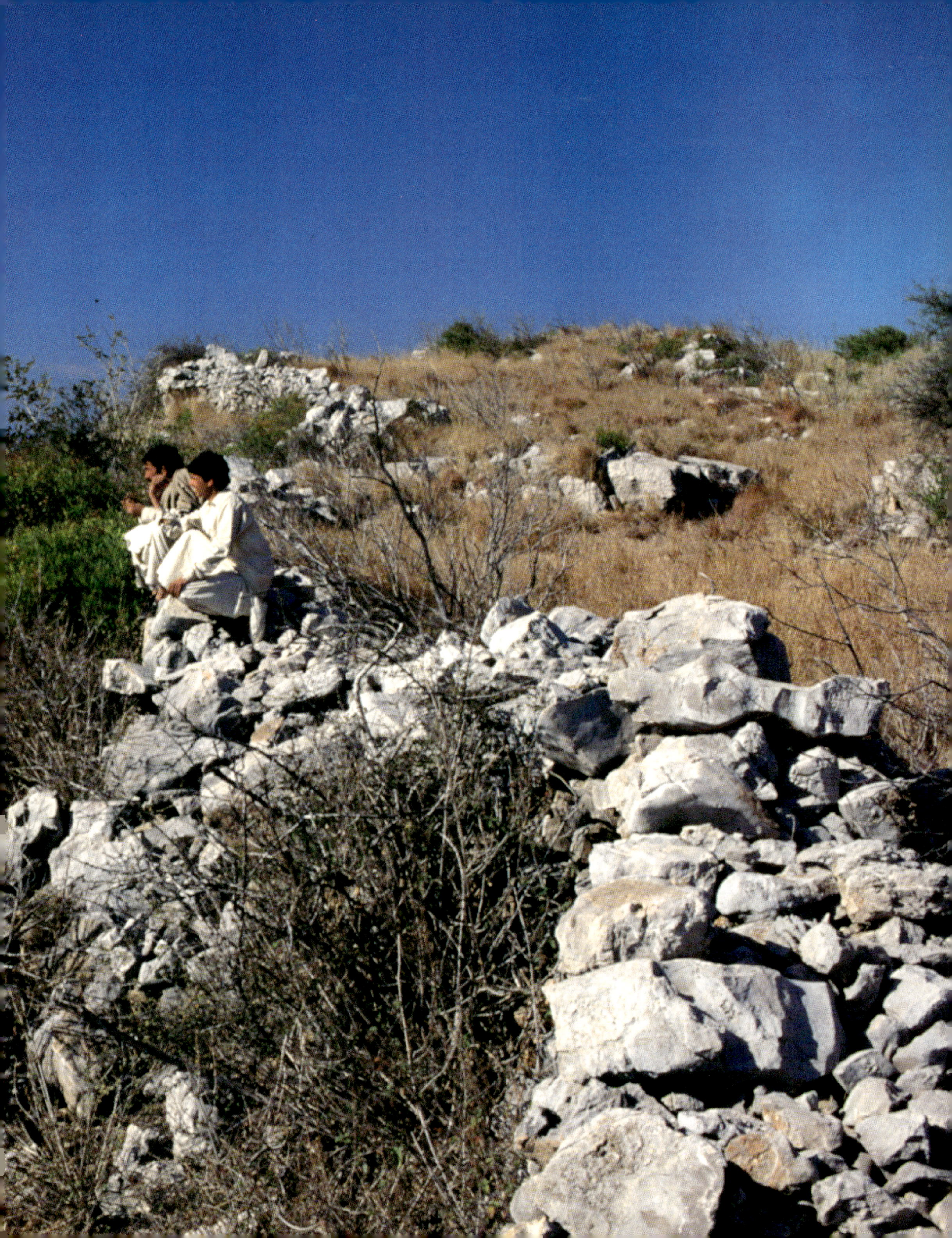

flank of the hill of the fortress, while we took the easier route up by the path on the south. Amir Khan said we would come athwart of the fortification wall – or whatever remained of it. This because they built, so he explained, 'the fortification only where assault was possible.' There was therefore no fortification above the sheer, hard-to-climb slopes, he said.

Two and a half hours after setting out of Gariala we were on the 1060 metre high hill within the walls of Rani ka Kot. Built by piling up dressed and undressed stones, without the use of mortar, the walls are now less than half a metre high and no more than fifty centimetres wide. But clearly they snaked around the highest flat part of the wind-swept hill enclosing no less than four square kilometres. The views all around were stupendous: to the north and west the sandy banks and blue-green water of the Sindhu could be seen; on all other sides the hills fell away to broken, torrent-scoured land sprinkled with tiny hamlets. An invader, whichever directions he approached from, would have been spotted a full day before he could assault Rani ka Kot.

There are some other foundations as well marking living quarters and the ground is liberally strewn with pottery shards most of which are the neck and lip of the traditional water pitcher. Some of these I inspected in the hope of telltale dating features. But my untrained eye saw none and I opted against taking any of them home to be checked out by archaeologist friends in Lahore – a decision that I was to rue later. My escort said coins were occasionally found on this hill. But sadly the people of Gariala seemed incapable of comprehending the importance of such finds because through indifference the coins were lost again.

Amir asked if the fortress could have been built by the *angrez*. I told him the *angrez* was yet a savage when this fortress was guarding the highroad that passed under its northern flank. Clearly that was its main function. I told him too that caravans benighted on these forested slopes would have stopped here for the night. And that the coins they occasionally found were perhaps reminders of those sojourners. Of course Rani ka Kot also doubled as a safe haven for some long-forgotten king who would have repaired to its vantage in the event of impending attack. But certainly it was not a residential fort, as they believed. Clearly the reason was the scarcity of water.

When did all that happen? They had no coins from Rani ka Kot to show. And those found at Gariala were all badly worn. Moreover, no archaeologist has thus far visited this site. Therefore there is no expert opinion. But as the fort lies athwart of an ancient route, I presume it has been there for a very long time. The question of how long can only be answered when the coins and pottery of Rani ka Kot are preserved and passed on to the experts.

GREEKS IN PUKHTUNKHWA

Revellers in Chowk Bazaar.

Greeks in Pukhtunkhwa

Upon taking over as the Deputy Commissioner of Bannu in the Northwest Frontier Province, my friend Jehanzeb Khan called me. Here was a city, perhaps the only one in the entire country, said he, whose old quarter was still circled by a wall punctuated with gates. These gates, I was told, were shut every day at sunset until the following morning – just as it would have happened in a past forgotten by most of us. It sounded like a town that had been left alone by the soul-destroying march of time and immediately a vision formed: thick, high town wall behind which rose tower houses of timber lattices and gloriously carved wooden balconies and doors, shuttered windows and rooftop parapets with lotus-shaped corner adornments. All closely packed together to look like the finest of all subcontinental walled cities.

Yet it took me two years to get to Bannu. The town wall is there all right. Some three metres

59

high, it is constructed entirely of the brick that was introduced to us by civil engineers of the Raj and that we still assiduously employ. The gate posts, topped by domes and finials too are constructed of the same bricks. But neither the wall nor the gate-houses possess the hoariness that I was expecting. They are, wall and every single gate-house, disappointingly new. Indeed, behind the city wall the old part, that European travellers would have called the 'native' part of town, is set out in grids, a layout that we of the subcontinent had forgotten after the downfall of the great cities of Moen jo Daro and Harappa.

The Aryan nomads who poured into the subcontinent as the great cities were dying of old age did not know town planning. They arranged their tents haphazardly around the tent or waggon of their leader and when they began to settle in the subcontinent they followed the same pattern. Their cities were random growths radiating outward from the central hub. The order of the grid layout was lost until it had to be re-taught to us by the Greeks in the 3rd century BCE. This we soon forgot again in order that the British might re-introduce this 'innovation' that our ancestors had known eight thousand and more years ago.

If the grid layout was disappointing, the houses of Bannu were more so. Lining the narrow, busy bazaars, they rose through two or

The interior of an inn near Phoori Gate. It serves as a carpenter's workshop.

three storeys of concrete plainness. Carved balconies, lattice windows, façades embellished with flowing curvilinear forms in stucco, and frescoes in cool interiors were singularly absent. There was only a newish austerity bordering on ugliness. The only embellishment was the bathroom tile exterior on a building or two. If architecture is an index of character, here was one of extreme dourness and poverty of the soul. Thinking we were not really in the right part of town, I annoyed my guide by repeatedly asking to be taken to the 'old quarter.' He repeatedly asserted that we *were* in the old city until eventually losing his cool and screaming at me.

At length, having walked every street in that part of town, I concluded that Bannu is a city absolutely, entirely devoid of any architectural pretensions whatsoever. It was as if as a community the people of Bannu were bereft of architectural aesthetics. For them houses were simply to be unattractive concrete blocks only to be lived in without bringing pleasure and joy to the spirit. Here functionability was not to be wedded to beauty as in, say, Shikarpur or Chiniot.

Of the ten gates that surround the old quarter, Lakki Gate is named after the town of Lakki Marwat in the southeast, while Preedy (pronounced Praiti) is named after some British civil servant. Qasaban Gate, they said, is so called after the butchers whose shops once lined the bazaar just inside. There is a Phoori Gate whose origin remains uncertain. The gates Sokarri, Miryan, Huwaid and Mundan are all named after villages in whose direction they face. The self-evident Railway Gate looks in the direction of the now defunct railway station. Standing outside the derelict building, its walls plastered with ugly graffiti and posters, I found myself wondering if a hundred years from now the Bannuchis (as they call themselves) will at all remember that time was when their city was connected to the main railway network by the Narrow Gauge line to Mari Indus one hundred and thirty kilometres away.

Taking up to nine hours for the journey, the service was far too slow to compete with road transport that took at most three hours. With little freight to haul, the line was a constant drain on railway resources and was closed in the early 1990s. The derelict station was now a dusty playground for local children. Sooner or later the building will be auctioned, torn down and replaced by an ugly, characterless concrete block. Then only the name of Railway Gate will remind Bannuchis that their city once had a railway connection.

Of the ten gates of Bannu that comprised of heavy planking reinforced with steel braces on the inside and steel plates outside, all, save two, have been burnt down. In the two that survive, the planking is heavily charred. Adjacent to each gate, inside the city wall, was a police post that too was given up to arson. It all happened late last year[*] when a young boy, rejecting the gay overtures of a policeman, was shot dead in cold blood by the frustrated suitor. The town erupted in righteous indignation. A week later, when the gunfire and the flicker of arsonists' fires died down, the gates and with them the police posts had all been burnt down and a few lives had been lost. So violent was the disorder that Bannu

---

* This would be 1998.

was placed under curfew – the first ever, they say, in its long history.

In its week-long disturbance the city had destroyed an integral part of its culture, its very *zeitgeist*: the gates that were closed daily to prevent passage after sunset. From the minute I set my eyes on the scorched or missing gates, one question rankled: why should anyone wish to destroy something like their city gates? In the four days I spent trying to discover old Bannu I found my answer. Nobody belonged to the city. Ask anyone and they will tell you they come from the mountains of Waziristan or from some village in the neighbourhood of town. No one, so it appears, is native to Bannu. And by that relationship, Bannu perhaps does not belong to anyone.

I became increasingly aware of this alienation between the city and her children when I asked why there were no beautiful old buildings. Always the answer was a dismissive reference to the juvenescence of Bannu. For most people it was a city established in the late 1840s after Lieutenant Herbert Edwardes (who gave his name to that first-class alma mater in Peshawar) first arrived as a revenue collector on behalf of the inept Daleep Singh, son of the great Maharaja Ranjit Singh. In pointing out that the part designated the 'old city' was still sometimes referred to as Edwardesabad, there was the oblique reference that earlier there was no city on the site, even less the name of Bannu. Similarly the sprawling mud fort of Daleepgarh, ordered by Edwardes and now held by the Pakistan army, too was said to have been built on virgin land. Indeed, both fort and city stand on flat ground, not on the eminences of earlier habitations.

Was it then really because Bannu did not exist until the middle of the 19th century that it has neither an architectural culture nor a population that calls it its own?

From classical writers we know of the great 'Royal Road' that existed as early as the 4th century BCE. Leaving its eastern terminus of Patliputra (Patna), winding across the great Gangetic plain one of its branches crossed the Sindhu at Kalabagh and followed the valley of the Kurram River in which Bannu is situated. Though the busier road bore north from the Salt Range to Taxila and crossed the Sindhu at Hund (Swabi district), a reasonable amount of traffic went along this southern route as well and it was only natural for a town and a staging post to arise. On pain of being screamed at again, I delivered this song and dance to my guide.

'*Voh yara ji!*' he said, 'If that is what you want to see, you say so.'

He drove me out some ten kilometres southwest of town to the famous mounds of Akra outside the village of Bhurt. The main mound rises some thirty metres above the picturesque fertile plain portioned out in neat squares of cultivation with a meandering stream cutting through it. Together with its auxiliary mounds Akra sprawls over nearly thirty acres. Finds of coins ranging from 3rd century BCE Bactrian Greek issues through the Kushans and Ghaznavid kings down to those of Shams ud Din Iyultimish of Delhi represent the age of Akra. In 400 CE Faxian, a Buddhist monk from

Bannu railway station. Until about 1991, the narrow gauge train operated out of Bannu for Tank on one side and Mari Indus across the Sindhu River on the other. At the time of this visit, the line was in the process of being uprooted. If not already, the station will soon enough be auctioned, razed and replaced, very likely, by a tawdry shopping mall.

China, having come through the mountains crossed a country whose name he rendered Pona in Chinese phonetics. Linguists believe Pona signifies Bannu, a belief reinforced by the fact that Faxian tells us the country lay three days journey west of the 'Sintu' River.

We also know that in 645 CE on his return journey from India the ever so delightful Chinese pilgrim Xuanzang paused in a city whose name he rendered Falana from, it is believed, Varna or Varnu. This name we first hear of from Panini the great scholar who lived in Taxila in the 6th century BCE. In the two and a half centuries between Faxian and Xuanzang, Buddhism had suffered greatly. While the former had found three thousand priests engaged in the service of their lord, the latter could record only three hundred in Falana. Buddhist temples, Xuanzang observed, had been taken over by heretics and the religion was in decline as a result of the depredations of the savage Huns under Tor Aman and his son Mehr Gul just a hundred years earlier.

This densely populated and fertile country, our pilgrim tells us, was vassal to the kingdom of Kabul. The people, some of whom were

Buddhists, were 'rough and fierce [and] persevering in their habits, but their purposes are low.' This last observations surely hints at the thieving propensities of the people, reference to which we find again in early British travellers. Xuanzang furthermore tells us that they 'did not care about literature or the arts* and their language was 'somewhat like that of mid-India' signifying that it was certainly not Pukhtu. In the 7th century CE Bannu must have formed the western limit of an older version of Seraiki that is still spoken as little as thirty kilometres to the eastward. The kingdom of Falana, we are told, was almost eleven hundred kilometres in circuit, most certainly an exaggeration. But the city itself, writes the pilgrim, was only ten kilometres around.

Having suffered the great setback of Hunnic raids, Varnu, as it might have been called when it flourished on the site of Akra, went into decline. The death blow came from the plundering raids of Mahmud Ghaznavi. Thereafter it took just another two hundred years for the city to be abandoned to the dust. The new city that grew up under the ancient name was a little way off on the banks of the Kurram River and from some early accounts appears to have been a collection of fortified houses – much like those seen even today in the tribal belt of the province.

That was what Babur would have conquered in 1505. This was long before he had looked upon himself as an empire builder and was merely a far-ranging freebooter. Having defeated the Khattak and Bangash tribes of Kohat, Hangu and Thal and raised piles of their severed heads, he set upon the 'Kiwi' Pukhtuns of Bannu. The slaughter was horrendous, and yet more skull pillars were erected until Shadi Khan, the Kiwi headman, came into Babur's presence in the Pukhtun posture of submission: without his weapons and with a tuft of grass stuffed in his mouth to signify that he was but cattle for the victorious Mughal.

It was this same collection of forts that Edwardes levelled in 1848 and laid out the walled city of the ten gates that took his name. The *Imperial Gazetteer of India* records that it was after the establishment of Edwardesabad that trade and commerce that was headquartered in neighbouring Bazaar Ahmed Khan moved into the new town. Now but a nondescript village, an interesting light is cast on this business entrepot by two early 19th century maps. Thomson's map of 1817 and Allen's of 1842 do not register Bannu on the highroad from Punjab to Ghazni, rather Bazaar Ahmed Khan which was where all passing caravans would have broken journey. Not being the result of physical surveys, these maps included place names familiar to travellers from whom the cartographers gleaned their information. Bazaar Ahmed Khan the bustling commercial centre thus made its way to the maps while the khaki cluster of mud forts called Bannu that was bypassed by the caravans went unnoticed. In Bazaar Ahmed Khan lived the wealthy merchant class while neighbouring Bannu was the military headquarters that invaders would have aimed to neutralise before the richer prize could be theirs.

After British intervention, trade would understandably have shifted to the newly laid

---

* Talk about perseverance! Their houses show that the Bannuchis have faithfully abided by this trait to the present day.

out town and since the volume of business is represented by the number of caravansaries a town can boast of, I was not disappointed. The bazaar inside Phoori Gate flaunted some half a dozen inns built in the traditional eastern style with high, arched gateways leading into large courtyards lined on two sides with small cubicles. The rooms were either single or double-storeyed, the latter having a woodwork balcony with rooms set behind a veranda.

The legend above the gateway of one of these revealed the ownership and the year of construction: Chaudhri Deep Chund Chawla, September 1891. Now every single one of the inns are carpenters' workshops. With the development along the Grand Trunk Road, trade through Bannu was seriously effected until it died out after independence when the sizable Hindu population that controlled it left the city – the children of Mr Chawla surely among them. In the context of trade Bannu was relegated to the status of a backwater. So many years have passed since the inns have been redundant and put to other use that none but the older residents remember seeing them frequented by travellers. These disused caravansaries are, nonetheless, reminders of a time when trade and commerce did indeed pass through the city.

Jehanzeb Khan, my friend the DC, had said that the older people of Bannu sometimes called their city 'Bannu Gul' – the Rose. In 1826 Charles Masson, that enigmatic deserter of the East India Company army, also noticed the phrase 'my own dear Bannu' being frequently used. But that is passé, changed by the new materialistic sensibilities of the end of the millennium. Now there is only a detachment from the city. To me it appears to be a misreading of history that has impressed upon every mind the newness of Bannu: it has no hoary past to be proud of; it was only established a century and a half ago. This impression was not helped when in August 1947 Bannu was, according to a Revenue Department official, virtually emptied of its population.

This misconception also arises from our national lack of reading. Those few who do read, confine themselves entirely to the superficial district gazetteers. Consequently stories are invented. Not strange then that I was told that the Pukhtuns being invincible, Babur had never invaded Bannu. Even stranger – and something they could rightly be proud of, they did not know that while neighbouring districts were yielding to the army of that upstart Nadir Kuli of the Turkish tribe of Kirklu a.k.a. Nadir Shah and subsequently Ahmed Shah, it was only the Bannuchis who put up a most resolute resistance. Forgotten too were the depredations of the Sikhs under Ranjit Singh who, unable to annex Bannu, mounted periodic plundering raids that went under the euphemism of 'tax collection.'

I was in Bannu at the wrong time of year for my friend Jehanzeb Khan had said the festivals of Eid were special occasions. Nowhere but in Bannu, it was said, could one see such exuberant revelry. Nevertheless, there was the festivity of Chowk Bazaar to be seen that takes place every evening round the year, but in the month of Moharram. In the tradition of Bannu this gala is the bridegroom's wedding celebration. On the day of his wedding a man is required to bring to this bazaar as many friends and acquaintances (men only, of course) as he can boast of. Then, adorned with garlands, the men give themselves over to an orgy of confectionery eating that leaves them rather in a state of stupor.

True to their frontier tradition, the men wore their rose and marigold garlands across their chests like bandoleers: over one shoulder and under the other arm. Others wore them around their foreheads. They jostled, laughed and played the fool as the cardboard boxes of sweetmeats were passed around. Then the drum and pipe music struck up and each group led by its beaming groom surrounded by dancing, flower-bedecked friends went its merry way. As I watched, I suddenly recognised in this very innocent carnival the traces of an ancient Bacchanalian spree of garlands, dance and music. Only women were missing and the orgy of drinking was replaced with ordinary confectionery.

Here was a tradition whose earliest echoes lie buried under the layers of dust smothering ancient Akra of the Bactrian Greeks. At that time wine would have flowed as freely as the little cardboard boxes of *gulab jamun* and *burfi*. Perhaps *bhung* would have been used at another time, but then Islamic sensibilities required the banishment of intoxicants. No one could tell me how ancient the nightly festival of Chowk Bazaar was, but they all said it had always been a part of the city's culture. And here was a facet that the Bannuchis were clearly very proud of. Unknown to them, this was their one living connection with a past otherwise forgotten, and I found it very odd that early British writers should have missed commenting on such a lively and unique festival.

One of the last few buildings that can boast of any age at all, it preserves the fine taste of some well-to-do Bannuite of yore. The picture having been taken in April 1999, it is more likely than not that this fine building has already been pulled down and replaced by a characterless blockhouse.

The disappointment of the beginning was finally redeemed. Bannu did indeed have a connection with hoary history. Only her children had forgotten the past and lost their sense of belonging. Perhaps time will change that once again.

Punjabi Bazaar where all the old timber fittings on store fronts have been replaced by tin shuttering.

Chinar City

I arrived late in Parachinar. About twenty years too late. It was once among the most picturesque towns in Pakistan, and certainly *the* most charming little place in Pukhtunkhwa. But now it is almost as ugly as any old city. But it did match the mental picture I had of a town surrounded by vast numbers of Oriental Plane (*chinar*) trees. While the streets of the old town afford no room for trees, the broad avenues of the newer part laid out by the British after annexation in the last years of the 19th century, are all shaded by what I love to believe is the subcontinental cousin of the Canadian maple.*

---

* After publication of this piece which I had then titled 'Maple City' Rohil Nana, my late and much lamented environmentalist friend, called to say the two trees are different genera.

The Governor's House.

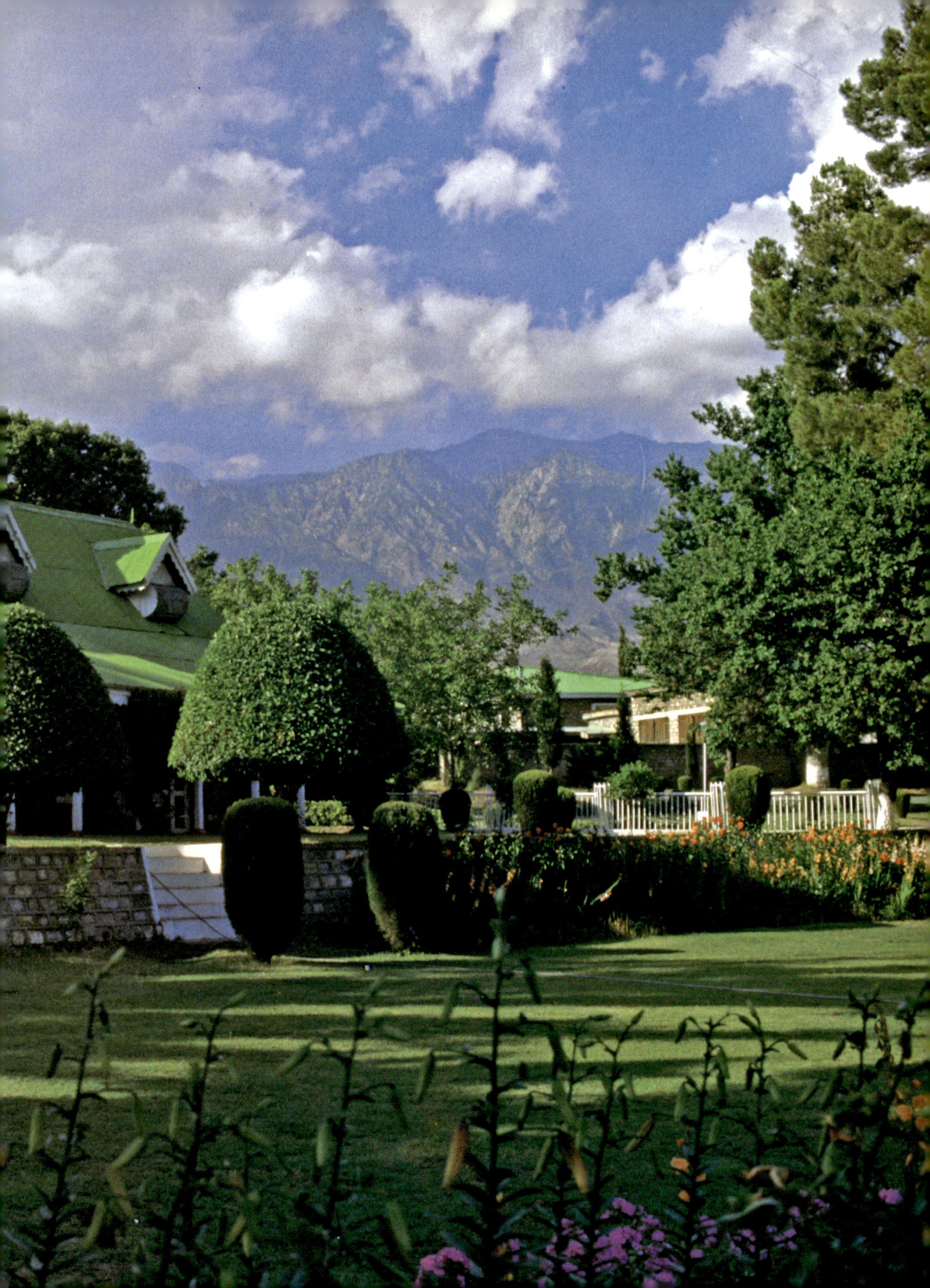

Though its height of about 1700 metres above the sea makes Parachinar a delightful summer retreat, the thing of beauty here once was the exquisite woodwork of its buildings. Here were two or three-storeyed houses with timber and wrought iron balconies screened by wooden latticework so that no outsider may lay eyes upon the women of the household. Here were store fronts protected not by the roll-up, roll-down ugly steel shutters that we now know, but by broad wooden slats, intricately carved on the outside that went one above the other into slots to close the arched doorway. The doorways, made of seasoned timber, were wooden pillars of Mughal design rising up to multi-cusped arches whose spandrels were adorned with the rosette, a common enough feature of vernacular architectural embellishment.

In the mid-1970s came the inflow of petro-dollars from the Gulf and things started to change as people with money and no understanding of architectural beauty carried out crude renovations. Catastrophe, however, struck in February 1980 when fire broke out in a store in Punjabi Bazaar, the busiest commercial centre of Parachinar. No one knows what exactly happened. Some believe it was an electrical malfunction; others are of the view that it was a minor explosion in an Afghan refugee's establishment. Once the fire began, it was fed by the very woodwork that was the aspect of beauty in Parachinar.

Everyone remembers how the fire raged uncontrolled for almost twelve hours in a town that did not possess any fire-fighting facility. Though owners tried to remove what they could, the conflagration, when it finally burnt itself out, had destroyed goods and property worth millions of rupees. There was, fortunately, no loss of life, but the blaze had completely destroyed more than half of the once picturesque bazaar. When reconstruction began it only threw up ugly concrete blockhouses with flimsy steel windows and, where the owner could afford, bathroom tile façades. Gone were the wrought iron balconies and lattice blinds, gone the Mughal arches and pillars rendered in timber, gone, too, were the intricately carved doorways.

In Parachinar I was introduced to Abbas Ali Turi: in his early thirties, middle height, slim, long-haired and bearded with a tranquil air about him and a degree in graphic design from Lahore's National College of Arts. An artist from the very depth of his soul, caught in provincial Parachinar with no market for his skills, he was teaching in the local government school. A gentle restlessness and the dreamy, far-away look in his eyes gave away that he was not altogether at peace with his world. But family obligations put him where he was while he yearned to be in Islamabad or Lahore where he could work the craft that nature had bestowed upon him and that he had trained four years to hone. To keep his sanity he painted in a small Spartan studio on the top floor of his father's restaurant in Punjabi Bazaar. Parachinar, as I was to know it in the next five days, was the one that Abbas introduced me to.

The Parachinar of his childhood was a walled city with four gates. The two, Man Singh and Ather Singh gates were named after prosperous local merchants, while Shingak and Thal gates were named respectively after the towns in whose direction they faced. Abbas remembers

Remains of the fabled chinar tree under which the Para Chamkani elders met.

the eventual pulling down of the gates in the early 1970s when the town started to expand and spill outside the walls. The great event about that time was the arrival of the first television set in town and how it mystified the people: a radio that showed pictures was beyond the imagination of many. Soon afterwards, some restaurateurs acquired television sets and put them in separate rooms to charge half a rupee for a customer to come in and watch the tripe. Naturally a cup of tea enhanced the indulgence of the novelty and the first ones to install TV sets did pretty good business.

The great fire of 1980 in Punjabi Bazaar is still fresh in his memory. With it hordes of people from adjoining villages had descended on Parachinar to take advantage of the chaos. They came not to help put out the fire and offer assistance, Abbas explained, but to take advantage of the victims' plight and plunder what they could lay their hands on. When it was over, Punjabi Bazaar was rebuilt, but the neighbouring Khwar Bazaar suffered from a conflagration two years later.

'We don't know if it was set alight on purpose or otherwise,' says Abbas sarcastically.

He points out that the two bazaars lying at right angles to each other have interesting names. Punjabi Bazaar, so called because before independence nearly all of its traders were Punjabi Hindus and Sikhs, was the more prosperous of the two. Consequently the other one was called Khwar (Wretched) Bazaar in comparison. Its other name, he says, was Kurmi after the Kurram River that waters the valley of Parachinar.

Though most of the Punjabi traders had left Parachinar long before Abbas was born, the name stuck fast to the bazaar. He knew, however, of one family and he took me to see young Charan Singh who runs a grocery store. Blue-eyed and fair-skinned, Charan who spoke Urdu with a heavy Pukhtu accent, could have easily passed for a Pukhtun. Beardless and turbanless, he was uncertain of the family's religious persuasion. Somewhat hesitantly he said that he was a Sikh because his family visited the shrine at Hasan Abdal. But then, he admitted, the family also visited Hindu shrines. He spoke no Punjabi. Neither could anyone else in his family, he said. Parachinar was the only home he knew and Pukhtu the only language he could comfortably speak. From all outward appearances, and so far as he was concerned, he was as good a Pukhtun as the next man.

It was a full sixty-eight years before independence, in 1879, that the masterful artifice known as the Treaty of Gandamak (after a village near Jalalabad in Afghanistan) took the Kurram Valley from the Amir of Afghanistan and made it part of British India. Two years later, the Miranzai Valley that provides access from Kohat to Thal and thence to Parachinar was taken over. In 1892, the British army under General Frederick Roberts moved in to occupy the valley of the Kurram.

That was a time when the turbulent and warlike Shia Turis, believed not to be true Pukhtuns but of Turkish extraction, had long been at loggerheads with their neighbours, the Sunni Bangash. Though the struggle between the Turis and the Bangash appears to have been for possession of the best agricultural land, the fact that the former were staunch Shias to a man, and the latter Sunnis, gave their conflict a sectarian complexion. Local lore asserts that the Turis wearying of the endless strife invited the British to take Kurram Valley under their control. This is confirmed in Olaf Caroe's book *The Pathans* with the hint that the Turis quite blackmailed the British: 'Finally the Turis' own plea that the only alternative to [British] occupation was their submission to Afghan rule led to the setting up of a loose form of administration...' And so, in 1895 Kurram became an agency directly under British control, to become one of only two tribal agencies with a land settlement and revenue system. The other being a part of Waziristan.

But that is recent history. Four thousand years before that, the Kurram Valley was known to the blue-eyed, fair-haired singers of Vedic hymns. In verse whose magnificence has never even been remotely matched by any other poetry contrived by man, they worshipped the great Sindhu River as a benevolent giver of life and prosperity. They celebrated too the lesser rivers that paid tribute to the mighty Sindhu. Among these, one was the Kramu. To know this river enough to be able to honour it, they would have journeyed through its valley as far as its junction with the Sindhu. The valley of the Kurram was therefore a travel route even in that remote age. In the 10th century CE, it formed the 'Lower' route between Lahore and Ghazni by way of Bannu, Kalabagh, and the Salt Range, while the 'Upper' was through the Khyber Pass. Henry Raverty, the erudite translator of the epic *Tabkat i Nasiri*, tells us that in the time of Subuktigin of Ghazni (late 10th century) the Kurram Valley, then pronounced Karma, was yet under the sway of the Rajput kings of Lahore. Barring the reference in the *Rig Veda*, it is the *Tabkat i Nasiri* that first mentions this place in history. But that was a time when the town of Parachinar did not exist.

The major centre in the area has been variously named in the histories as Sankuran or Shanuzan. This, according to Raverty, is the modern village of Shalozan some kilometres to the west of Parachinar on the highroad to Afghanistan via Peiwar Kotal (Pass). Set smack upon the banks of the wide, pebbly Kurram River, it is a delightfully embowered spot where myriad flowers bloom along irrigation ditches and birds sing in vast mulberry trees. It was here during the Second Afghan War that General Frederick Roberts had tarried long enough to build a house for himself and lay out a garden that is to this day known as Roberts' Garden.

Roberts, however, wasn't the first one to be attracted to this sylvan spot. In the late 12th century Taj ud Din Yalduz, the Turkish slave turned general, governed Sankuran on behalf of his king and mentor Muiz ud Din (a.k.a. Shahab ud Din Mohammed) Ghori. History relates that the Ghorid king having been murdered in his sleep by the doughty Khokhars (or was it the Gakkhars?) of the Salt Range was being carried home to be buried in Afghanistan. When his bier reached the vicinity of the capital of Yalduz, the man rode out many kilometres to escort it into Sankuran en route to Ghazni where it was eventually buried. Subsequently we hear from Taimur the Lame of his passage through this valley.

History amply demonstrates that the Kurram Valley formed an important route, but it does not name a town called Parachinar (the first *r* being a hard, palatal pronunciation) in it. My friend Abbas Ali and others assured me that this is a modern name that became popular after the setting up of the Agency. The Para Chamkani Pukhtuns living in the nearby mountains habitually held their *jirgas* under one of the most magnificent *chinar* trees here. And so it came to be Para Chinar – Plane Tree of the Para Chamkanis. It is certainly not a far-fetched story, and to substantiate it, they have an age-darkened stump of a plane tree to show right outside the offices of the Kurram Militia. Since the tree had historical value for giving the town its name, its stump was preserved after it died of natural causes.

However, before it came to be called after the Para Chamkanis, Parachinar was Tootkai – Mulberry Orchard, a name that is still popular with the older residents of town. Once again history provides support to this title for we learn that the Kurram Valley produced a respectable amount of reasonably fine silk until the beginning of the 19th century. By the time the British annexed Tootkai and gave vogue to the new place name, this trade had all but died away. Today the Government of Pakistan has a

Parachinar tea shop.

sericulture department struggling to bring back the silk-producing glory of Parachinar. But as most government endeavours go, this one, too, has nothing to show for itself, except a green signboard with white lettering announcing its presence in Parachinar.

From the 10th century CE, we returned to present times: Abbas complained of the pollution. In the 1970s, Parachinar had just two busses that had to be hand-cranked to get them going, and there were a few decrepit lorries. Now mini buses and cars vie for space with humans. The air was cleaner then, the summers were much cooler and people had no notion of electric fans in the home. Parachinar received its share of winter snow regularly in those days. And the scenery was different for the dark mass of mountain looming to the north and west, has for centuries been called either Spinghar by the Pukhtuns or Safed Koh by Persian speakers. It is a misnomer now, but once the mountain did indeed remain a glistening white the year round.

'The last two winters brought no snow to Safed Koh and now we jokingly call it Siyah Koh – the Black Mountain,' said Abbas.

Not long ago this mountain was covered with fine stands of juniper and pine, but now it is largely denuded which may have played a part in reducing winter snow. Abbas said Parachinar used to be a busy mart for timber coming out of Afghanistan – a business that has been dead for about twenty-five years now. I suspected that all of it may not have come out of Afghanistan, that some or even most of it could have been stolen from the slopes of Safed Koh.

My friend Sarwat Ali in Lahore who knew Parachinar from about the mid-1960s had instructed me to be sure to visit the Shia Jamat Khana. This, he had said, was a priceless building with excellent woodwork. He was talking of a memory more than thirty years old. Sadly, it was no longer as he remembered it. The 'renovation' had been done so long ago that Abbas did not remember anything but the dreadful building of marble mosaic floors and pillars that now stands in place of the beautiful original.

The Jamat Khana was the Shia headquarters in the sectarian riots of 1986. The nearby Sunni mosque with its single minaret was the counterpart. I had taken the gaping holes in its tall minaret as the beginnings of new windows. No, said Abbas, these are reminders of some of the rockets that had found their mark in that war. Closer inspection revealed that the minaret was completely pocked. But we could not go into the Sunni mosque because the militiamen at the entrance were paranoid about my camera and so we walked about outside examining the damage.

'We had grown up together, Shias and Sunnis, as friends, playmates, business associates,' said Abbas. 'Then suddenly one day we were enemies. It was like open war.' Of course there were examples where neighbours assured each other that they were above the madness and standing by their word did indeed remain aloof. But when a people are misguided in the name of religion, these little exponents of sanity go unnoticed. They went unheeded even in Parachinar. Sanity did not return until many good lives had been wasted. Even then it was, and still is, a somewhat uneasy peace.*

One thing that I found rather strange in Parachinar was the total absence of a social event that could be termed typical of the place. The one small garden adjoining the Political Agent's residence was deserted most of the time and the teahouses were largely peopled by older men. Young men (no question of women!) seemed to have no more to do than to walk hand in hand in the bazaars or meet in the homes to chat over tea. Parachinar must certainly be the only town of this size not even to have a cinema house.

Before they had television, Parachinar had a daily event and so Abbas took me to Radio Bagh. Now almost completely built up with only a central open lot the size of half a football field, it once was a garden complete with trees and shrubbery. Here, men congregated daily after the evening prayer. The municipality brought out a transistor radio and broadcast news and songs for the benefit of a pretty sizeable congregation of all and sundry. Then, long after the broadcast was over, men would lounge around in groups and chat. But then along came television. From a couple of sets in the beginning it spread like a disease shutting people away in their homes and in the few restaurants that charged fifty paisas for one to sit and watch. Radio Bagh became redundant. In a society that lays no premium on open spaces, it did not take long thereafter for it to be turned into a housing colony.

In his studio Abbas had a painting of a tree-lined avenue with sunshine cascading out of one side. It was not out of his imagination. It was the road that leads north past the army and militia officers' messes. We saved it for our last evening together. It was just the way he had painted it. Only the magic was added to by the fluty whistles of golden orioles streaking about like darts of gold and black in the canopy above. In the burnished late afternoon light we paused to photograph ourselves. 'For remembrance,' Abbas said. Conversation turned to why Parachinar that could have been a successful summer resort was not known even within the province, let alone the rest of the country. The guilty, it was said, were the provincial and federal and provincial tourism development corporations. That is perhaps the reason that the town does not have single hotel.

Surely one day they will wake up to Parachinar. Developers will come teeming in. The great building rush will demolish whatever little of the town's old architecture remains to replace it with tawdry hotels and inns. Noisy, mindless tourists will arrive to pollute and corrupt. Her residents will make money and Parachinar will forever change. Then it will be just any other place in a long roster of ugly resort towns. That is the price of opening up to tourism.

---

* For this madness as well as the Sunni attacks on Gilgit, we have to thank that most malicious of dictators, Zia ul Haq.

MYSTERY ON AN ANCIENT HIGHWAY

The ruined arch.

Mystery on an ancient Highway

'Bamaar's blow was so violent that it clean struck off Sultan Mohammed's head, and sent it rolling down the hill,' said the old man that my friend Abbas Ali had enlisted to show us the purported jailhouse and palace on the crest of the low eminence of Bamurg Kandao just two kilometres due east of Parachinar town.

The jailhouse was no more than a natural cutting in the limestone hill and the palace was

77

simply the foundation of three or four rooms whose antiquity I could not guess. Whoever had lived here in whichever period of time, enjoyed an indisputably magnificent view along the Zeeran stream, a tributary of the Kurram. Below us lay neatly parcelled squares of cultivation, across the river were the houses of Yusufkhel village and far away to the north the dark line of the Safed Koh range dissolved into storm clouds that sparkled with lightening every now and again. Parachinar was sprinkled in the middle ground to the west; a range of low hills blocked the view to the east. And to the south the Zeeran cut through more farmland.

They buried the Sultan where his head came to rest under the hill, said our guide. But neither the period of the Sultan nor of Bamaar, the wicked Hindu (what else!), is known. Finished with the story, he led us down the hill to the ruined shrine of the Sultan: a raised plinth strewn with dressed stones that were once part of the whole building, and a single arched doorway. The only telltale sign that the ruin was ancient was its level in relation to the ground. Repeated flooding in the Zeeran had raised the level in the lee of the hill, burying the doorway so that one had to stoop low to get through it.

The old man brought me a coin and a small terra-cotta figurine, both of which, he said, he had found in the vicinity. Broken off at the neck the figure measured forty-five millimetres with its peculiar elongated headdress. Its disproportionately large nose and beard reminded me of faces seen on Kushan coins of the 1st century CE, and the novice in me immediately assigned it that period. The coin that I was unable to read was later identified by an expert at Lahore Museum as a Ghaznavid issue of the 11th century.

In Lahore, Dr Saifur Rahman Dar, the pre-eminent archaeologist, gave proper perspective to the ruin. The arch, he says, is the transitional form of arch from the Hindu Shahya to the Sultanate style of architecture that came into vogue in the latter 10th century CE. That was a time when the Muslims were yet unsure of the strength of such a true arch and reinforced it with a wooden beam. This timidity in arch construction extends into the 13th century that brings us from the time of Subuktigin through to the period of Sultan Shahab ud Din Mohammed, the Ghorid king who was killed in 1205 by the doughty Khokhar Rajputs of the Salt Range.

Could it then be this same Sultan Mohammed whose shrine nestles under the hill of Bamurg Kandao outside Parachinar? The *Tabkat i Nasiri* recounts how Taj ud Din Yalduz, the Turkish slave turned commander, upon hearing of the death of his king and mentor rode out to receive the bier. Yalduz was then the governor of Sankuran (identified with modern Shalozan some kilometres to the northwest of Parachinar) on the highroad to Ghazni and we know from history that he attended the funerary procession all the way to that place for burial.

Since the Sultan died during the hot weather, there is a small likelihood that he was buried here on the banks of the Zeeran stream as *amanat* for some time before eventually being escorted to Ghazni. Alternatively, it could be that the

The mysterious figuring from Parachinar. Notice the technique of applying the circular eyes and the beard made by scratching with the sharp object.

corpse, now beginning to rot, was eviscerated and the insides interred here. We know of the similar case of Emperor Jehangir's entrails being buried outside Gujrat town and being worshipped to this day as a saint that answers prayers. Then again, we also know that Shahab ud Din Ghori also has a 'shrine' at Dhamiak near Sohawa in Jhelum district. It is therefore more likely that the viscera were buried at Dhamiak and the corpse as *amanat* at this location.

The temporary burial as *amanat* appears plausible in the light of history. The *Tabkat i Nasiri* tells us that the Sultan's nephews and a brother or two came out of Ghor at the head of an army for possession of the corpse. Yalduz had to fight and win a hard battle to retain it. In the course of this struggle and certainly because the corpse was now stinking to high heaven, it would have been buried here temporarily. Even after it was removed to Ghazni, the reverent Taj ud Din Yalduz commemorated the site with the shrine that still exists.

So far as I am concerned, neither the shrine of Sultan Mohammed nor the coin given me by our guide is a mystery. For we know both from the *Rig Veda* and from later history that the Kurram Valley was a much frequented route between Ghazni and the Punjab plains. Countless feet trod this dust over the centuries. All sorts of people, great and small, could have left their mark here. What is mysterious is the small figurine. Dr Dar says that it is unique for it has no parallel in the historic period. Nor is it modern. Which makes it prehistoric – but even there we see no correspondence. Besides the lack of a parallel, it is the strange elongated headdress, a feature not seen elsewhere, that denies it assignation to a specific period – or even an area.

The large nose and ears were made by pinching a very well levigated blob of clay, the eyes were a unique appliqué moulded into circles and pierced. The beard was scratched on by a fine instrument. But an even finer instrument, a needle, was used to make two perforations running from the front to the back just below the eyes. Through these holes, according to Dr Dar, ran a thin thread to suspend the figure either as an ornament or an amulet. The figure, however, lacks the beauty of an ornament, and to my mind it seems more an amulet or the representation of a god. Dr Dar also points out that in prehistory a thread so fine as to go through the holes could only have been produced with some difficulty. The figure was then fired well and applied a red slip.

Where did this figure come from, and what was its purpose? Did the fair-haired singers of the Vedic hymns bring it with them four thousand years ago? In those hymns they celebrate the 'Kramu' (Kurram) River and how it pays tribute to the mighty Sindhu. To know so much of its geography one of their groups surely had to come over the Peiwar Pass at the head of the Kurram Valley and journeyed down the length of the river to its junction with the Sindhu.

But for at least six millenniums before those fair-skinned nomads arrived, the people of the Sindhu Valley were living in great cities. They had perfected agriculture, domesticated cattle and the dog and were making fired pottery. Such civilised people could not have existed in isolation: they would have travelled for trade, pleasure and in search of knowledge. The mysterious figure could then have also originated in the great cities that follow the sinuous path of the Sindhu River.

The question that rankles is: why has no parallel ever been found? Is this the representation of an esoteric god known only to a chosen few and jealously guarded? Was it lost here by a priest who must have then had to face severe penalty? Or is it the guardian of the traveller and the trader – a minor god? Or even, perhaps, of the hunter? Was it placed here in a temple that has long since returned to the dust? But as the lower part is broken off and lost we do not know its real aspect, and it could just as well have been an insignificant toy.

I do not have the answers to these questions. But one day my queries will surely be answered by great minds.

Sikaram blooms. Paraquilegia microphylla *grows in a cleft in a rock to shelter from the chill breeze above 3300 metres.*

Seat of the Gods

Safed Koh – White Mountain, once glistened with snow the whole year round. The mountain is so named, wrote Babur the Mughal, 'because its snow never lessens.' Having made himself master of the Kabul valley in 1504, Babur described the range as running south of Ningarhar (Afghanistan) dividing that province from the country of the Bangash Pukhtuns. There were, he wrote, no 'riding roads' across the mountain – only narrow, precarious footpaths. Little has changed since the time of the Mughal, except that global warming has put paid to the everlasting snow. In grim jest the educated of Parachinar, the quaint little town at the foot of the southern slopes of Safed Koh, now call it

Siyah Koh in Persian or Torghar in Pukhtu – Black Mountain.

I arrived in Parachinar with hopes of climbing Sikaram, at 4761 metres (15,620 ft), the highest peak in the Safed Koh range. There on the peak, it was said, was a shrine and also great views not only into Paktiya province but also Ningarhar right up to Jalalabad. Friends in high places made arrangements that introduced me to Major Dil Nawaz Khan of the Kurram Militia. A full-blooded Yusufzai with a stern, hawkish face and small body, he had climbed the mountain only three weeks earlier and was meant to brief me on the route to be taken.

Ten minutes into it, he abruptly brought the discussion to an end by saying there being no proper guides, he was taking me up himself. He said he would make necessary arrangements and I was to call him later in the afternoon for details. And so it was ordained by the good major that we depart Parachinar at 2.00 AM in order to get to the end of the jeep road early enough to be able to climb the mountain and return in time for dinner. He had, moreover, arranged for 'the old man' who knew the mountain well, to be our guide. The Old Man of the Mountain: shades of Hasan bin Sabah, the infamous 13th century leader of the Assassins! Now, that sounded good to me.

We drove out at just after two in the morning. Forty-five minutes out of Parachinar on the old road to the Afghan frontier (by Peiwar Kotal) we picked up our guide from a militia post. With a serious deficit of teeth in his mouth, Juma Khan, a Kharote Pukhtun, seemed about sixty, but was perhaps no more than fifty and as fit as any mountaineer can be. He said he knew the mountain well from the days of his youth spent roaming its wooded slopes both as a shepherd and in search of game. The way to the shrine he could find blindfolded, he added for good measure.

Thirty minutes later, in the quickening light at about 3.30 in the morning, we halted on the banks of a dry stream by the summer settlement that goes by the unpronounceable name of Vachakharwalasar* – with more letters to its name than the sum total of its population. Besides the major and Juma Khan, our party consisted of Captain Shahid, chubby and seemingly rather ill-conditioned and Aqeeq Bangash, a geologist, with his languorous face and easy, unhurried manner. Corporal Dildar Hussain and Lance Corporal Lal Hakim made up the escort. Cups of tea, the only breakfast that day, were passed around, Major Dil Nawaz apportioned out some dry fruit and toffees and we were ready to go. I asked what we were doing about lunch.

'We forget it!' said the Major with simple finality.

The mountain rose darkly against the lighting sky. Pointing out the ridge and the *kandao* (pass) through which we were to ascend, Juma strode out at the head of the party. Across the dry steam bed we went up the slope, climbed the ridge and turned north along its crest. High above us the peak of Sikaram rose in a jumble of jagged crags. To the west the contours fell to a valley floor still swathed in darkness with a few pinpricks of light marking human habitation.

---

* The name means Hill of the Emaciated Ass. If there was ever an evocatively beautiful name, this was it. The height of this place was, if memory serves, 2300 metres.

That was Paktiya province, said Juma Khan, and if we took the path winding down to the left we would be in Afghanistan in less than thirty minutes.

Paktiya, an ancient land, culturally rich in prehistoric and Classical times, reverted to savagery in the name of religion by sub-humans who have neither an understanding of religion nor of the norms of humanity. Paktiya, first mentioned by Herodotus, the Father of History, in the 5th century BCE, was just beginning to wake up far below us. In Chapter 102, Book III of *The Histories*, Herodotus writes of this land of 'warlike people' as the 'country of Paktyika; [whose] people dwell northward of all the rest of the Indians, and follow nearly the same mode of life as the Bactrians.' Our historian apparently gleaned this information from the work of the Greek admiral Skylax who was ordered by Darius the Great, the king of Persia, to reconnoitre and map the river that my ancestors called the Sindhu and which the Greeks transliterated into Indus. Skylax undertook his journey in the year 512 BCE – a full fifty years before Herodotus wrote his *Histories* in which he quotes a portion of the Greek sea captain's undertaking and findings.

It does not take great scholarship to connect modern Paktiya with the classical Hellenised Paktyika. From there of course flows the word Pukhtun, making this unarguably the earliest mention of the name of a people in trans-Sindhu territories. It must be conceded that there are scholars who disagree with the connection between Pukhtun and Herodotus' Paktyika – on flimsy and uninformed grounds too, but to my mind the link is substantial and very real. However, since Herodotus did not travel to this part of the world, but wrote from hearsay, I have forever been intrigued by the identity of that unknown writer of the Classical Age who would have mentioned this place name the first time ever. The question of who that was can only be answered if assiduous archaeological exploration or some great miracle of science places at our disposal the lost works of classical Persian, Indian and Greek scholars who pre-date Skylax. Until then, we can only thank Providence for preserving for us the works of Herodotus.

Ever upward we went through juniper bushes and what was once thick pine forest, now reduced to a jungle of ugly stumps. Crossing the 3200-metre mark we were beyond timberline. The path petered out and we picked our way over a shingly slope that, at places, fell sharply away at a nearly dangerous angle. The major and Juma Khan danced on ahead, followed by the two soldiers. I puffed along in the middle with the captain and Aqeeq bringing up the rear a couple of hundred metres behind.

The ridge that we were climbing ended at the foot of a sheer slope and as we paused to catch our breath Major Dil Nawaz pointed out the rock face he and Captain Shahid had climbed only three weeks earlier. That they had made it to the top that way and back within the span of single day said a lot for their tenacity. The jagged, friable slope shooting up at an angle no less than sixty degrees told me that they would have scrabbled up on all fours.

As we started up the sheer slope, the valley

Juma Khan, Major Dil Nawaz Khan and the two militiamen at the supposed grave. Once pagan Pukhtun ancestors very likely worshipped the earth goddess and performed fertility rites here. Then came Rama, and much later the present quasi-Islamic belief.

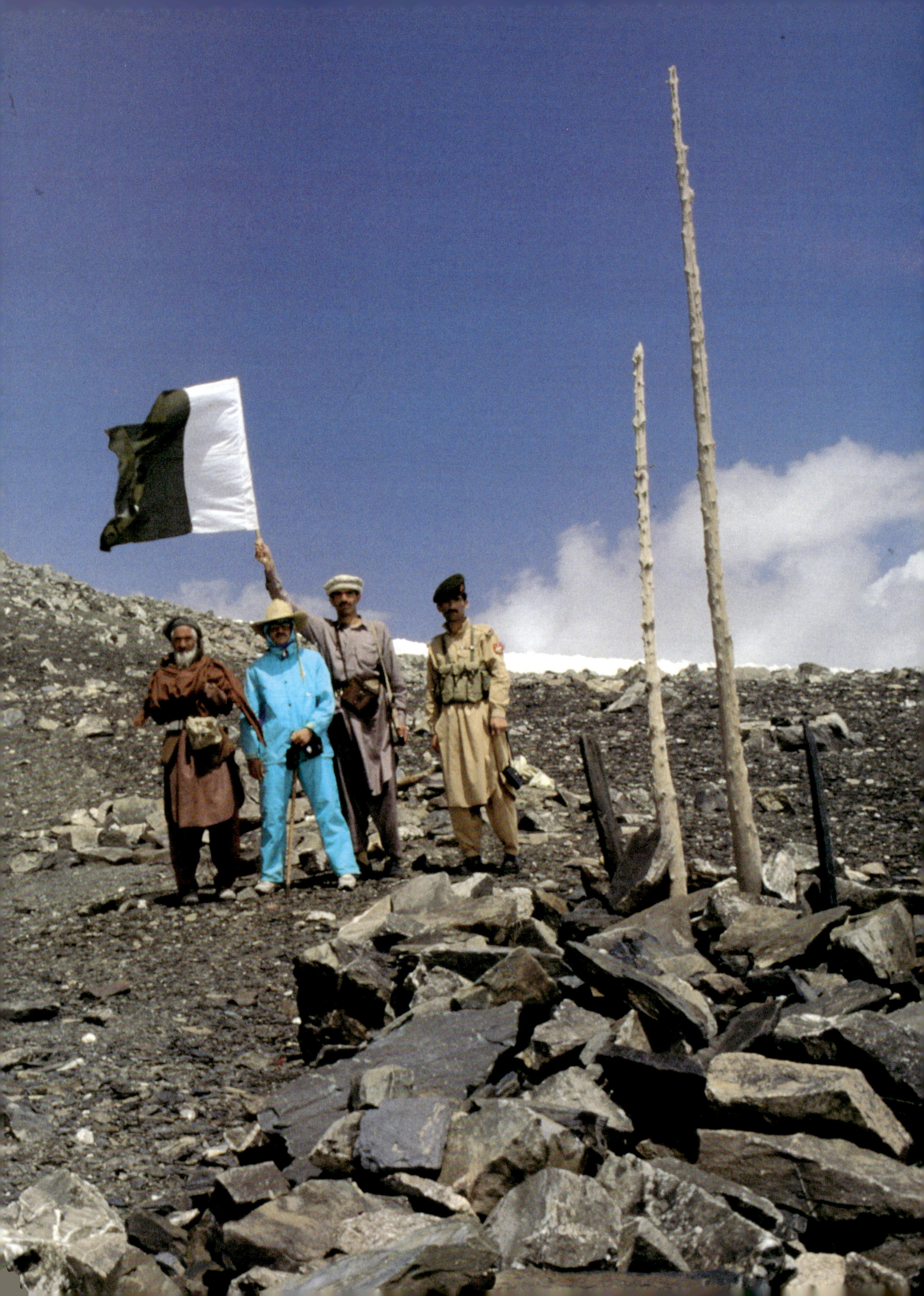

of Paktiya lighted up and we could clearly make out two villages. Not long after that the clouds rolled in from the south shutting off our views. At 3800 metres a veritable squall set up bringing with it a stinging spray of freezing sleet. My heart sank for I had not brought any inclement weather mountain gear and getting wet at that height could have consequences rather more serious than just being miserably cold. Thereafter it alternately cleared up and clouded over on regular twenty-minute intervals. Meanwhile, Major Dil Nawaz who had earlier chatted every time I caught up with him had grown quiet, almost sullen, with a very grim set to his mouth. It was only at the end of the day that I learnt how he had suffered severe nausea all along – a common enough problem at high altitudes.

We passed an area strewn with large grey plates of rock; a little farther it was long, thick pencils of dark slate. At 4000 metres the temperature variation between daytime maximum and nighttime minimum can be as high as eighty or ninety degrees centigrade, and moisture caught within the fissures of the porous sedimentary rocks alternately freezes and boils. This sequential cooling and heating works the rocks loose and over time shears and shatters them into these unusual shapes. And so, six hours after having left the jeep we struggled up the shingly slope and onto an oblong plateau laced with large drifts of gritty snow. A couple of hundred metres to the north was the shrine, an elongated heap of stones with a couple of upright poles. To our left was the peak of Sikaram. Over large shattered rocks we clambered to the precipice.

In Parachinar I had been told that an officer of the Raj, having climbed this peak was so impressed by the views into the valley of the Kurram River (of which Parachinar is the principal town) that he gave to a poetic burst of eloquence. Pointing in that direction he said, 'See Kurram.' Over the years his utterance was corrupted, so they said, to Sikaram. This officer must have been seriously verbally challenged. Very likely he was autistic, or suffered from Down Syndrome or both to have been capable of saying nothing more profound or even richer in syntax.

Frivolity aside, this is just a naïve fable invented to conveniently explain away a name that goes back to our pagan prehistory – a prehistory that we in our converts' zeal vehemently disown. For one, Kurram is not the only way one can see from the peak. When the clouds cleared we could see all the way into Paktiya and to the northwest was the red and sienna gorge of one of the putative nine rivers that wash the northern slopes of Safed Koh to feed the Kabul River in Ningarhar. To the north, beyond the shrine and snowfield, was yet another narrow river valley that led straight down to Jalalabad obscured in the clouds. Secondly, the name of the peak predates the first arrival of the British.

The major unfurled the national flag and waved it on the peak to mark the success of our little enterprise. As we savoured our few minutes of brilliant sunshine, I marvelled at the similarity of the topography of Safed Koh to that of the great Himalayas. Like a miniature of that greatest of mountain ranges, Safed Koh too stretches

SEAT OF THE GODS

Juma Khan, the Kharote Pukhtun, who led us up the mountain.

on an east-west axis but is a meagre sixty kilometres long as opposed to the almost two thousand kilometre length of the Himalayas. As if making an irrefutable statement of finality, the Himalayas ends in the magnificent Nanga Parbat, which at 8128 metres is its second highest peak. So too does Safed Koh fulfil itself in a great paroxysm of vanity with Sikaram rising to 4761 metres, high above all other peaks in the range. Westward of this high peak, Safed Koh, like the mighty Himalayas, dwindles and fades away into the wind-scoured, eroded valleys of Paktiya.

Done with the flag-waving we headed for the shrine. No one knew who was buried under that pile of rocks, but the militiamen had no doubt in their minds that it was a holy man. This, however, was not Syed Karam who, according to another legend, was the eponym for Sikaram and whose last resting place, so the militiamen said, was on the slopes to the Ningarhar side. The frenzy to invent a history that is removed from a pagan original is characteristic of conversion to Islam in our part of the world. Takht e Suleman in Balochistan and Musa ka Musalla in Kaghan, both prehistoric pagan shrines have been similarly converted and their original names lost. While the former very likely was dedicated to the same deity as Sikaram – both being situated in the Pukhtun heartland, the latter was sacred to an earth deity of the nomadic cattle-owning Gujjars. Subsequent to conversion Takht e Suleman became the tomb of Qais Abdur Rashid, the purported progenitor of all Pukhtuns, and Musa ka Musalla the prayer mat of either the prophet Moses (Musa) or a god-fearing Gujjar of that name who followed the creed of Islam*.

In my mind there is no doubt that Sikaram was sacred to the earliest ancestors of the Pukhtuns who lived around this magnificent snow-draped mountain three or four thousand years ago. Periodically they would have trekked up its then forested slopes taking with them their offerings of blood and flesh to appease their gods, perhaps to entreat for better harvests or successful hunts, or more offspring, or for the prosperity of a trading enterprise, or perhaps for the success of a long journey. For long millenniums Sikaram, the snow-covered seat of the gods, was sacred for the people that lived around it. And so even with the coming of Islam it remained sacred in the collective memory of the first converts.

It did not take long thereafter for the origin of the name Sikaram to be lost. With that loss the altar where ancient worshippers had made their offerings was adjusted to become a Muslim grave. Only one aspect was overlooked: while the Muslim grave is set in a north-south alignment, the one on Sikaram is out of kilter! With an innocence born out of a purity of belief, the early converts did not bother to properly adjust their shrine in keeping with the norms of the new religion. All they wished was to retain and incorporate into the new belief system the site that had been sacred to their ancestors before them. And so the pagan shrine of Sikaram lives to this day.

An attractive proposition – that occurred to me in a moment of solitude by the shrine, with

---

*   For both these stories see my book *Prisoner on a Bus*.

respect to the name is its possible connection with the Vedic god Rama. For ages the valley of the Kurram River that lies under the southern slopes of Safed Koh has been one of the main routes between Central Asia and the Indian subcontinent. Surely when they first came this way four thousand years ago, the singers of Vedic hymns, those carriers of the swastika emblem, would have thought the glistening white heights of Safed Koh a suitable sanctuary for one of their gods. Now, the ornate spire of the Hindu temple is called '*shikhara*,' a word that in classical Sanskrit also signifies 'mountain.' Could it be then that those early travellers named this mountain Shikhara Rama – the Mountain of Rama? Thereafter the passage of time and a profusion of usage neatly abbreviated the name to Sikaram.

Postscript: It took us six hours to the top. All that had powered us was the little dried fruit and some water that each one of us carried. On the way back energy levels began to run low. By three in the afternoon when the jeep became visible way below us, with yet another hour's slog ahead, my legs had turned to jelly. I wished for no more than to lie down in the mellow sunshine and sleep. Major Dil Nawaz Khan was clearly unwell. Only toothless old Juma Khan continued to remain as sprightly as a mountain goat running back and forth to give a hand first to the major and then to me as we stumbled downhill.

Moreover, he kept a watchful eye on the slope behind us where Captain Shahid and Aqeeq Bangash were struggling down after having been delayed by storm clouds and low visibility in reaching the top. Though the Major had ordered the two militiamen to remain behind to guide the stragglers down, the trustworthy Juma Khan considered it his sole responsibility to get us all down the mountain in one piece. That then was the kind of man one could put one's trust in.

In the event, all went well and we were in Parachinar dog-tired and famished but satisfied with the success of our scramble. But one thing must be said: if this adventure was anything, it was a penance. Ideally, we should have carried tents, sleeping bags and a day's rations to spend the night at the shrine and return the following morning. From his earlier experience Major Dil Nawaz had known it was indeed a punishment, yet he had led us all into it. To me it now seems that he had taken us up in the spirit of those forgotten ancestors who would have visited the Sikaram shrine with their sacrificial rams and bulging wineskins to propitiate their gods.

We did not bear the same offerings. But considering that we had pushed ourselves to our utmost limits to reach the abode of ancient gods, we had not done so badly either.

SEA MONSTERS AND THE SUN GOD

The main square at Nagarparkar. Sometime after August 1999 when this picture was taken, Nagarparkar was ravaged by an earthquake. It was reported that the tremor razed the double-storeyed building to the right of the picture.

The enigmatic George Tyrwhitt

'Turwutt came to Nagarparkar at the head of an army in 1858 when Rana Karan Singh ruled over the place. A great battle was fought here in which the English were roundly defeated and had to flee for their lives. The Rajputs went in pursuit, and Turwutt was only able to get away with his life after a Meghwar tanner hid him under a pile of cowhides. Returning subsequently with an even greater army, Turwutt was finally able to overcome the Rajputs of Nagar. And not the one to forget the Meghwar, Turwutt allotted him a vast *jagir*.'

Nawaz Ali Khosa, the elderly teller of tales from Nagarparkar fell silent. The tap-tap-tap of his steel-tipped cane on the street became more pronounced. From afar the *koel* called, the moisture-laden monsoon wind gusted down the corridor of the street and the old man sat down in the veranda of the ruined hulk at the west end of the old Nagarparkar bazaar.

'I have never read of any great battle between the British and the Ranas of Nagar,' I said.

'But of course there was a battle,' Khosa corrected me. 'It is part of the lore of Thar Desert.'

There were, he said, even the ruins of the fortress to show for the eventual defeat of the Nagar Rajputs. At the very end of the bazaar, past the ruined storefronts and houses of the rich Hindus of Nagarparkar's glory days, past the impressive Jain temple now a sad ruin, Nawaz Khosa walked up the slight incline. There in front was a length of wall and further on, a subterranean opening that looked like a large water conduit. The wall, according to my guide, was all that remained of the Rajput fortress and the opening led into its basement where a cache of gunpowder was stored.

After the defeat while the Rajput chiefs hid in the surrounding Karonjhar hills, the valiant General Roopa Kohli stole into the fortress to remove the cache. He was discovered, however, arrested and tortured. But he gave nothing away, and so he was hanged to death. Khosa offered to walk me to the east end of town to the site of the hanging. There was some fragment of historical truth here. We know of Roopa (or Roopla) Kohli, a great resistance leader of the middle 19th century celebrated in local folksongs even today. But the granite blocks of the purported castle and the entrance to the

Nawaz Ali Khosa, the keeper of the tale. In this meeting (August 1999) and one six months later he would say, 'My papers are ready. Any day now I'll receive my marching orders.' He said this with the satisfaction of a man who had lived his life as well as circumstances permitted. Now word is that he has indeed passed on from this life.

underground vaults were cemented together with modern cement that would have been introduced in Nagarparkar by the British. If it existed in Roopa's time, this building must have been redone after British annexation.

Sixteen years ago while free-wheeling around Thar Desert I had been told that no trip to the picturesque little town of Nagarparkar at the south-eastern edge of Pakistan was complete without visiting *Turwutt jo Thullo* – the Pedestal of Tyrwhitt, for that was how the Welsh name had been translated into the Sindhi and Parkari languages. The stories Nawaz Ali Khosa told me at that time made out Tyrwhitt as a saint and a demon in equal measure. Here was a man who pursued his official duties, whether to bridle contumacious Rajputs or to provide justice to the aggrieved, with single-minded madness. Tyrwhitt, it was told, was a fun-loving man as well who would climb the hill daily to sit on the pedestal especially prepared for him on the windy peak in order to enjoy his drink in the remarkable scenery of the Karonjhar hills. But, it was also said; he was ruthless in his attempts to bring the recalcitrant Rajputs to heel and carried a pair of binoculars with him daily to actually keep a watchful eye on his domain between sips on his whisky.

In 1858 the district of Tharparkar was detached from Bhoj and placed under the Hyderabad Collectorate. Owing to the more regular system of administration, the Ranas of the desert lost some of the independence they earlier enjoyed. Consequently, true to their Rajput spirit, they raised the Kohlis to revolt. On 15 April 1859 a mob burnt down the telegraph office at Nagarparkar, killed a number of the police guard and took possession of the town. That is when we first hear of Lieutenant George Tyrwhitt who accompanied the army with a force of six hundred police levies to restore order.

Order was restored, but the miscreants made off to spend the next year as fugitives. When they eventually did surrender, the Rana and his principal abettors were awarded lengthy jail sentences and deprived of their properties, while those who had assisted the government were granted *jagirs*. The passage of nearly a century and a half had embellished and romanticised the story of a failed revolt with tales of a valiant Kohli general trying to spirit away a cache of ammunition and the defeated white man cowering in fear under a pile of stinking uncured hides.

The authorities now saw the difficulties in keeping a vast desert region under the control of a distant administrative headquarters. Consequently in 1860 the area that now forms the districts of Mirpur Khas and Mithi was detached to form a separate Political Superintendency. The man to head it was George Tyrwhitt. E. H. Aitken's *Gazetteer of the Province of Sind* (sic) notes that here was 'an officer whose memory is associated in the traditions of Sind with many eccentricities.' Whatever those eccentricities may have been, at the time of his appointment as the Political Superintendent of the district of Tharparkar, Tyrwhitt was reputed to be 'able, energetic and possessing an astonishing degree of insight into the characters, habits and feelings of the border tribes.'

The man must have done well to hold his appointment for a full thirteen years until 1873. But it is intriguing where and how he acquired his 'astonishing degree' of knowledge when we do not hear of him in Sindh prior to his appearance on the scene with his force of six hundred police levies. However, we do learn from the illustrious Mirza Kalich Beg that both his father and grandfather enjoyed friendly relations with Tyrwhitt and that the young Mirza was given

THE ENIGMATIC GEORGE TYRWHITT

My guide, Nawaz Ali's son, sits on Tyrwhitt's pedestal. The views from the pedestal all round were great.

an English education on the exhortation of the Political Superintendent.*

Among the legends regarding the man's singularity of purpose when it came to the job assigned him, one legend still lives. A con artist of his day impersonating as a district administration official, complete with his train of clerks and peons, visited Tharparkar. There, right under the nose of the Political Superintendent the impostor received some money from a certain party and gave it possession of a block of land that was another man's rightful property. Even before Tyrwhitt

---

* Two years after this journey to Nagarparkar, I was in Karachi visiting my friend Syed Abu Akif, then the Additional Commissioner. In a storeroom below his office, he showed me an old incumbency board that bore, among others, the name of George Tyrwhitt. My notes from that trip were subsequently lost, but if memory serves Tyrwhitt served in Karachi as the assistant or additional commissioner in 1859-60 for about a year's time.

could get wind of the carrying on, the swindler and his party, pockets bulging with ill-earned moolah, made tracks.

As soon as word reached him, Tyrwhitt saddled up and rode hell for leather after the tricksters, and, it is said, after riding non-stop through the night came upon his quarry at the edge of the desert just as the eastern horizon started to light up. The impostors were arrested, tried and sentenced to life imprisonment in the island fortress of Manora outside Karachi.

If Tyrwhitt left anything in writing, all or much of it is lost. However, rather unlike other officers of the Raj, he certainly did not leave many photographs: there is but a single portrait of the man on record. This surely is evidence of his shy, reclusive nature. And so we know next to nothing of this mysterious person. But there are oblique references to his falling from grace toward the end of his service in Tharparkar. There is no official word on how or why he left his position of Political Superintendent in 1873. There is only the reference that he came heavily under debt – a circumstance rather difficult to attain for a man seemingly as reclusive and retiring as Tyrwhitt. It seems that it was the pressure of this debt that occasioned his departure for home the same year as he was removed from his superintendence.

The Raj apparently protected its officers' secrets well for we get no inkling of the nature of Tyrwhitt's humiliation. We know that he sailed away for England sometime in 1873. Mirza Kalich Beg wrote that Colonel George Tyrwhitt died 'after 1874' in England. If there was a wife and children, there was no mention. The man who had brought order to the vast desert district of Tharparkar and ruled judiciously over it for thirteen long years disappeared from official record because of some unknown indiscretion. But for the people of Nagarparkar where he had held court, Tyrwhitt's pedestal on a wind-scoured hilltop outside town even today remains very much a tourist attraction. They still flaunt it not without a shade of pride even though his memory is confused with the accretion of time.

The dearth of official record makes it difficult to chronicle the accomplishments of Colonel Tyrwhitt in any detail, but whatever little is available does make one thing clear: here was a man no less in stature than John Jacob or Bartle Frere. But here was a man who missed the Role of Honour because of his reclusive nature. Here was a man who missed out on glory because of an impropriety that led to bankruptcy. Now, one hundred and twenty-five years after his death let as acknowledge him as one of the able empire builders that he really was. With these words do I celebrate Colonel George Tyrwhitt of the former desert district of Tharparkar.

'No one believes the Professor'

Orpheus Augustus Marks, the Professor.

I first came to know of the 'Professor' from friend Farjad Nabi's documentary film whose title I have borrowed for this piece. The film features an aging, square-faced rather good-looking man with long hair – the kind of face that belongs in an action film. The impression I got from the first few minutes of the film was that this was an attempt in absurdity in the tradition of Jonathan Swift. But it turned out otherwise. When the show ended, I shook the hand of Orpheus Augustus Marks, who featured in the film, and whom I had earlier noticed among the audience. It was an honour, I told him, to make his acquaintance.

Here, I thought, was a man that needed to be discovered. And so recently one morning around ten I arrived at his second floor flat in Lahore's Rivaz Gardens. In response to my knock, he opened the door a mere chink and said he was busy in his worship and would appreciate if I could come back after an hour. I returned at the appointed hour to be shown into a cluttered, unswept room with a charpoy (woven with synthetic tape) without bedding, a couple of chairs, a table and a settee all piled with books, old newspapers, unwashed items of clothing, old film posters and assorted stuff. A leaking blue plastic water cooler lay in a puddle on the floor – Professor* Marks' only modern convenience that was any good.

He ushered me onto the balcony saying electricity had been disconnected for he had been unable to pay his power bills and it would be better in the breeze. Like the room this too was cluttered: a room cooler, a broken charpoy, and a couple of broken chairs. We sat on the charpoy for a while and made small talk before the Professor decided we would be better off inside the room without the breeze than balancing ourselves on the broken charpoy on the balcony. I asked if that was all the room he had and Professor showed me the spare room: more broken furniture, books, old newspapers and disintegrating items of household linen. But there was no place to sit, much less to repose. So I asked him where he slept.

'On the balcony, because it is an airy place.' It was a simple statement of fact. There was no apology or self-pity. On one side of the small balcony was the toilet and next to it the kitchen. The latter was disused and locked for he always ate outside. It was 'stuffed full of books,' said the Professor.

In the spare room the high shelf had a copy of Ameer Ali's translation of the Koran. I asked about it, and the Professor took it down, kissed it and handed it to me. It was a well-thumbed copy and he said he read the Koran as he read his Bible. As a child in school in Tanda Mota near Gujrat he had won a prize in a school festival for singing a Sikh hymn better than the Sikh students. By his own admission, he was equally good with the *Gita* as well.

'I respect all religions, will kiss all religious books, but have never, will never, prostrate myself to a graven image,' he said as he reached over and pulled out a laminated sheet from under some stuff. It was a letter from Libroitaliano, an Italian publishing house, informing him of the inclusion of one of his poems in an anthology of twenty poets from around the world.

For the first time I realised that the line between reality and delusion was not only thin but also obscured by a turbid mist. The Professor said that he must get to Italy to sign the contract before the book can be published. But there being no money to pay the fare, everything was on hold.

'You do understand that I am one of twenty international poets – the only one from Pakistan,' he said with felicitous sadness. 'And I cannot get out there to sign the contract.' When the contract has been signed and the book published, his work will be read in all the major libraries of the world. But for that Orpheus Augustus must wait. He did not explain however, why he must travel to Italy to sign a contract for the publication to go ahead.

Poetry, writing and painting were creation, he said. And so he was a creator. But he was a creator because he was acquainted with the works of those greater creators like Homer, Aristotle, Plato, Shakespeare, Tennyson and Elliot. Not only was he acquainted with their work, he said, but he also acknowledged them

---

* He was known as Professor, it turned out, because of his looks and persona that most Pakistanis would associate with a teacher – and of philosophy at that.

as his masters and mentors. When one did not follow great men, one was removed from greatness for just the mere fact of following them is edification.

'It is improper to call poetry just poetry. There is much more in it,' he said. 'And so too in acting. I have always wondered what goes on in the minds of those great film actors when they are doing a part. Is it a latent desire to become the part they are playing?'

The answer to this question came to the Professor when he read Greek mythology where the gods changed shape at will. Acting, the art of becoming someone else, was thus in a way the apotheosis of man. But apotheosis is not for everyone who playacts. It is in the purview of only the perfectionist, and in perfection lies madness.

'So I thought it was better to be mad for a certain length of time. And I chose to be mad. I plunged into the world of insanity and for a time I thought I will never be able to return to normal life.' In his intensity he broke off from his beautiful Lahori Punjabi into English. The art in his madness, he said, was to break into dialogue as he walked the streets of Lahore. (For my benefit he delivered his lines on madness and burst into laughter). It was all impromptu and it could go on and on. But those who shared the streets with him did not share his enthusiasm for art. They stoned him, threw rubbish at him and children followed him about screaming *Paghal ee oye!*

This seeker of apotheosis would however be too engrossed in his performance to be aware of anything. One day he nearly drowned. He was deep in dialogue as he walked past the old Beco factory in Badami Bagh. Nearby was a ditch filled with waste oil from the factory and the Professor walked right into it as he struggled aloud with the nature of truth and falsehood, of madness and sanity. He was up to his middle when someone grabbed him and hauled him out. Angrily the Professor turned on his saviour.

'Why have you done this?' he asked.
'I've just saved your life.'
'You fool, didn't you realise I was doing something far more important than life itself?'
'But,' persisted the life-saver, 'the ditch is very deep and you could have drowned.'
'Deep it might be, but not as deep as my thoughts or me!' retorted the Professor.

This man, it turned out, was an old student of the Professor's father from the time the family lived in Misri Shah. In regard for his erstwhile teacher, the man took the son home where he spent two hours washing the viscous muck from the Professor's clothing.

When it came time to end the madness, Orpheus Augustus prayed together with his religious mentor (whose name he did not deign to disclose) and the madness was over. This must have been in the late 1950s. Sometime later (the Professor does not talk of years) he completed his Master's degree in English Literature. General Fazle Raziq, a good friend of the family, suggested he join the Army Education Corps as an officer. Orpheus Augustus scoffed the idea: he was an artist and his goal was Hollywood and the Oscar

Awards that he believed would naturally follow.

'Had I accepted, it would have been another life,' he said and I just discerned a touch of rue.

To be a film star was an abiding dream. When still a child he was once asked by his father what he would like to be when he grew up. There was no thinking, no ambiguity: he wanted to be in the movies.

'I used to go to the cinema and then copy the likes of Spencer Tracy and Paul Mooney.' It was in the 1950s that he read of Yul Brynner winning the Oscar and cabled him a challenge. Brynner wasn't the greatest, he wrote, it was unknown, untried Orpheus Augustus Marks of Lahore, the uncrowned king of acting. Alys Faiz herself, he asserts, sent the message from the teleprinter at the offices of *The Pakistan Times*. Back came the reply that it may well be true that he was indeed the greatest actor of all times, but had he been tried?

The dream called Hollywood became an obsession, but unable to get there he joined the local film industry in 1975. The dream receded further into the distance when all he got were part roles. Even to face the camera for a minute brought him untold happiness.

'Each minute in front of the camera was the brick that was to build the great edifice I dreamed of.' But for a performer of his class there was little work in the studios of Lahore and its only reminder is a black and white picture or two of him posing as a soldier with a spear. The fantasy of Hollywood nevertheless refused to die. Even today when he says that he will eventually get out there to win an Oscar, the conviction is tangible. He is clearly not just saying it.

The line between the real and the imagined disappears when the Professor recalls his meeting with Ava Gardener come to shoot *Bhowani Junction*. She was in Room 9 at the Faletti's, he recalls. There he dazzled her with his thespian skills. She offered to take him home to Hollywood, but his family got in the way. They would not permit him to leave and he lost his chance to fame and glory. He relates his meeting forty years later with Robert Feuchtman who publicly acclaimed him the greatest living actor. But again it is difficult to separate the grain of truth from the chaff of unreality.

When he wasn't concentrating on the Hollywood dream, he was practicing cricket. In the late 1950s he was, by his own admission, the greatest fast bowler Pakistan could produce. He played first class cricket and claims there was no test cricketer in those days that he hadn't bowled out for naught. Once again the family got in the way of the rise to glory and he had to give up cricket to resume studies that had been interrupted some years earlier. Later he tried short and long distance running – his spikes rest in one corner of the room. Had there been money for a proper athlete's diet he could have won Pakistan laurels. And so yet another dream died.

The one dream that lives and is still real is the epic he is composing – an epic to end all epics. A work to surpass that of Firdausi, Dante and Milton. Running into thousands of verses, the poem, yet incomplete, is a dialogue between

God and Satan. We do not know when we shall ever benefit from it.

They say the name affects the life of the person; to be named after great personages is to acquire greatness. But Augustus, the adopted son and successor of Julius Caesar, who ruled over Rome for almost fifty years, seems to have been defeated by Orpheus, the tragic hero of Greek mythology. Orpheus, the singer, musician and poet who played the lyre and the cithara. Orpheus whose song was so sweet that wild beasts followed him tamely when he sang; Orpheus who, being on the good ship *Argo* when it was struck by a storm, becalmed the sea and comforted the Argonauts with his song. When his much loved wife Eurydice died, the inconsolable Orpheus followed her into the Underworld to bring her back. There he charmed the monsters and gods of darkness with his lyre. Persephone and Hades, moved by his great love for his wife, granted him the desire to return to the World of Mortals with her.

But on one condition: he was not to look back until Charon, the ferryman of the Underworld, had rowed him across the Styx River and he and Eurydice were again in daylight. Just as he was reaching the light of day, seized by a terrible uncertainty, Orpheus turned to see if his beloved was indeed following close behind. She was, but the condition being violated, Eurydice died a second time and was returned to the Underworld. The unfortunate Orpheus was denied a second entry and expelled to the world of the living unconsoled, unaccomplished.

There is a parallel of sorts here. Orpheus Augustus, a man of many talents, lives clinging to his dreams in the Underworld of rejection and failure. Surely he is responsible, in part, for bringing this sorry pass upon himself. But in a country where talent is not always acknowledged such is the natural end for many gifted but unconnected dreamers. The son of a school teacher and a nurse of the Army Medical Corps, our hero, unknown even in his own city, much less the rest of the country, wanders into the evening of his Underworld forever seeking daylight. Unaccomplished, unsung, unconsoled.

'Chup Sha! Hari Singh raghle!'

In the first week of January 1836 an aristocratic Austrian visited Gujranwala: the botanist Baron Carl von Hugel. Having spent some considerable time in Kashmir, and subsequently having sojourned at Wazirabad with the Neapolitan governor of that city, the wily and cruel Paolo de Avitabile, he was now on his way to the durbar of the aging Maharaja Ranjit Singh.

Gujranwala was then the domain of a man called Hari Singh Nalwa, a native of the town. A Rajput by caste and follower of the great Guru Nanak by creed, he was the ablest general that the Punjabi Maharaja could boast of. It was this man who had taken Punjabi arms across the Sindhu River and into the Pukhtun heartland. Such had been his terror that for nearly a hundred and fifty years after his death Pukhtun mothers were to restrain recalcitrant children with a whispered, *'Chup Sha! Hari Singh raghle!'* (Be quite! Hari Singh comes!).

It was to the house of this man that the *yekka* provided by Avitabile bore the Austrian from Wazirabad. The Gujranwala of 1836 had a population very likely of about five to six thousand and the streets that are today teeming would have seemed reasonably wide avenues, perhaps with trees lining them. Hugel's *yekka* was surely driven right up to the arch over the side-street that gave access to the house in what is today called Kasera (Coppersmith's) Bazaar. Today one can scarce walk a yard without being jostled; to go in by *yekka* is simply out of the question.

The house stands to this day, now known as Anyan di Masjid (Mosque of the Blind). Long after the demise of the Sikh empire, with the birth of Pakistan, this house became the property of a certain Maulvi Yasin who had emigrated from East Punjab. He set up a seminary for the visually impaired and gave the *haveli* of Hari Singh Nalwa its new name.

I was returning after eight years. The narrow bazaar was even more crowded, the shops looking well-stocked as ever, the teeming shoppers unfazed by the slump in the economy. A shoddy steel fixture had replaced the beautifully carved wooden arches of the second floor windows;

the simple façade was ruined by an ugly great tangle of power and telephone cables. It had been rendered photographically unattractive. The cusped arch over the side street was, thankfully, still intact. There was little else that remained unchanged.

On the first floor a *tundoor* busily turned out *naans*. To the left was a neatly swept room with a large sign on the door announcing it as the last resting place of Maulvi Yasin. Inside I could see the green satin-draped grave that, I imagine, will by and by become a busy money-making shirne.* Across the central courtyard the arched woodwork was blocked by a steel and timber door and another sign said this was the seminary of Maulvi Ghulam Rasul.

On the second floor several blind men groped there way about the sunny courtyard where the woodwork arches leading into the rooms were still intact. A group of women waited by the south windows, where ugly steel had replaced the beautiful woodwork I had photographed in 1991. Here Maulvi Yasin once tended to their spiritual (and sometimes superstitious) needs, but now there was nobody. I asked a man sitting in the veranda on the right. He blinked his unseeing eyes and told me that a grand-nephew of the late maulvi now filled that post.

The floor above was the private residence of the successor of Maulvi Yasin and therefore out of bounds for visitors, as it surely would have been in the time of the Austrian's visit. Then it would have been home to Nalwa's family. Instead of the old brickwork, it now showed grey cement plaster and seemed to have been either

The plaque that habitually appears and disappears.

completely rebuilt or extensively modified.

The second floor was very likely where Hari Singh Nalwa would have entertained von Hugel with, as the European tells us, twenty-five different platters of confectionery and over a dozen different fruits. This fact reflects on the efficient communication that existed at that time to make it possible for the Punjabi general to have on hand such a choice of fruit. In mid-winter Punjab, then as now, can only produce some citrus and guavas.

Carl von Hugel was impressed by Nalwa's good taste. Here were expensive and very fine carpets from Kashmir and Kabul adorning the floors as well as the walls. Though he does not comment on the furniture and other fixtures, he does tell us that every room was well-appointed and comfortable. And when the traveller complained of the bitter cold of the previous days, a clap of the general's hands brought in glowing braziers. But today most of the rooms are derelict, the plaster peeling, the walls and the floors bare and dusty, except for the inexpensive cotton rugs spread where the seekers of solace meet Maulvi Yasin's successor.

---

* Maulvi Yasin was alive when I first visited in November 1991.

The present masters of the *haveli* of Hari Singh Nalwa were only vaguely aware of their illustrious predecessor. That also only because of the inscribed marble plaque put up by the British when they first took over Gujranwala. This plaque was removed many years ago and dumped in one of the rooms. Today it is no longer to be seen for such is our regard for history.* For a people for whom history began in 1947, there is no sense of connection with Hari Singh, a son of Punjab, because he was not a Muslim. I wandered about unhindered trying to conjure up the spirit of Hari Singh and wondering where he would have entertained von Hugel and in which room the Austrian would have slept the one night that he remained in 'Gusraoli.'

With rapidly expanding population, the warren of narrow alleys and closely packed two or three-storey houses grew up to obliterate the walled-in garden that greatly impressed von Hugel. Tended by the general himself in his spare time, the Austrian said the garden was 'the most beautiful and best kept [he] had seen in India.' Here were plane (*chinar*) trees and stately cypresses imported from Kashmir to ease the heat of the Punjabi summer, here too were citrus and other fruit trees. Among them did Hari Singh lead his European guest showing off his green thumb. The flower beds, too, were rich and well arranged and von Hugel found the fragrance of the narcissus 'almost overwhelming.' The general was indeed no mean gardener.

But today the garden of Hari Singh does not exist. It is all but forgotten, living only in the memory of the oldest of the inhabitants of the old city of Gujranwala. Several elderly men remember the walled-in garden that existed until the early 1950s. None, however, know that the *chinar* trees in whose shade they had lounged as young men were the very ones planted by Hari Singh Nalwa. None even know that the garden and the *haveli* had once belonged to this great general, able administrator and keen gardener.

Instead of the garden there is today an ugly, unplanned maze of narrow streets and boxy houses devoid of the least architectural pretences that rise two or three floors to give a feeling of claustrophobia in the streets below. Surely in Hari Singh's time much of the area would have not been built-up and there would have been trees also beyond the boundary of the garden. But the mad rush to build has consumed all the open space. It has devoured the garden that was once the most beautiful in the whole of India.

That is not the irony. The irony is that within fifty-two years of independence we have destroyed what could have been a beautiful green space, the lungs of the old quarter of the city of Gujranwala. The irony is that in this process we have also forgotten a part of the history of Punjab. I wonder how long the *haveli* where Hari Singh lived and which is now the Mosque of the Blind will escape the demolition squad.

When that happens, another man following up in the footsteps of Baron Carl von Hugel will not even have a building as a point of reference. Then one part of our history will finally and irrevocably have died.

---

* The plaque alternately disappears and reappears. On my last visit in 2001, three years after the visit to write this piece, when it had been found again, I requested the son of Maulvi Yasin to install it in one of the rooms on the second floor. I do not know if that was ever done.

NOT A SOUL WAS LEFT LIVING

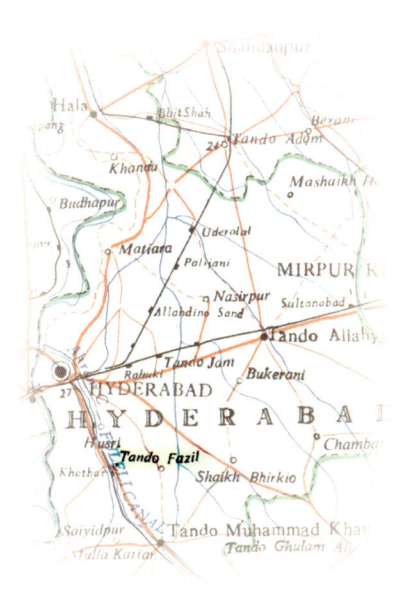

All that remains of an opulent mansion. The eagle owl roosts in the wall on the left.

'Not a soul was left living!'

The deep-throated double hoot of the Indian Eagle Owl rising from the ruin they call the *mari* (mansion) rode the gusting wind across the undulating *peelu*-covered terrain to me on the roof of the derelict mosque. Other than that haunting call and the sigh of the north wind it was silent as it has been for over two hundred years. From my perch on the roof of the mosque I could see the full extent of the ruins of Dhonra Hingora sprawling over perhaps a hundred acres: two mosques, a domed mausoleum, remains of houses, the four corner columns of the *mari*, and massive brickwork that appears to be the remains of a bridge. And

103

One of the mosques among the Dhonra Hingora ruins.

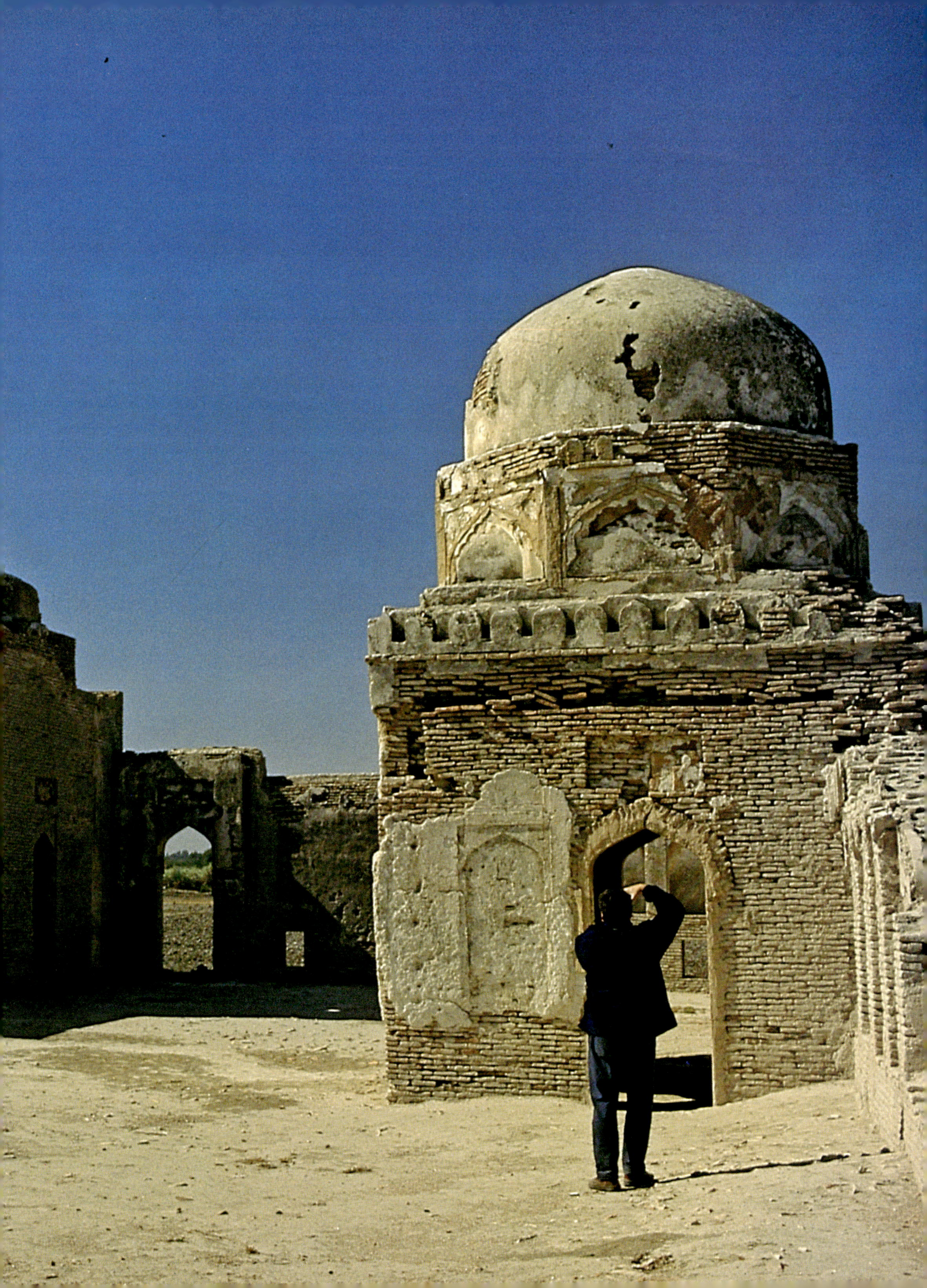

everywhere amid these ruins, shards and shards of glazed and unglazed pottery badly eroded by the saline soil.

Lying outside the small village of Tando Fazal, twenty-five kilometres southeast of Hyderabad on the road to Sheikh Bhirkio, Dhonra Hingora, or the 'Ruins of Tando Fazal' as the sign of the Department of Archaeology calls them, commemorate the lost majesty of a once thriving centre of trade and commerce. Legend recalls a holy man who lived here and took time out from his ecclesiastical duties to prepare and drink vast libations of *bhung*. Indeed so given was he to this narcotic drink that he always had several pitchers brimming with it, ready to be imbibed.

Now the Kalhora ruler of nearby Hyderabad disapproved of this iniquity and one day sent out a troop of soldiers to arrest the man and confiscate his hoard of *bhung*. But when the soldiers arrived the holy man said he only had yoghurt in the pitchers. And sure enough, so the legend goes, when the soldiers looked there was only yoghurt. From that day on, they say, the town of Hingorani has been called Dhonra (yoghurt) Hingora.

The *District Gazetteer* of Hyderabad gives a brief account of the village of Tando Fazal and almost in passing mentions the nearby ruins: '[The village] has in its vicinity some striking ruins, the most remarkable being a *mari* or storeyed house of which one wall, almost intact, rises to a sheer height of forty feet. These are the remains of the town of Hingorani, the former seat of a family of powerful Syeds, which was among the places wrecked by the Afghan Sardar Madad Khan in or about 1775.'

The mosque whose roof I had climbed to survey the surroundings has had a facelift. Its three domes were white washed and the high plinth atop which it sits had a facing of dressed stones. I sent up a silent prayer for whoever had made this effort. Past the mosque I paused in the undulating ground at the massive brickwork. A detached portion, clearly an arch, told me that the whole must have once been a bridge. The winding course of the dry waterway in which I stood gave further credence to my deduction. A minor stream, prone to flooding, must indeed have flowed here for that is the only logical explanation for the ruined bridge as well as the high plinth of the mosque.

As I stood there a *tonga* arrived. Driven by an elderly coachman with snow-white eye brows and hair, it ferried a distinguished looking gentleman of equal age. They paused and we talked of Dhonra Hingora.

'Oh yes, it was indeed that accursed Madad Khan Pathan that had destroyed this city. He plundered it and set it alight. So great was the conflagration that for a full day it was impossible to pass nearby for the heat and for a full night the eerie glow lighted up the landscape. And when the man withdrew, not a soul was left living,' said the coachman. But neither he nor his fare knew the reason for this savage visitation.

Inspection of the eroded site shows several layers of successive occupation and the topmost layer does indeed show signs of a conflagration. Though each layer had an ample sprinkling of animal bones – a common enough phenomenon

Vine and grapes on the façade of the mosque recall the nostalgia of the Central Asian workers who would have crafted this building nearly five centuries ago.

in the case of an omnivorous society, I even perceived human bones near the top. These were surely the grotesque reminders of the abominable Afghan's savagery.

I passed the domed mausoleum with its single grave and paused at the *mari*. The eagle owl glared down at me from its perch and not wishing to disturb it, I walked on. The other mosque, perhaps a little older, had no facelift, yet it seemed to be holding its own well enough. This architectural style is sprinkled all over lower Sindh and having seen several similar buildings I knew that the mosques were built not later than the middle of the 16th century. I knew, too, that such extensive ruins could only recall a city of great wealth and opulence: Hingorani was no mean little provincial town. Part of her wealth would have come from agriculture, perhaps fruit-farming – for that is the kind of country it is situated in. The rest would surely have been a result of assiduous trading. Who knows if Hingorani merchants would have vied with competitors form Shikarpur renowned for their diligence in business and commerce?

The Syeds have always been powerful in Sindh but we do not know which family ruled over Dhonra Hingora or Hingorani and when. But the layer upon layer of occupation of the

The coachman and his fare.

site reveals a long history. What we do know, however, is of the fateful end at the hands of the marauders.

Following the death of Aurangzeb, the uncertainty at Delhi gave the opportunity to Mian Yar Mohammed Kalhora to seize independent power in Sindh in the beginning of the 18th century. A judicious man himself, he was followed by two wise successors, Mian Nur Mohammed and Mian Ghulam Shah. But then came a long line of petty quibblers ending with the weak and inept Mian Ghulam Nabi Kalhora.

The Talpurs who had for over a century looked up to the Kalhoras as spiritual masters represented the only sanity in the court of Sindh in that troubled time. Encouraged by the weakness of the rulers, jealousy was rife and intrigue followed intrigue resulting in the futile murders of some of the best Talpur generals and administrators. In order to stem the surge of conspiracy and artifice, Mir Bijjar Khan Talpur contrived to install the spineless Mian Abdul Nabi, a brother of Ghulam Nabi's, on the throne of Sindh. But he who was taken as a pliable ruler open to advice, proved to be a rare breed of villain who engineered the dispatch of Bijjar Khan at the hands of two Rajasthani mercenaries.

Abdullah Talpur who replaced his father as the head of the clan remained stoically passive.

Driven by guilt, Abdul Nabi was alarmed by this quiet equanimity, which he took to be the sign of a brewing storm, and sought to remove the Talpurs from their powerful position with military aid from the Khan of Kalat. A series of battles ensued in which the Talpurs defeated the Kalhoras and Abdul Nabi fell back on Taimur Shah, the king of Afghanistan. The scourge called Madad Khan was dispatched at the head of a vast army to the aid of the Kalhora feudatory. The price to be paid to the Afghan was a portion of the Kalhora treasure.

Arriving in Sindh, the Afghan demanded his wages, but greed taking the better of him, Abdul Nabi advised the Afghan to make good his expenses by looting the country. This the dastardly Afghan did with his heart and soul and he brought down upon the country a bane the likes of which had never before been witnessed. Cities were plundered and sacked, the living were put to the sword in vast numbers and the dead were left to rot and feed the vultures and the jackals. Seized by a frenzy Madad Khan tore across Sindh leaving in his wake smouldering ruins where opulent towns once stood. He withdrew from the country only when he received news of Abdullah Talpur's preparations for battle.

This was in the year 1781. Such was the slaughter that a terrible famine accompanied by pestilence swept across Sindh and the country was to struggle for years to recover from the effects of the mad Afghan's visitation. Surely the great Shah Latif had envisioned just such an eventuality when he had said that the gravest danger to Sindh was from Kandahar.

One of the towns that the Afghans destroyed that year was Hingorani. Once the pride of its inhabitants, it is now the haunt of the eagle owl and the jackal. No longer do its impressive mosques ring with the call of the muezzin. Now, only the wind sighs through their empty chambers. Somewhere in those forgotten ruins lies a secret that tantalises: why and how did prosperous Hingorani manage to miss the full glare of history?

SEA MONSTERS AND THE SUN GOD

'Here lies Helen of Troy, one of the wives of Alexander.' The tomb of Ali Beg outside Helan village.

The unsung Hero

I set out of Lahore early. Northbound on the Grand Trunk Road, I took the slow passage through Gujranwala and Wazirabad, rather than the faster bypasses and stopped at the old 'Chenab Road Bridge' as the metal plaque says. A hundred metres upstream was the impressive Alexandra Bridge commissioned in January 1876 to carry the first Metre Gauge railway line across the Chenab. Inaugurated by the Prince of Wales (later Edward VII), it was named after his royal consort. But some railwayman called A. A. Qureshi knew only one similar sounding name and that appended with the title 'The Great.' And so it came to pass that this good Qureshi had a sign put up to give out the history of the bridge. The second sentence tells us, without punctuation, that the structure was named 'after Mr Alexandra the Great the then Chief Engineer of North Western Railway.'

I sent up a happy prayer for Qureshi and for that conscientious officer of the future who will have the peeling sign repainted and ordered in three columns to make it easier to read and possible to photograph so that it may enter the realm of history. The contribution of Pakistani railway engineers to the history of British royalty must never be forgotten. For me it was an appropriate diversion for I was on my way to revisit the field of that epic battle fought on the field outside nondescript Mong in May 326 BCE between Raja Paurava* of the Punjabis and Alexander from distant Macedonia.

At seven in the morning Gujrat was still barely awake as I took the road to Phalia. A bustling town, sitting high atop a mound, it is believed by some to be the site of Bucephala, the town Alexander established and named after his much-loved horse Bucephalus. This of course isn't original local research, but what they have been fed by visiting archaeologists. There is no explanation for the apocope of the first two syllables but the last part, they tell you, has been corrupted to Phalia. Brave attempt, and could have been true for the town's antiquity is confirmed by the finds of Greek coins of the period immediately following Alexander's. But Phalia still begs a thorough archaeological survey and the tomb of a horse is yet to be discovered to prove that it is indeed that ancient place named after an unruly horse that was famously tamed by a ten year-old prince in distant Epirus in a far off time.

There are, meanwhile, kernels of doubt. In saying that Bucephala was on the 'spot where [Alexander] crossed the [Jhelum]' Arrian, who wrote the authoritative *The Campaigns of Alexander* in the early years of the 2nd century CE implies that the town was built before the crossing. Also the historian's assertion that the horse died of old age and not from wounds suffered in battle would indicate that it died before the crossing of the river. Plutarch, writing barely sixty years before Arrian, tells us of Bucephala being on the east bank of the Jhelum – which is where Phalia is. Strabo, in the 1st century BCE, also places Bucephala on the west bank of the river and might have been the source for Arrian. Consequently, whenever I am told Phalia is that ancient city named after the horse, I smile and talk about the weather.

Ten kilometres northeast of Phalia is another place that recalls possible Greek influence. Marked Helan on Survey of Pakistan maps, the name is pronounced with a nasal ending. The town is today known for the 16th century tomb of Mirza Sheikh Ali Beg, one of Emperor Akbar's noblemen who was killed here in a skirmish with the doughty Gakkhars. I arrived just before the terrible wind and rainstorm broke, and as I was pottering about the tomb, two elderly men joined me.

Having established that I was just an ignorant bumpkin of a passing traveller they proceeded to educate me.

---

* This is the learned pronunciation. The average man would have referred to the king as Pora, which was rendered Porus on Greek tongues.

'Do you know that the town was established by and named after Helen of Troy, one of Alexander's wives?' asked one.

First Mr Alexandra the Great was a railway engineer; now Helen of Troy was a wife of the Macedonian prince! Boy, my education was really getting along. I asked them if either of these two persons had, perchance, served on the North Western Railway. They looked at me pitifully and added that Helen, being a woman could not have worked and Alexander had lived before they had railways.

The ornate sarcophagus of Ali Beg's tomb came under discussion. On it the name of the nobleman was given in flowing calligraphy, yet the two did not know who was buried therein. They wondered, very gravely (no pun), if the tomb could also date from Alexander's time. But then the calligraphy on the cenotaph prompted them to overturn their own idea. They nevertheless decided that the tomb was very old, very old indeed.

'How about Akbar's time?' I suggested.
'Akbar was yesterday!' the spokesman for the pair said scornfully.

Sometimes coins were found, they told me and after the rain let up we walked into the village to check if we could see some. Parking us at the teashop my guides dispatched a youngster to see about the coins. He returned about twenty minutes later with one 1907 Government of India one-anna issue to show for his labours. The real ones, the spokesman said, were always sold off to collectors. No gold coins had ever been found, only silver and copper. Some of those had writing that 'no one could read.' Others were marked with strange figures. But all their descriptions were so vague that it remained impossible to know what they were talking about.

I thanked them for making my visit such an enriching one and walked back to the car. Through Dinga, past the Chillianwala monument, I headed for the village of Mong. A kilometre or so from the Jhelum River, this village also sits on a mound that rises no less than thirty metres above the surrounding plain. While the eastern flank of the mound is gradual and covered with modern habitation, the western and northern flanks, facing the Jhelum River, are sharply defined. Here can one see ample signs of past occupation rising through layer upon layer: animal bones, perhaps human as well, pottery, ashes and then the houses on top. It is undoubtedly an ancient town, believed by many to be the Nikaea – Victorious, that Alexander established to celebrate his victory over Paurava.

At the teashop I asked for the local historian and soon I was talking to a rather disagreeable piece of work. I offered him tea, which he accepted after an argument. But that did nothing for his mood. He did not know if Mong was Nikaea, but he did know that the battle was fought just by the town. He spoke proudly of Alexander's triumph over Raja Paurava sounding quite like the usual rave about all battles of Islam against the Rest.

'It was a great win,' I observed.
'Oh, it was indeed.'
'Are there fathers in Mong who celebrate that

victory by naming their sons Sikander?' I asked.

'Of course there are! What manner of absurd question is that?' I could just discern his chest expanding with pride.

'But are there fathers here who name their sons after the great Paurava?'

The man, indignation personified, looked at me as if I had uttered the most condemnable blasphemy.

'Porus was no Muslim!' he said contemptuously. 'He was a *Hindu*! The man almost spat out the last word. I was not surprised that my repeated reference to that great king by his real name did not impress the man sufficiently for him to follow suit. I very nearly blurted out that once the rest of us too were Hindus – all of us who have since conversion invented illegitimate Arab fathers for ourselves. Thanks heavens for discretion, however.

'But then neither was Alexander,' I pointed out instead.

'Alexander is named in the Koran, and that is reason enough to name sons after him.'

This was interesting. In Iran where Alexander defeated that cowardly Darius who did not once stand and fight but fled from one ignominy to another, the Macedonian is a villain. For the Iranians Darius, who was not even from the line of Persian kings but a usurper placed on the throne by the intriguing vizier Bagoas, is the great hero. Alexander, the foreigner, is the violator of all that was Persian and thus sacred. The myths overlook Darius' shameful cowardice and lionise him as the defender of Persia. They also overlook Alexander's chivalrous behaviour towards the defeated king's mother, wives and daughters and villianise him.

But in Pakistan, Alexander becomes almost an Islamic hero worshipped for overthrowing the infidel Paurava. The Punjabi kings' admirable gallantry in combat and his magnificent conduct in defeat does not raise Punjabi admiration for this great king for he was not a Muslim and therefore not for them to honour. It matters little to these people that he lived almost a thousand year before the advent of the religion they profess to hold so dear to their hearts.

As for the name of Alexander being contained in the Koran, that too is no more than fable. The name Zulqurnain – the Two-Horned, is what we translate to signify Alexander. Now this king, according to the Koran, was a great conqueror who brought under his control all the countries from the rising to the setting sun. In the course of these adventures he also came upon a barbarous people, the Gog and Magog, against whom he built a wall. The Two-Horned king could have been Alexander who wore the ram's horns with his diadem. And it could also be Cyrus the Great, the Achaemenian conqueror who lived two hundred years before Alexander, whose conquests were no less than the Macedonian's and who also wore a double-horned helmet. If greatness be measured by the longevity of one's kingdom, Cyrus was indeed the greater for his kingdom survived him by two hundred years. Alexander's, on the other hand, did not make it beyond his premature death.

I did not tell my ignorant guide that I had come to celebrate my hero Paurava. I did not tell him that it was this king and this king alone that won Alexander's unstinting admiration in all those years of campaigning in the east. Neither Darius, nor Oxyartes, the father of Roxane, the mother of Alexander's posthumous son, nor any king of the Scythians or of the Pukhtuns, nor of the Sindhis won such unyielding respect from Alexander as Paurava, king of the Punjabis of Chaj Doab, did.

Just outside the town of Mong, where the freshly harvested wheat fields still looked like gold, Paurava had stood at the head of his army against the horde that Alexander mustered. Some eighty thousand fighting men against each other, the one side fighting to defend the sanctity of the land of their forefathers; the other in search of glory and riches. Thence did I go to celebrate my hero exactly two thousand three hundred and twenty-six years after his heroic stand against the Macedonian. It was a day in the month of May when the foreigners, having stolen a night passage across the storm-swollen River Vitasta – Hydaspes to them and Jhelum for us, clashed with the Punjabis.

One wonders if at the moment of his stolen passage Alexander's mind went back a few years. In September 331 BCE, the Macedonians were arrayed against the Persians under the cowardly Darius on the plain outside Gaugamela (Tell Gomel midway between Mosul and Arbil in northern Iraq). In view of the overwhelming disparity favouring the Persians, one of Alexander's generals suggested a night attack. With unusual brusqueness Alexander returned, 'I do not steal victories.'

Young as he was, Alexander did not lack the ability to judge human character: he had full measure of Darius from earlier encounters and knew he was faced with a poltroon. On the Jhelum, he had heard stories of the man he was soon to meet in mortal combat. And these were no mean yarns.

Reading Arrian's pages is like watching a film. The din of the onset, the neighing of horses, the trumpeting of elephants, the wheeling cavalry, the stolid phalanxes of Greek heavy infantry, the thundering chariots, the twang of the Punjabi longbow and the swish of clouds of arrows, the clash of steel upon steel, the cries of the wounded and dying filled my mind in the field outside Mong. From break of day until well into the afternoon the engagement continued. The tide of battle turned against the Punjabis only when their tired elephants could no longer sustain their charges. With the battlefield hallowed with the blood of twenty-three thousand of their dead brothers, the Punjabis began to withdraw.

'Throughout the action Porus proved himself a man indeed, not only as a commander but as a solider of the truest courage. …. his behaviour was very different from that of the Persian King Darius: unlike Darius, he did not lead the scramble to save his own skin … [but] fought bravely on.' No greater tribute could be paid to Paurava than these words of Arrian.

Deserted by all his units, Paurava, bleeding heavily from a grievous wound in his right shoulder – the only part of his torso unprotected by armour in order to permit him to freely draw his bow, at last turned his elephant around and began to withdraw. Then did Alexander send

Ambhi the king of Taxila (who had submitted earlier and was part of the Macedonian retinue) galloping after him with a message. But Paurava and Ambhi had long been at loggerheads and the proud warrior hurled his lance at the approaching messenger who quickly withdrew. Then it was, Arrian tells us, Meroes a much respected friend of Paurava's who came to plead that the king present himself to Alexander.

Paurava, 'much distressed by thirst' asked for a drink. Then, revived, he mounted his friend's chariot and permitted himself to be driven to Alexander's camp. As the Macedonian saw the Punjabi approaching, he rode out with a party of soldiers to meet his opponent. Alexander reined in his horse, writes Arrian, and 'looked at his adversary with admiration: he was a magnificent figure of a man, five cubits high and of great personal beauty.' The cubit being variable in various parts of Greece, this figure would yet mean that Paurava was over seven feet tall – perhaps almost eight and a half. Alexander of middling stature would have had to look up into those dark eyes and the sweat-streaked face.

It was then that the dramatic and well-known exchange took place between two great kings:
'What,' asked Alexander, 'do you wish that I should do with you?'
'Treat me as a king ought,' replied the Punjabi.
'For my part your request shall be granted. But is there not something you would wish for yourself? Ask it.'
'Everything is contained in this one request,' said Paurava the Punjabi whom we are ashamed to claim as our own.

Alexander was so moved by the dignity in defeat of this king that he declared friendship. Subsequently, he did not only return Paurava's kingdom to him but also helped him annex the country between the Chenab and the Ravi Rivers. As for Paurava, he was the only king of the Sindhu Valley who remained steadfast in his loyalty to Alexander even after the latter had left the country – indeed even after he had died in Babylon.

Across the stubble on the rain-drenched ground – very much like Paurava would have found it for the battle was fought after a heavy shower of rain, I walked wondering where Paurava would have dismounted from the chariot of Meroes and where Alexander would have stood somewhat in awe of the towering battle-stained giant. Perhaps on the very spot where I now stood. Repeated readings of Arrian played out the scene in all its grandeur in my mind's eye. I could almost hear the dialogue: Greek into Persian into Punjabi and back the same way through the interpreters. I could see the gigantic Paurava, his massive corselet-covered chest still heaving from the exertion of his blood-letting, standing tall and Alexander arch an admiring eyebrow as he glanced at his generals upon hearing the king's response.

I also saw Alexander reach out and clasp the brown blood-soaked hand in his own. Then, as the import of the king's words sank in fully, I saw him raise himself on his toes and embrace his vanquished adversary, his blond head reaching as high as the Punjabi's breast. Here was a man worthy of admiration and friendship. Here was the only king whose grace and majesty were to find their way into the official histories. Alexander might have eulogised Paurava's conduct in one or more of the frequent letters to his mother Olympias and his tutor Aristotle. Perhaps the king's conduct came repeatedly under discussion among Alexander and his generals in those pre-prandial drinking bouts. Eumenes, the royal secretary, would have made elaborate note of his king's observations on the defeated adversary. It was these letters, diaries and discussions, now lost, that formed, among other material, the basis for the works of Strabo, Plutarch and Arrian.

They tell me a monument has been raised to Paurava, or at least to the battle. I could not find it, nor was there anyone at hand to tell me where to look.* But less than six kilometres to the east of this battlefield, there was a monument. Not to Paurava and his magnificence in adversity, but to the fallen of another battle. Outside the village of Chillianwala, hard by the road, the red sandstone obelisk marks the site of the British field ambulance that served the wounded of the Battle of Chillianwala in January 1839.

There the Sikhs had rallied for the last contest as the British closed in. It was a sanguinary struggle and the plaque on the monument acknowledges the inordinately high number of deaths – especially among British officers. Few people visit this monument, and fewer still understand that the Sikhs fighting for Punjab were standing on ground barely two or three kilometres from where Paurava would have marshalled his forces two millenniums before them.

The Chillianwala monument does not acknowledge the valour of the Sikhs. But then the monument was raised by the British to honour their own. Surely Paurava would have raised a monument too, but that would have crumbled long ago. Paurava, however, would have acknowledged Alexander's superiority in battle. This I can say with impunity for I know from the work of Apollonius of Tyana, a 1st century CE Greek visitor to Taxila, that Paurava did indeed do so.

The king, Apollonius records, had copperplate murals put up in two temples in Taxila. Both plates depicted scenes from his encounter with Alexander. Both showed him the vanquished and Alexander the victor. Both were installed as an acknowledgement of the Punjabi raja's friendship with Alexander some time *after* word arrived from Babylon that the great conqueror had died. Alexander was no more, his Greek garrison in Taxila had deserted along with its officers and Paurava was free to re-write history. He could have painted himself the destroyer of Alexander. That he did not and that he chose to tell the truth, even though unsavoury, is a measure of his greatness.

More than his valour in combat and his dignity in defeat, it was this character and greatness of Raja Paurava's spirit that had brought me to the battlefield of Mong to celebrate my hero. Yet for us who abhor our own pre-Islamic history, he is just a shadow on the periphery of Alexander's radiance. Nothing could be more unfortunate and unjust. It is now time to commemorate the greatest ever king of Punjab.

---

* I have since been to this monument on the west bank of the Jhelum. It lies between the village of Jalalpur and the hill of Mangal Deo.

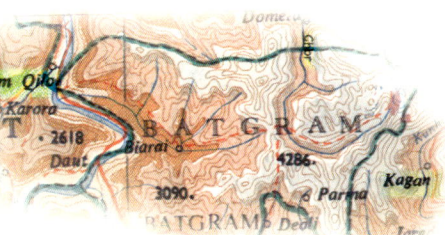

Rashung skies clear up after a shower.

Stranger in Alai

'You want to *walk* through Alai to Kaghan?' The young man asked incredulously. I nodded. 'But it's hard and you're too old!'

Grey hair (even if it is a week old stubble returning after a head shave) certainly does not inspire confidence. The crowd gathered to ogle me at the only hotel in the village of Rashung in Alai Valley snickered and nodded knowingly.

No, I could not do it, they all agreed. I was too old for this sort of thing. One said that since there was every danger of my guide-cum-porter having to carry me over the intervening passes, they would charge a preposterous five hundred rupees per day to go with me.

Having driven all the way from Battagram through Thakot in the Sindhu Gorge to this

SEA MONSTERS AND THE SUN GOD

remote little village in the heart of Alai, it seemed it would after all be impossible to trek across to Kaghan. In my mind, I was already beginning to formulate alternate plans when Maqbool, the Forest Department ranger in whose charge I had been placed at Battagram, intervened. I had done a good deal of mountain walking in my life, he told our audience. For instance, said he, I had climbed K-2.

Never in my life had I been nearer than twenty-five kilometres from this great mountain and never had I climbed higher than 5900 metres (19,300 ft) – a full 3000 metres less than K-2. I hurried to correct him, but he nudged me to shut up. I shut up and if Maqbool had hoped to impress this lot, he failed badly. They made some rude remarks about how I must have reached the summit of K-2, laughed and ordered the next round of tea. Meanwhile, a wild sort of red-beard joined the party. Taj Mohammed, a native of the village of Gungwal further up the valley, said he was interested in portering for me. But on the condition that we pause to shoot all the ibex and musk deer that we meet on the way.

I stood for the conservation of wild species not for senseless extermination, I said. He'd give me more meat to eat than I could imagine, returned Taj Mohammed. I told him I was a vegetarian and the good man looked at me as if

Taj Mohammed and his mates. Before setting off from Gungwal, my guide purchased a pair of new running shoes. While one friend holds his gun, the other threads the laces on the shoe.

I suffered from AIDS, cancer and all other incurable afflictions. Meanwhile, the bucketing rain that had forced us into the inn in the first place let up and Maqbool said we ought to head for Gungwal where we were to spend the night in the Forest Department rest house. There, he said, the deal could be finalised with Taj Mohammed.

The walk was easy in the course of which Maqbool laid on his oratorical finesse to impress upon Taj Mohammed the need to escort me across to Kaghan. At the rest house, however, the man left us without any commitment and Maqbool sauntered off after him into the village to 'look for another porter.' He returned after dark to say that tomorrow, God willing, there would be someone to porter for me. In plain-speak this meant that not having been able to muster anyone, he didn't know what to do next. And so I went to bed in a state of uncertainty.

On the morrow, well before sunrise, Taj Mohammed arrived with his red beard, an aged shotgun across his shoulder and a cartridge belt around his waist. For him this was to be no tame trek, but a hunting expedition. With his wide grin he animatedly told me of all the *kill* (ibex) and *raunce* (musk deer) that roam the high hills east of Alai. For the shikari that Taj Mohammed was, there would be more than sufficient meat that we could share and perhaps a pod or two of musk that would be his. There would be nothing of the sort if I can help it, I thought to myself as we bid farewell to Maqbool and set out on the trail leading out of the village.

Immediately east of the last houses of Gungwal, the forest encroached upon the maize fields. We were 1900 metres above the sea and it was largely coniferous with a few broad-leaf varieties. In the several valleys of Kaghan and Siran and in the surroundings of Abbottabad and Mansehra the only species of pine tree is what I call Toilet Brush Pine (*Pinus toilet brushicus*). This is the tall pine tree with its branches lopped off and burnt by the rapidly multiplying humanity that lives around it and has no other fuel. The little tuft of green left at the top to give it a semblance of tree, is also the little tuft that makes it look exactly like a toilet brush. Hence, *Pinus toilet brushicus*.

There are few sights more offensive than such a shorn and forlorn tree. But there is no way to prevent this crude topiary – except of course through a very special breed of infallible forest rangers. Since we do not have those, this great crime against the beauty of nature shall continue. Here in Alai, however, it was very gratifying to note that the pine trees were what pine trees should be: neat tapering cones of well-proportioned branches covered with healthy vegetation. There were, of course, some signs of felling, but the forest was, by and large, healthy and regenerating. Being in these hardwoods was like being caught in an ambuscade of birdsong: it shot out at us from all directions. It was after a very long time indeed that I was walking through what could be called, with a little overstatement, a 'primary' forest.

I had arrived in Alai three days after the worst storm in living memory had savaged the valley. Though it had not caused any loss of life but the gale that had swept through at an estimated

'Have gun will travel.' Taj Mohammed who wouldn't leave home without his shotgun en route to Ajri Kandao.

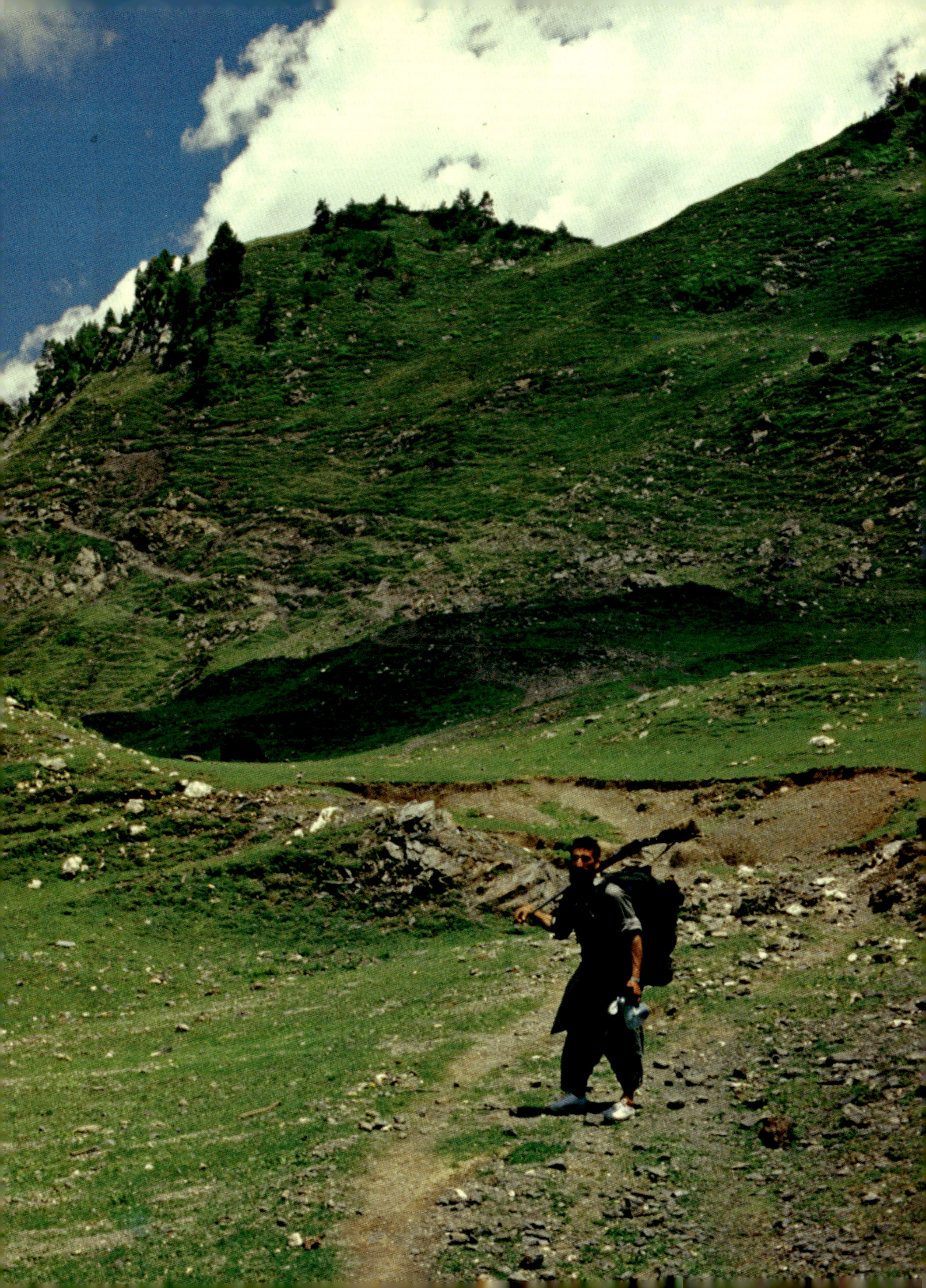

hundred and fifty kilometres per hour had snapped scores of hefty pine trees in halves or simply yanked them right out of the earth, roots and all. The dead trees littered the forest and lay next to our path or sometimes even across it.

Though this was what they call a '*guzara*' forest, that is, owned privately where local populations can utilise forest wealth for their own use, they cannot harvest it commercially. Consequently, even to get this storm-harvested timber to the market was illegal so far as the Forest Department was concerned. The procedure, Maqbool had earlier told me, would be a long drawn-out hassle of reporting the number of damaged trees to ask for a survey to be carried out before the timber could actually be removed to the market. But surely this is the only way to prevent greed from taking over and beginning a wild scramble to take down even healthy trees under cover of storm damage.

Climbing up the high ridge that separates Alai from the Chor Valley that lies on the route to Kaghan, Taj Mohammed pointed out the footbridges destroyed by the recent storm, five in all. Three hours of an easy walk brought us to Jabr where they have a couple of houses and the last watering hole before Ajri Kandao (Pass). Such an establishment in the Alps would have served up some fine German Weizen Bier, but here in the Western Himalayas we had to fortify ourselves with cups of very sweet tea. The innkeeper, a smiling , friendly Alaiwal (as they call themselves) insisted that we spend the night in his care. But we had places to go and having tarried long enough took our leave.

A hard climb of two and a half hours brought us to the top of the pass at 3050 metres above the sea. On the other side an hour's descent betook us into the plain of Chor. The first houses that we saw in the valley below were the settlement of Larray Kus,* the summer home of the nomadic Gujjars who come up to this fertile grassland from Alai. All along the descent Taj Mohammed had been carrying on about the wild and lawless Kohistanis who come up the valley from Palas to rob and vex – and sometimes, even kill. They were evil people who knew no law, said he. He even had a story to tell of the Kohistanis who had kidnapped a girl from Alai, yet they persecuted any Alaiwal that came within range. He sounded as if the Kohistanis were mad at the Alaiwals for making available a kidnap-able girl! The story made no sense at all, but Taj Mohammed insisted upon its veracity.

It needs be clarified here that the Kohistanis of Palas, though they (like other Kohistanis) have assimilated the worst elements of Pukhtun culture, are ethnically distinct from the Pukhtuns. While their kinsmen, the Kohistanis of the right bank of the Sindhu speak Kohistani, these of Palas and other left bank communities speak Shina, which is also spoken in Astore, Gilgit and parts of Baltistan to the east. Linguists and anthropologists place both Kohistani and Shina in the Indo-Dardic group having a strong affinity with the classical Prakrits of northern India. Pukhtu, on the other hand, derives from archaic Persian.

---

* The name means Stream by the Wayside.

Looking northward into Chor Valley from the foot of Ajri Pass.

Interestingly, the Alaiwals all claim to be Yusufzais who migrated to Alai, according to one rather weak tradition, under pressure of the Karlugh Turks. Now these Turkish incursions that began with the advent of the 11th century CE and petered out after the death of Taimur the Lame, were all mounted in the glorious name of Islam. Yet, in reality, they were no more than plundering campaigns by bloodthirsty and impoverished savages. The histories of Mahmud of Ghazni and Taimur the Lame shamelessly gloat over the vast riches and number of slaves that the land of the Sindhu River yielded giving the lie to the purported religious purpose of these raids. Wearying from this periodic killing, plundering and enslaving one branch of the

Granite spires north of the glaciated crest of the pass whose name I never learnt.

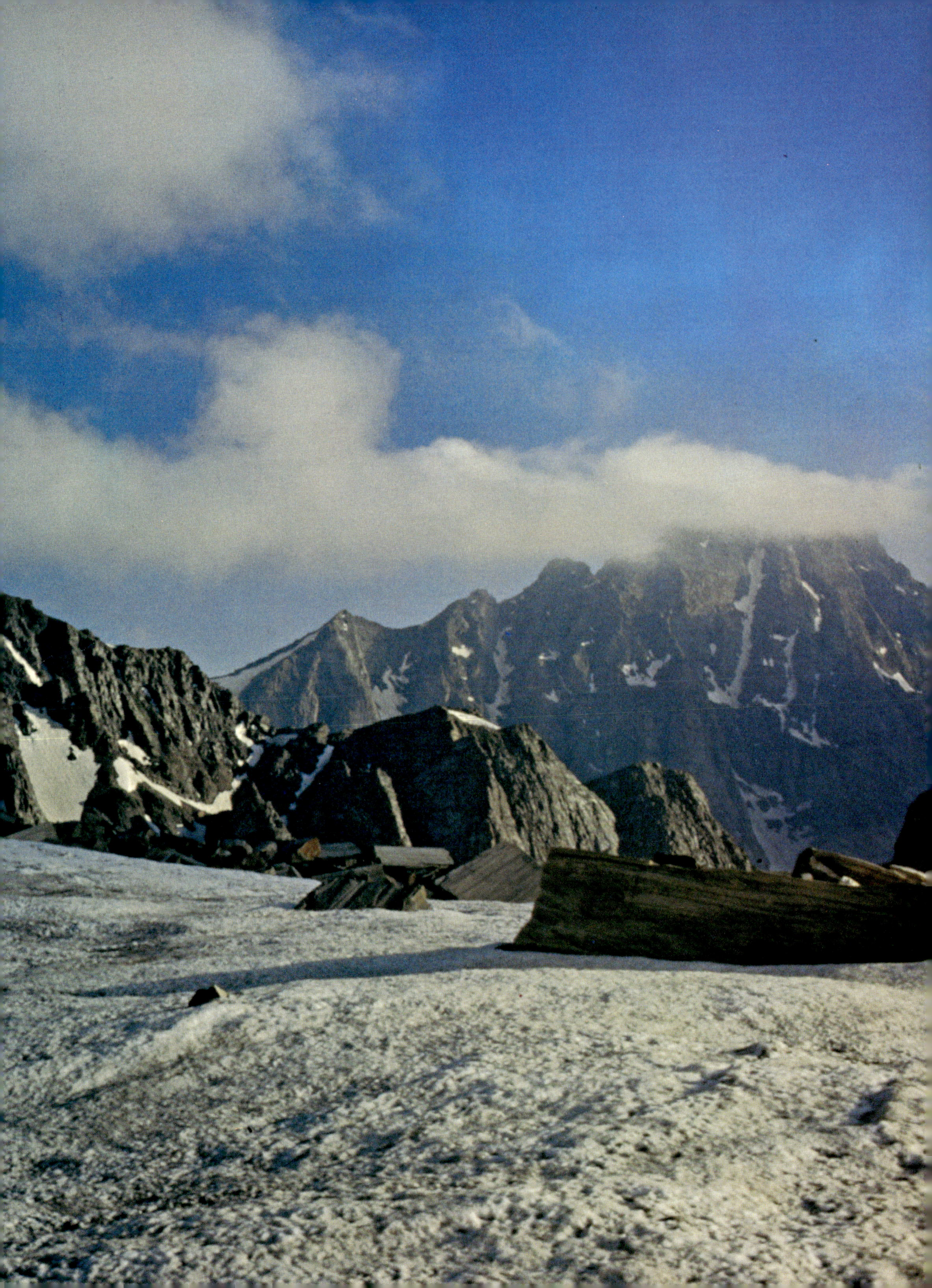

Yusufzais of the rich agricultural country of Mardan, goes the tradition, sought the new and relatively safer refuge of Alai.

My friend, Adam Nayyar, the renowned anthropologist, takes erudite and earnest exception to this argument however. The Alaiwals, says he, are not Pukhtuns but the original inhabitants of Swat who were pushed out by the expansion of the Yusufzais. Among other elements, they borrowed the language from their Pukhtun adversaries.

Since all subcontinental Muslims have either come from Arabia or Central Asia ('original Muslims', as they like to call themselves, and not converts), I am surprised no end that pseudo-intellectuals from Alai have not yet invented their connection with Central Asia which will make them better than the Yusufzais in their own eyes: there is in Kyrgyzstan a mountain range and a peak called Alai. And sooner rather than later some half-baked historian should assign to the Alaiwals a Kyrgyz origin.

We crossed a log bridge over the stream that we had followed down from Ajri Pass and were in what some trekkers have wrongly termed the Chor Plain. Chor is, in fact, the upper reach of the Palas Valley of Kohistan that stretches some seventy-five kilometres in a southeasterly direction from Pattan in the Sindhu Gorge. From its height of 3000 metres in its watershed, it eases down to 800 metres at its confluence with the Sindhu near Pattan. Since this descent of 2200 metres progresses through seventy-five kilometres, a very gradual drop indeed, the valley gives the illusion of being a wide, elongated plain. That it surely is not.

Another thing that Chor certainly is not is a part of Alai as claimed by the Khan of Alai. And I say this on geographical basis. Chor, as has been said above, is actually Upper Palas Valley of Kohistan. The river that flows north through it waters Palas before emptying itself into the Sindhu, while the 3000-metre high Ajri Pass forms the watershed between Chor and Alai. This topography separates the two valleys by a boundary as physically stark as stark can be. But being so distant, and with plenty of far more fertile side valleys nearer at hand in middle Palas, the Kohistanis never saw the need to travel the long distance to Chor in order to pasture their herds in summer.

Meanwhile, the Khan of Alai, who also was the Khan of the several Gujjar families that wintered in his valley, was receiving the annual tribute of *ghee* and goats from his herdsman subjects who availed of the bounty of Chor. Consequently he laid claim to this fertile grassland. This was easy enough, for it takes but half a day to cross the Ajri Pass from Alai into Chor, while the Palas Kohistanis had to travel at least three days to get to it. The Kohistanis, moreover, were not watching when the Khan of Alai annexed Chor. This, if you please, is then an older and miniature version of the Siachen conflict between Pakistan and India.

The volatile Kohistanis of Palas, finding the upper reaches of their valley attached by the Khan, took violent exception. The feud began in which the Alaiwals were largely discomfited. Among other losses, the great-grandfather of the present Khan of Alai was killed in one of the skirmishes. John Biddulph writing just over a hundred years ago was not wrong when he noted (*Tribes of the Hindoo Koosh*): 'One branch of the Alai Valley stretches up towards the head of the Palus (*sic*) Valley, from which it is separated by a low pass.' He went on to say that the men of Alai casting 'longing eyes on the Palus land' had given rise to disputes. So these quarrels continue down to our times and with a few lives lost on either side show no signs of early settlement.

The one help the government provided in this squabbling was the hare-brained idea of a hydel project on the Chor stream at Larray Kus. In a nutshell, it was to dam the waters and transfer them by tunnel into Alai. It was monumental imbecility to expect the Kohistanis to put up with it. They came down in force and kidnapped thirty-five staff members of the Karachi-based engineering firm working on the project. The government had to backtrack before the anarchy-loving Kohistanis of Palas released these people.

Adam Nayyar adds a hilarious footnote to this grand fiasco: in order to appease the Palasis, a brochure was prepared clarifying the matter. Unfortunately the visual was a photo taken against the sun with a polygonal flare showing up on the mountainside. This, the Palasis were convinced, was the 'hole' meant to convey the water from Chor to Alai. Nayyar, who had a part to play in all this, had a hard time convincing them that their fears were in vain.

Taj Mohammed, however, was unaware of the mass kidnapping of engineers. He told me of the

The honky-tonk man of Chor. The lute, fashioned out of a slat of wood and an empty plastic oil can, produced a wild, jangling tune. To this accompaniment, the man sang a soulful song.

helicopter nipping down just in time to pluck the 'three Germans' as the Palasi force was coming down. This of course was fable, for there were no foreigners on this project.

We made it to the mosque of Larray Kus well before sunset and settled down for the night. The end of our first day out of Gungwal was both dull and eventful in equal measure.

Taj Mohammed had exhibited, quite explicitly, that he was in nervous thrall of the Kohistanis. Going by his description, these people were the meanest pieces of work ever devised by God or the Devil. Killing and plundering was to them as breathing was to the rest of humanity. And having come over Ajri Pass and descended into Chor we were right in their territory.

While I was putting up my tent on the roof of the mosque there appeared, as if on cue, a young, lanky man with a Kalashnikov slung over his shoulder. He quizzed Taj Mohammed and I heard the good man tell him that I was a colonel surveying for the proposed road from Alai to Kaghan. How he had contrived this one, I shall never discover, but thereafter as long as we remained within range of the purportedly evil Kohistanis, that was the story Taj Mohammed told everyone.

Having told Taj that I ought to sleep in the mosque like the rest of them, the Kohistani came over and asked why we were travelling through Chor. Emboldened by the endowment of the title of colonel, and wishing to play the part well, I brusquely asked the man if there was anything the matter with his ears. A little confounded the man said no, there was nothing wrong with them.

'So, didn't you hear what my man said to you? Why do you want to hear the same thing twice?' I asked, pleased with my role of the colonel. The man withdrew. Later he told Taj Mohammed to get me to sleep in the mosque because other Kohistanis, not being as God-fearing as him, were likely to come down in the night and finding me alone in my tent, rob me. There was also the added excitement of a knife being run across my throat. Years ago I had learned that one thing the Kohistanis feared more than the God they daily worship five times, was an officer wearing the uniform of the Pakistan Army. I was therefore not being overly gutsy by remaining in my tent.

Early the next morning this man saw us off, and this thankfully was the last we saw of him. In an hour we were passing the houses of Marria where we stopped by the mosque. Kala Khan Gujjar, the head of this group, offered tea and we accepted. As we waited, Taj Mohammed delivered his little spiel about the 'surva' we were carrying out to push the road through to Kaghan. For good measure he added that this road was to go on to Chilas and eventually connect with Siachen Glacier. It was just as well that none of these simple folks were proficient in Himalayan and Karakorum geography or they would have drummed us out of their valley in return for this not very bright bit of fibbing.

Not only did we get away with it, but the information also delighted Kala Khan. Why, this was the best thing to happen to this area, and after the road was through, he could even take his herd to sell in Kaghan. We were both good men, he declared, to have taken upon ourselves this arduous task and would we like to stay until lunch? We said tea was just fine and, having done with that, we were soon by ourselves again.

Three hours later we passed another mosque (roofless this time) and a couple of houses. Taj Mohammed suggested we should wait in the mosque and ask the householders to send us some food. He repeatedly hailed the house, but no one turned up. A couple of young women peered shyly from behind the walls and a bunch of children arrived to sit on top of the mosque wall and gape at us. Taj tried his Pukhtu and then his Urdu with them. They giggled back at us. I tried Punjabi. They giggled some more and whispered to each other in Gujri. Presently, a young bearded man arrived. He was the mullah who serviced the religious needs of the widely spread out households of this area called Sar Kus – Stream at the Head of the Valley.

It was apparent that he wielded considerable influence for shortly after his shout two girls came out to ask what we would like to have. And so fortified with tea, chapattis and a large bowl of yoghurt we thanked the mullah and set out again. Having told me for the hundredth time that he had once killed a musk deer in the hill on our left, Taj Mohammed now had to say that a friend of his had been even luckier. In a single outing this man and his two partners had slaughtered a total of nine of those animals! He assured me for the hundredth time that we were sure to bag at least one musk deer or ibex. Then he proceeded to shoot my plan to bits.

I had hoped to trek over a low pass (about 3300 metres) and reach the rest house of Sharan in a minor side glen of the main Kaghan Valley. Since I had booked this rest house in Abbottabad, I was looking forward to a bath and a day of relaxation, reading and bird watching. But Taj Mohammed thought otherwise. As we passed by the mouth of the gorge that would have led us to Sharan, he said we had the choice of leaving Chor by Chumber Pass a little farther up the valley. Once over that pass, it would take us an hour to reach Kaghan town, he assured me.

I wasn't exactly looking forward to the walk from Sharan into the main valley, and this proposition sounded pretty good to me. I asked Taj Mohammed again and again if he was certain about the route and the travelling time. Of course he was, said he. He had done it only the previous winter. Further up the valley Taj Mohammed paused to ask another Gujjar if Chumber Pass was open – and I foolishly continued to believe that he knew the route. The man said it being past midday, we would not be able to make it across if we went the regular way. In any case, a bunch of dangerous people was camped right under the pass and was likely to attack us in the night.

'Is it Jehangira from Kala Dhaka?' a visibly alarmed Taj Mohammed asked.

'Yes,' said the man. 'It is indeed Jehangira Dakoo.' For the past seven years I have heard of Jehangira every time I have gone walking in or around Kaghan. If one were to rely on the current stories, there must be at least a dozen clones of this most dangerous man running wild simultaneously in Kala Dhaka west of the Sindhu River and Kaghan in the east.

'But Jehangira is dead.' I said trying to put Taj Mohammed at ease. 'I heard that in Kaghan six years ago.'

'No, he cannot be dead. Evil such as Jehangira lives on forever.' Taj was past comforting.

My travel companion somehow seemed aware that this particular clone of Jehangira would have no qualms in running the knife across the throat of a road surveying (counterfeit) colonel and his orderly.

'So what are we to do?' I threw the question

without aiming it either at the Gujjar or Taj. The Gujjar pointed out the ridge in front of us and the path zigzagging up it. If we took the path, he said, in two hours we would be at the top and over on the other side, cunningly having skirted the camp of Jehangira and his not-so-merry band.

The ridge stood straight up. I balked at the idea for at my age I have nothing to prove, no heroics to perform, no records to set and want to be in camp well before sunset with the pot bubbling on the stove. Moreover, I had planned an easy walk to Sharan and an easy, relaxing day there, not some struggles up rock faces. Briefly the thought of backtracking to the original plan passed across my mind. But then, foolishly, I again considered the wall that stood athwart of our line. I estimated it was at least six hundred metres high. That would make it about 3500 metres above the sea, and even though I was not acclimatised (it was my second day in the hills), I told myself we would be over it in less than two hours.

And so we went zigzagging up the sharply rising path. In an hour and a half we reached an elongated grassy shelf that was about five hundred metres wide. Beyond it there was no path and the slope seemed to rise at a gradient of sixty degrees or so. We literally had to heave ourselves up the contours as a spanking great storm came billowing out of the north. Soon we were engulfed in the wet mist with great flashes of sheet lightning tearing up the clouds above.

I told Taj Mohammed his stupid shotgun sticking above his head was a veritable lightning conductor and he ought to turn it around or cover it up or, better still, dump it. He dismissed my warning with a casual remark about God being his preserver. With every flash of lightening I repeated myself and so did Taj Mohammed. I fell back a little so as to be out of range of the lightning strike and thought how I would best dispose of his charred body and whether the police would come looking for me when he failed to return home.

It was just as well that the rain came teeming down before the lightening strike and we sought shelter under a rock overhang. An hour later with the storm having passed we were again hauling ourselves up the hill with me noisily reviling Taj Mohammed for having got me into this situation. By five in the afternoon, almost five hours after we had left the valley floor, we were in the glaciated pass at an altitude of 4050 metres. We had climbed not 600 metres, as I had estimated, but a full 1100 metres. So much for my estimation of heights!

Across the decaying, cracking glacier we stepped gingerly not knowing how deep it could be. The fear of it breaking to engulf one of us was intensified because we had no rope, so essential in such a situation. We crossed over without mishap, however. The descent was over a vast jumble of moraine material, great chunks of shattered rock, the harvest of the glacier that would have once choked this valley as little as two or three hundred years ago.

By nightfall we had reached a grassy meadow at 3450 metres to quickly fix dinner and turn in before the inky darkness of the moonless night swallowed us up. The next morning found us walking a full five hours to reach Kaghan against the one hour that Taj Mohammed had promised from the crest of the pass. Yet he insisted that he knew the route well!

Encounter with a lovelorn Poet

We met him on our way up the Ajri Kandao. He sat by the path whittling away on a tiny piece of wood with an ungainly adze. Taj Mohammed said he was making a needle to apply antimony to the eyes and paused to greet him. The man looked up abstractedly, shook hands, mumbled a few words in Pukhtu and returned to his work. The faraway almost vacant look in his eyes gave the unmistakable impression that he was mentally deficient, but as we walked away, Taj Mohammed said, the man had 'two cupboards full of books' in his home in village Rashung. He was also a poet, he added.

As we lounged over tea in the little inn below Ajri Kandao, the poet caught up with us again. The haunting, faraway look was still there as he quietly came in and sat to one side of the one-room inn. Wordlessly cradling his cup of tea in both hands he started to sip without looking up at anyone. Wazir Mohammed who sports the *nom de plume* of Sha'ir Wazir Mohammed Zakhmi, had to be coaxed into speaking.

He did not know when he was born, but in 1959 when his 'beard had not yet sprouted' and with just two years of schooling he travelled to Karachi with an uncle to seek his fortune. Finding work in a textile mill, he worked by day and went to a religious seminary in North Nazimabad by evening. Under an able master he learnt the *hadith* and the Quran. He read the Book in translation and also perfected his Arabic recitation so that he could recite the complete

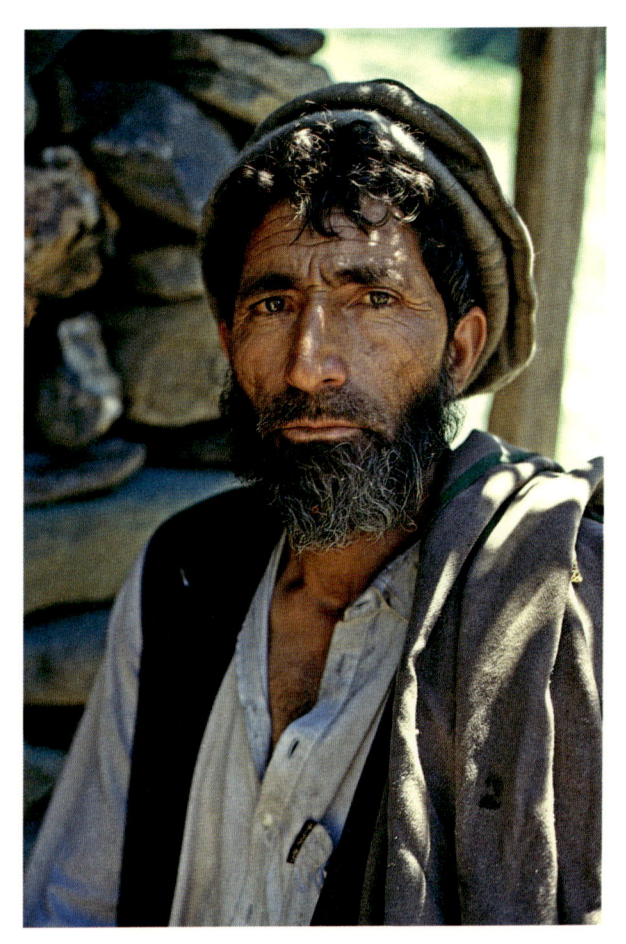

The wounded poet: Wazir Mohammed Zakhmi.

Quran in just over seven hours.

In 1963 he started to write poetry in Pukhtu, and a year later in Urdu as well. So prolific was his Urdu work that by the beginning of 1965 he was the master of a hefty manuscript. This work which was largely of a religious tone with a sprinkling of philosophy was unfortunately lost. Then love entered the life of Wazir Mohammed when, purely by chance, he set eyes upon Fauzia. A pharmacist by training, she was the daughter of a reasonably successful lawyer of Nazimabad. It was difficult for a mill working lovelorn poet to approach a middle-class educated girl. And so for eleven long years Wazir Mohammed daily stood by the way Fauzia passed on her way to work with a government laboratory.

By his own account, Fauzia became aware of his presence. They exchanged glances, but he never spoke to her; never was he able to tell her how besotted he was. For eleven long years from 1965 to 1976 this went on every workday. His poetry underwent a transformation. From addressing his God and the Prophet, Wazir Mohammed wrote mostly for the love of his life. Then one day the worst happened: Fauzia's family sold their house and moved away. Frantically the young lovelorn mill worker from distant Alai Valley tried to find their new place of residence. But he failed.

Though he seemed reluctant to admit, it may be that the lawyer's family had discovered this vain infatuation – as it may have seemed to them. Perhaps Fauzia herself reported the daily wordless encounter to her family. There might even have been a confrontation between Wazir Mohammed and the men of Fauzia's family. But the poet did not speak of all this. For him, the love of his life had suddenly vanished from his world. Though he knew where she worked and could have sought her there, Wazir Mohammed was reluctant to talk about any such endeavour that he might or might not have made.

This great catastrophe, he said, changed everything for him. It made him a *malang*. He wandered the streets of Karachi, searching, searching, searching. But it was all in vain: he never found the one he sought. It got more and more difficult for him to work. He became reclusive, crowds disturbed him, even the company of friends was oppressive. The poet became Wazir Mohammed Zakhmi (Wounded). At last, broken-hearted and in utter despair he left the city that had brought love to his life only to take it away and returned to his native Rashung in Alai.

In the course of these past thirty-five years or so, he has accumulated a total of one hundred and twenty-four hefty manuscripts, four of these have been published. The ones in Urdu were published by a firm in Karachi while the Pukhtu collection has come out from Peshawar. But Wazir Mohammed Zakhmi who has never received any institutional support does not care if his remaining work ever sees the light of day or not. He is certain that one day, when he is no more, it will all be published.

From wandering the streets of Karachi, Wazir Mohammed drifts through the Alai Valley, a ghost with vacant eyes who is always somewhere else. There is a tangible sadness about this man who never married and whom few have seen smiling. He carries the burden of an unattainable passion that the passage of almost a quarter century has not lightened.

He was travelling around Alai to assess the damage done by the violent storm of only three days before in order to record it in his poetry. There being no newspapers or other record in Alai, he hoped his poems would preserve for posterity the memory of this dreadful storm that many had thought was the precursor of the end of the world. 'I now write about everything between the earth and the sky,' he said.

Wazir Mohammed recited some of his Urdu couplets for me and I was impressed by his command over the language. It was as if he had a more than fair knowledge of Persian. Though he confessed he did not, he quoted freely from Hafiz Shirazi as well. For a man who had only two years of formal schooling he was unique. That he had gone on to become learned in theology yet keeping himself from descending into the depravity of intolerant fundamentalism is a measure of his intellect. An even greater measure of this mind from remote Rashung is the collection of some hundred books that fill the cupboards of his mud, stone and timber house.

On request he recited a Pukhtu poem (*lobha*) for us. His mournful voice made this ode to Fauzia almost a dirge, and I thought I even perceived a tear in his eyes. My Pukhtu being extremely basic, I was unable to judge the merit of the poetry. But if one were to go by his Urdu work and the fact that he has four published books, there surely is something to be said for his work. If nothing else, here is an extraordinary person born in a poor house with but two years of formal schooling who, when he is not roving God's earth, spends time with books. Will Sha'ir Wazir Mohammed Zakhmi then die uncelebrated, barely known outside his native Alai?

Sakhia, the sahib of Gori.

Sakhia Revisited

It was a balmy day in February 1989 that he came upon me sitting under a *kundi* tree by the side of the road skirting the small village of Gori in the heart of the Thar Desert. I was in no hurry for I was awaiting the westbound *kekra* (W.W.II vintage truck) to carry me out of the desert and so we sat together and talked. Sakhia in his Sindhi (or was it Thari?) and I in my mix of Sindhi and Punjabi. We got along like a house on fire and Sakhia, all of twelve years old, endeared himself to me like few people have in my thirty years of travelling.

I returned to Thar on a brief visit in 1995

but despite my wish, failed to get as far as Gori. Indeed in these past years I had often thought of Sakhia. What would a live wire like him be doing in the backwaters of the Thar Desert? Wouldn't he have moved on to a job in Hyderabad or Karachi? Or even to the Gulf? Would he have added to his two years of schooling? I even imagined young Sakhia, with his intelligent, active mind to be a sahib. Of course there was also the dreadful thought of him having got on the wrong side of the law. And so it was in quest of this remarkable person that I asked our convoy of three jeeps and twenty odd people to pause a while in the village of Gori.

Sakhia was a common enough name, I was told, so which Sakhia did I seek? He would be about twenty, said I. Two of them were that age, returned the man. He was a Bheel, I tried again. So was everyone else because Gori was a Bheel village. Sakhia, said I finally, was as bright a spark as the village of Gori could ever have produced; a right little devil was he. Ah, that one, said the man with a flash of recognition lighting his face. He worked the cotton fields near Mirpur Khas. That came down on me like a wet blanket: I would be unable to see my man. But he was visiting his family, said someone. And they went away to get Sakhia.

Back in 1989 Sakhia had told me of the Angrez doctor who worked in the local hospital

Pageantry in the dome of the main foyer of Gori temple.

The Jain temple of Gori which had first betaken me there in 1989.

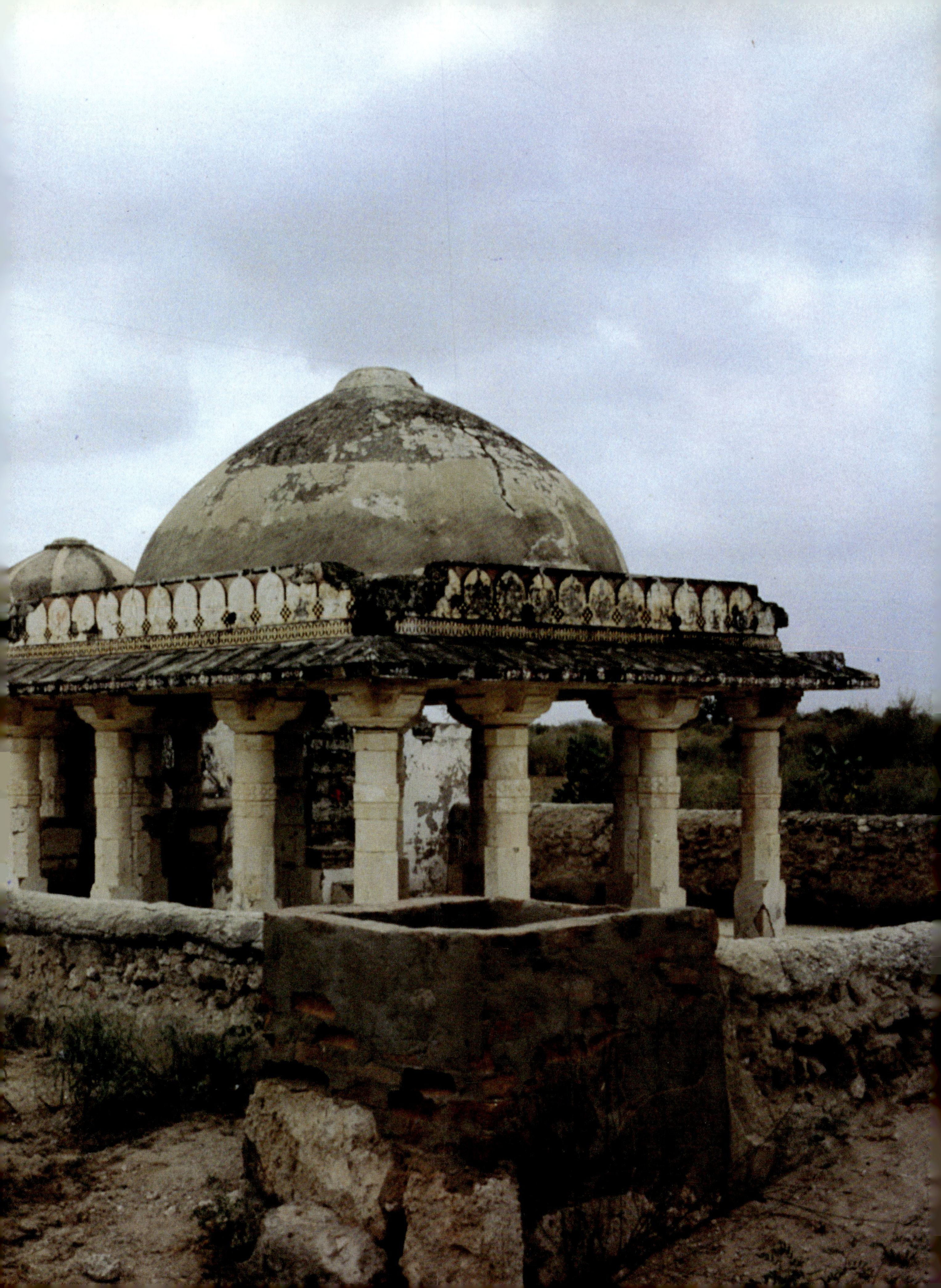

and whose wife had gone away 'with stomach.' His loud, naughty laughter had made it sound like a pregnancy of highly suspect origin. Going off tangentially he had then asked me if I knew Javed Jabbar. I said yes, and the little devil condescended to inform me that I of course did not know of the pretty girls he had brought with him on the *kekra* only the week before.

He asked for my socks, but later not liking them offered to sell them back to me. When I declined he said he would give them to me as a gift, for he worried what my friends in the city would think of me returning without my socks. Sakhia had made the act of being sock-less sound almost illegitimate and scandalous. Then, in the very next breath, with untainted, childlike innocence he asked me for my pants! I burst out laughing, and Sakhia, somewhat discomfited, wanted to know if I was laughing at him. His masterstroke, however, was inflating the goats. Inserting a stalk of sere grass about four centimetres long into a goat's teat he blew up the udder, and then milked it to produce a dry farting sound. Then he inflated the goat once again.

'Its owner will think the goat is full of milk,' he had grinned. 'But all he'll get tonight will be some old air.'

This time around, a full ten years and six months down the road, Sakhia was a stocky man, married and with children of his own. Working as a tractor driver on a farm near Mirpur Khas he had come home to visit with his family – entirely to my good fortune. Of course he did not remember me, yet from the outset he generously regarded me a friend.

'But I had taken your picture. And you still don't remember me!' I accused him.

'So had dozens of other visitors to Gori. None of them was important enough to be remembered,' he returned. I became unsure if I was talking to the right Sakhia.

'Did you like to drink goat's milk and then inflate their empty udders? Or were there other children who practiced this craft?' A jaunty smile cracked his angular face and his eyes shone with a cherished recollection.

'That,' he said with undisguised pride, 'was my art alone.'

I had the right man! There was no recollection of the socks, though. A little later he asked, somewhat thoughtfully, if these were white socks. Somewhere in the mysterious recesses of his mind was a trivial item filed away under the title: 'White Socks.'

In the years that I had thought of him and looked forward to seeing him again, I had always imagined him having done better than his peers. Of that he was confident: if his friends earned a rupee, he was making something more than that. I asked if the work of a tractor driver was good.

'If it weren't good, wouldn't I have been a dacoit?' Sakhia said with as straight a face as he had when asking to be given my pants ten years ago.

It is common knowledge that all paid drivers are crooks who steal fuel, oil and spare parts, so I asked Sakhia if he too could be so accused. Without pausing to think, he said that since all employees are necessarily crooks so too was he. He sold diesel sometimes to pay for his food, drink and cigarettes.

'You know, sometimes my *seth* does not have any money to give me for the day and he tells me to improvise. So I improvise by selling diesel.' That, he said, was not theft (*chori*) but something taken as a matter of right (*zori*).

Someone in the crowd sitting around us said that one day this improvisation will lead to the selling off of the tractor. Sakhia laughed out loud at the suggestion. That, he was quick to point out, would mean killing the goose that laid the golden eggs. I said if ever his landlord read my article and learned that he was selling diesel on the side, Sakhia was sure to lose his job, perhaps even get to see the inside of a police station. But he appeared entirely at ease for he enjoyed his Qaimkhani employer's absolute confidence. This is manifest in the fact that every year, just before the monsoon rains, Sakhia brings out his landlord's tractor to rent it out to small farmers in Thar. Never does the landlord or a supervisor accompany the man to keep an eye on the number of hours he works and the money he turns in.

'I have worked for this same master for six years.' Sakhia said with visible pride. 'If he didn't trust me, I wouldn't have kept this job so long.'

'Sakhia, I am a bit disappointed for I had imagined you to be a sahib.' I said.

'No need to be upset,' said he, 'I am a sahib in my home and in the village. I don't have to be in an office to be a sahib.' The spirit of the child I had met ten years ago, was still living.

'Can any of your children inflate goat's udders?'

'No. Is it such a great thing that they should?' Then without waiting for a reply he added, 'I could teach them if you say.'

But more important than that was their education which was clearly low priority. I appealed and he solemnly nodded his head in favour of schooling. I could not tell how seriously he was taking my exhortation.

As we were parting we talked of the possibility of our next meeting. 'As long as friends live, they are bound to meet again, even though it may take twenty years.' Sakhia gave his own words to an ancient Persian dictum. We shook hands and he walked out of the hospital compound where we had parked ourselves at the head of the crowd gathered to witness our meeting – a very sahib leading his entourage. Outside the gate the shout went up about the inflated goats' udders. I smiled.

For ten years Sakhia had kept his little game to himself, that day he would have to teach it to the youngsters of Gori. But another twelve year-old showing it off to future travellers would surely lack the spontaneity that I had witnessed. And when, perchance, they tell me of it, I shall sit back and gloat for I had the good fortune of waiting under the *kundi* tree outside Gori for a *kekra* on that long ago February afternoon. I had the good fortune of seeing the original show.

SEA MONSTERS AND THE SUN GOD

History's forgotten Page

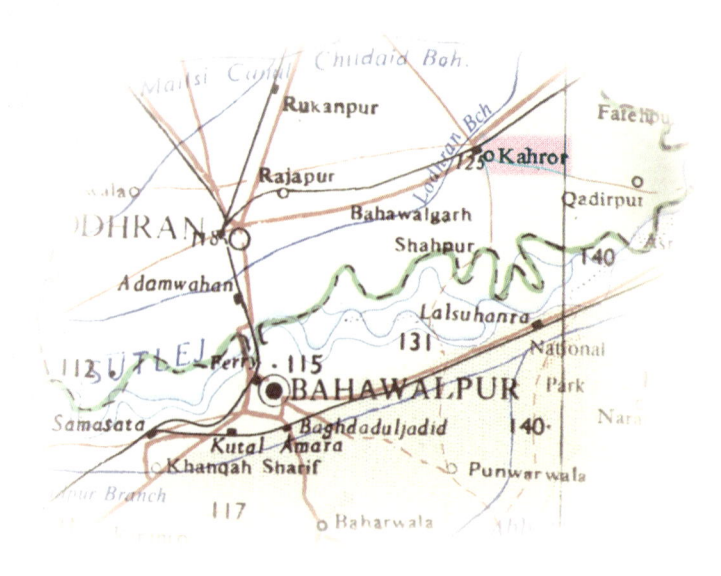

It was the middle of the 5th century CE. And it was a time of despair for the lands now called Afghanistan, Pukhtunkhwa and Punjab. The bleak, windswept steppes of Central Asia, fertile only with destructive storms of savages, had unleashed yet another howling monster: the White Huns. From the same stock that had set Attila on Europe only decades before, these savages under a man called Tor Aman (Toramana of English texts) had destroyed all that was sacred in the land of the Pukhtuns. With smouldering ruins of once great cities and rotting carcasses of man and beast littering their wake, these barbarians were poised to cross the Sindhu.

Cross this great river they did. Taxila and her monasteries were sacked, the populace was put to the sword, only the lucky ones escaped with their lives to hide away in unknown mountain fastnesses and God's earth trembled as the Huns moved on deeper into the Land of Five Rivers. By around 510 CE Tor Aman was dead, only to be replaced by his even more barbarous son Mehr Gul (Mihiragula). Soon it was that the Huns' reputation preceded them. Kings and chieftains deluded that surrender to the Huns would spare their lives laid down their arms without a struggle and were ruthlessly put to death. Their armies and subjects were either drowned in the rivers or distributed amongst the savage soldiery. None were spared. Armies that chose to resist, simply folded against the superior mobility and tactics of the Huns.

The *Rajatarangni* (Chronicle of Kings) written *circa* 1150 by a Kashmiri pundit of great learning gives graphic descriptions of the Huns' progress across the land. We learn from its pages that these savage killers of 'three crores'

The tomb of Ali Sarwar Lodhi is the only claim to fame of Kehror. The heroic stand of the Rajputs against the White Huns is obliterated from memory.

knew no pity either for women or children or the aged. And we read too of the dark cloud of crows and vultures that advanced with the Hunnic army to feed on the corpses left behind. None that crossed the Huns' path lived and there was no recourse, neither to leniency nor to help from any quarter. It seemed that all India lay at the mercy of these dreaded fair-skinned warriors.

The long and unbroken string of victories (including a successful raid against Sri Lanka, as reported in the work of the Chinese pilgrim Xuanzang) filled the savage head of Mehr Gul with illusions of his own invincibility. And so while ruling from the Punjabi city of Sangala (possibly Sialkot), he heard of the gathering of a numerous confederacy of Rajput warriors far away on the fringes of the southern desert. Those who had dared to face his military might had not lived to rue the day. And neither would these supposed warriors. He set out for the desert dreaming of yet another victory.

Records are scant, but we learn of two Rajput princes, Yasodharman the king of Mandasor and Baladitya of Magadh, raising the confederacy. As patriots, the unfolding of events in the face of the Huns would surely have dismayed them. Without doubt they would have fretted about the safety of their own thrones, but surely the thought of saving the land of their forefathers from these northern savages would also have been prominent in their minds. It was the beginning of the year 528 CE, a time when the sun was yet mellow and when our ancestors would celebrate the spring festivals to honour the fertility of the Earth. It was, according to some records, February when the Rajput army gathered 'in the region of Kehror between Multan and the castle of Loni,' writes the 11th century intellectual Abu Rehan Al Beruni.

Now, there is at least one Loni (or Looni) in Rajasthan. Between Multan and this desert settlement lies Kehror, a sprawling town some thirty kilometres northeast of Bahawalpur. Once just a little village, Kehror now sprawls in an irregular, dusty jumble over a mound that rises about thirty metres above the surrounding plain – its only attestation to antiquity. Once it was celebrated for its block-printers and its courtesans. Today only the former flourish. The courtesans to whom the rich of the Seraiki belt resorted not only for their own pleasure but also for their sons' education in etiquette, civility and the norms of conduct for high places, are a sorry tale. Today their 'bazaar' is no more than a sad-looking brothel.

We were driving to Kehror to commemorate the great victory of the Rajputs over the Huns. For my friend Kashif Noon, himself a Rajput and a native of Kehror, it was a pilgrimage of sorts: he was on his way to celebrate the signal triumph of his ancestors. For me it was a journey to see if they remembered that history did indeed unfold here even before the light of Islam blessed our land.

In the light of early morning the jumble of houses sitting atop the mound looked neat. But it was no different from any other Pakistani town with scarcely a building older than thirty years: Gulf oil money and the upstart mentality of replacing everything ancient with new blockhouses had taken the toll. The tall 16th century brick dome of Ali Sarwar, a Lodhi governor of Kehror, dominated above the sprawl of packed houses. Since the domed mausoleum was at hand, the crafty machinations of the man's descendents (supposed or real, we shall never know) have turned the dead man into a great saint, replete with stories of the miracles he wrought in his time. They now grow fat on the monetary harvest of this fiction.

Kashif had warned me earlier that nobody would remember, or even be interested in, the battle fought almost fifteen hundred years ago. Nevertheless, as Kashif was parking his car I asked a shopkeeper what his town was famous for.

'Nothing. The town is famous for nothing,' he said with a laugh.

'The block printers.' I suggested.

'Scarcely a reason for renown,' he countered.

'What of the courtesans then?' I asked somewhat diffidently. He set up a song and dance about the depravity of that business and that as a Muslim he would have nothing to do with it. How we just love to parade our sham religiosity.

The only claim to glory for poor old Kehror was the looming dome of Sarwar Lodhi where one's heart's desire was fulfilled, the man said. Even for him who, by his own admission, prayed five times a day, Allah was not a suitably proficient Provider. He needed the so-called saint to reinforce Allah's work. I pointed out that our worship of tombs was as un-Islamic as harlotry and therefore equally unfavourable in the eyes of God. Pat came the response that as a person of great godliness, such a one as the long dead Sarwar Lodhi, enjoyed direct intercession with God on behalf of us sinners. Thus the power to get God to fulfil desires.

The man listened intently as I told him of the epic battle of February 528 that delivered Punjab from Hunnic oppression.

'Yasodharman would be a Hindu?' he observed solemnly when I had finished.

'He was indeed,' I said.

'And Mehr Gul a Muslim?' It wasn't really a question; it was more a statement of known fact. I very nearly called him an ignorant bloody idiot.

'He couldn't possibly have been a Muslim. There was still over a century to go for the advent of Islam.'

'How can that be?' he said incredulously. 'Mehr Gul is a Muslim name!'

The retrogression of the Pakistani intellect, carefully planned at the highest level of the State and brought about from the grass roots upwards, leads us to believe that even names have religions. But names evolved long before modern religions were contrived and Mehr Gul (Sunflower, or Sun Rose) has been a man's name in Persian-speaking countries for a few millenniums if not longer. My friend, the shopkeeper, was unable to comprehend this. He insisted on posthumously converting Mehr Gul to Islam and a Pukhtun to boot. So far as he was concerned mankind did not exist prior to the coming of Islam to the subcontinent.

When my man was half convinced that the battle did indeed predate Islam, I asked if the fact that a desert prince, perhaps even his own ancestor, had defeated the foreigners warmed his heart. Indignantly he told me that no Hindu could be his ancestor for his line came from Arabia with the conquering army. There is no Muslim worth his or her name in the subcontinent today that will admit of a local origin. We have all invented Arab ancestries and the shopkeeper was no exception. Mankind really must not have existed in this great and wonderful land of the Indian subcontinent prior to the Muslim conquest!

The only history the people of Kehror know is that their town has nothing to do with 'crore' (ten million), but that it is named after a long ago king of that name. And that the suffix of 'Pukka' does not signify it was famous for its burnt brick buildings, but that it comes from the suburb called by that name. Like no one knew of the Rajputs' struggle against the Huns, none could tell me when Raja Kehror lived. These details were not a part of our history. They were from a pagan past, they were not to be remembered and commemorated.

On the periphery, the houses of Kehror straggle out into the surrounding fields. I knew there would be no memorial to that battle, yet I asked to be driven around. Fifteen centuries muted the sounds of battle and dulled the vision, yet it was not difficult to see it as it would have happened. The scantiness of historical record permitted the imagination to run wild: the Rajputs, dark of skin with upturned moustaches and colourful turbans, in their chain mail on their ponies were a vast multitude. The fair-skinned Huns with their pointed helmets astride lightly on their bigger horses, their buff-coats sewn on with metal plates as armour. From under the helmets that concealed shorn pates, the hair of their fringes hung in ringlets. The Rajputs brought into the field longbows, swords, axes, javelins and maces. The Huns came armed with their shorter, multi-cusped bows that permitted rapid fire from horseback. For close quarters they carried broadswords and lances.

For the Huns it was a battle to gain yet more slaves and women to sleep with. For the Rajputs it was a fight to the finish for they would have left behind in their cities and villages their women and children awaiting word of the outcome of this struggle. Were the Rajputs to fail, those at home, rather than face the savagery of the victors, were to destroy themselves to the last person. That was the way of the Rajput; it had always been done, and it was to be repeated this time as well should the tide turn against their fighters.

The contest was hard fought. Even in the face of unfamiliar Central Asiatic tactics, the sons of the desert rallied to the exhortations of their leaders and held their ground. The Rajputs were troubled most by the wave after wave of archers that came galloping in to release their volleys just as they began to wheel away. The Rajputs would surely have expected a charge. The wheeling away must have come as a complete surprise, and it would have taken a couple of waves for the Rajput archers to be prepared to let lose with their longer shafts of greater range. And only when many Hunnic archers were lost would Mehr Gul have ordered a closing in for hand-to-hand combat. The

Huns fought hard; the Rajputs harder still until the blood of the Rajput and the Hun, kinsmen from an ancient past, mingled to drench the dunes surrounding Kehror. That fateful day the arrows flew as thick and dark as Bhadon clouds across the sky and the clash of swords and the yelling and screaming of the contestants rose to one mighty and ceaseless ear-splitting roar. The sun had barely crossed its highest point when the Huns faltered. They fell back. The Rajputs closed in. And then the rout began.

For the Rajputs mortal combat had always been as sport in the arena: it was never their way to pursue and slaughter a vanquished and withdrawing enemy. As the Huns retreated, the commanders of the confederacy held back their warriors to wait and see if the enemy rallied around a second time. But the Huns only receded in headlong rout. The Indian trumpeters were ordered to sound the cessation of battle. In triumph Yasodharman and Baladitya turned homeward at the head of their host.

Smarting under the humiliation of defeat that he had until then never known Mehr Gul made straight for the cold climes of Kashmir. There he wrested control of that kingdom. But even that signal defeat in the desert did not temper his cruelty, for the pages of history are rife with stories of brutality. One in particular tells of how a war elephant fell over the precipice as his army was negotiating the Pir Panjal Pass. The beast's terrified trumpeting as it plummeted to its death so delighted the barbarian that he ordered dozens of elephants to be driven over. The spot of this macabre sport is to this day commemorated as Hastivanj.

Mehr Gul lived on until about 542 CE. Then, decrepit with age and disease, he ordered his own funeral pyre. As the flames licked around his body, one wonders if he would have thought of the agony of those he had burnt in some of the greatest cities of the Sindhu Valley. That is something we will never know, but at least we know that he met his deserved end – even if it was of his own making.

SEA MONSTERS AND THE SUN GOD

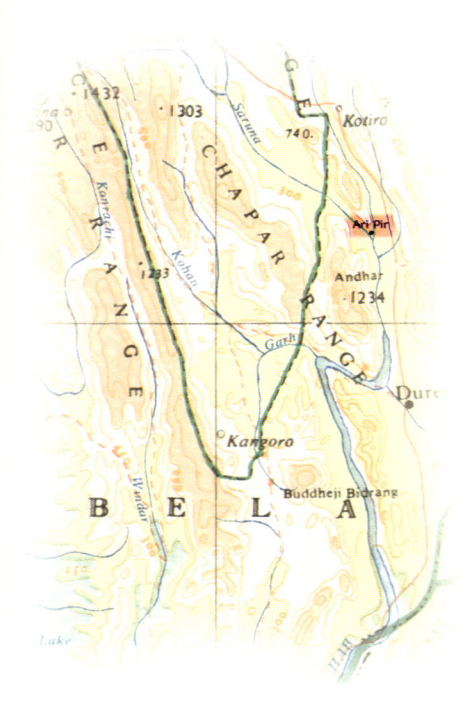

Until the mid-1990s it was just a simple grave. Evidently income was good enough to pay for this fancy edifice.

Return to Ari Pir

I first saw this magical place in February 1987 when a friend and I trekked from the mouth of Hub River to its source. Here, one hundred and forty kilometres due north of Karachi in the district of Lasbela (Balochistan), the Saruna River breaks out of its confining rocky gorge and spreads out to form a deep tarn just before it runs into the Hub. On the one-inch map that we were using at that time the place was marked 'Ari Pir' giving us the impression that it was a village of sorts.

But all it had was a grave (or two) on a rocky eminence and a solitary shack all but lost in the wide-open landscape that typifies the Khirthar Range of Sindh and Balochistan. The shack was

146

RETURN TO ARI PIR

the local inn where pilgrims could rest on their way from the shrine of Shahbaz Qalander at Sehwan, several days' journey (by foot) to the northeast, to that of Shah Noorani in the Lahut Valley a day's march to the southwest. Since the festival at Lahut follows a couple of weeks after the Sehwan celebrations and because the followers of the one are also devoted to the other, there is a great once-a-year traffic of *bhung*-quaffing pilgrims along this route. There is, besides, the incidental traffic of occasional *malangs* back and forth as well. The inn serves them all. Otherwise it's very quiet.

Back in 1987 Ahmed, the innkeeper, served up an excellent chicken curry and rice and told us stories. There were crocodiles in this gem of a lake attracting occasional pilgrims from Karachi who, he said, sacrificed goats to Ari Pir and fed the innards to the crocodiles in the Saruna. We had never seen crocs in the wild and Ahmed led us up the rocky slope to see. As we noisily clambered over the top we just managed to spot four or five of the brutes slithering from the sandbank into the emerald green water on the far side of the pond.

In all these years, having read of mindless hunters shooting up all our wild crocodiles, I had always wanted to return to Ari Pir just to check out the welfare of the lake's inhabitants. Always it was one thing or the other that prevented the expedition until recently when my friend Marvin drove me out of Karachi early one Sunday. Past Hub Dam we headed across wide-open country for the village of Dureji where we hoped to visit my friend Saleh Mohammed Bhotani, the chief. But we arrived to be told that he was in Karachi and I missed his hospitality yet another time.

Another half an hour and about twenty kilometres farther north and we were at Ari Pir. But the prospect had changed altogether in the thirteen years since my last visit. Ahmed's solitary shack was replaced by two rows of mud-and-wattle huts that are rented out to pilgrims and travellers. The tomb itself now had a green dome striped with white like a melon. Ari Pir has since risen high in holiness. By coincidence we had arrived on the day after the three-day *urs* had ended on the fifteenth of the lunar month of Rajab and found groups of stragglers waiting for transport to return to Karachi. Their detritus of discarded plastic packaging was strewed amply around what was, in my memory, a pristine landscape.

Although I knew the disturbance would have driven the crocodiles into the gorge of the Saruna, we climbed up the same rocky slope as thirteen years ago. We saw no crocodiles. But floating on the water were several sets of intestines and one dead white goat that had so far failed to interest the satiated reptiles. The practice of ceremonially feeding the animals obviously still continues.

The man who offered us tea was surprised, and pleased too, that I remembered Ahmed from so many years ago. Ahmed had moved on and had been replaced by this man. Like his predecessor, he kept not only the inn but also had charge of the collection made by the shrine. The dome, he told us, had been constructed about four years ago. Donations for Ari Pir have obviously not been slack. That was also about

Where only a shack masquerading as an inn once stood, there is now a veritable complex of hostelries. The shrine of Ari Pir is visible in the middleground to the right.

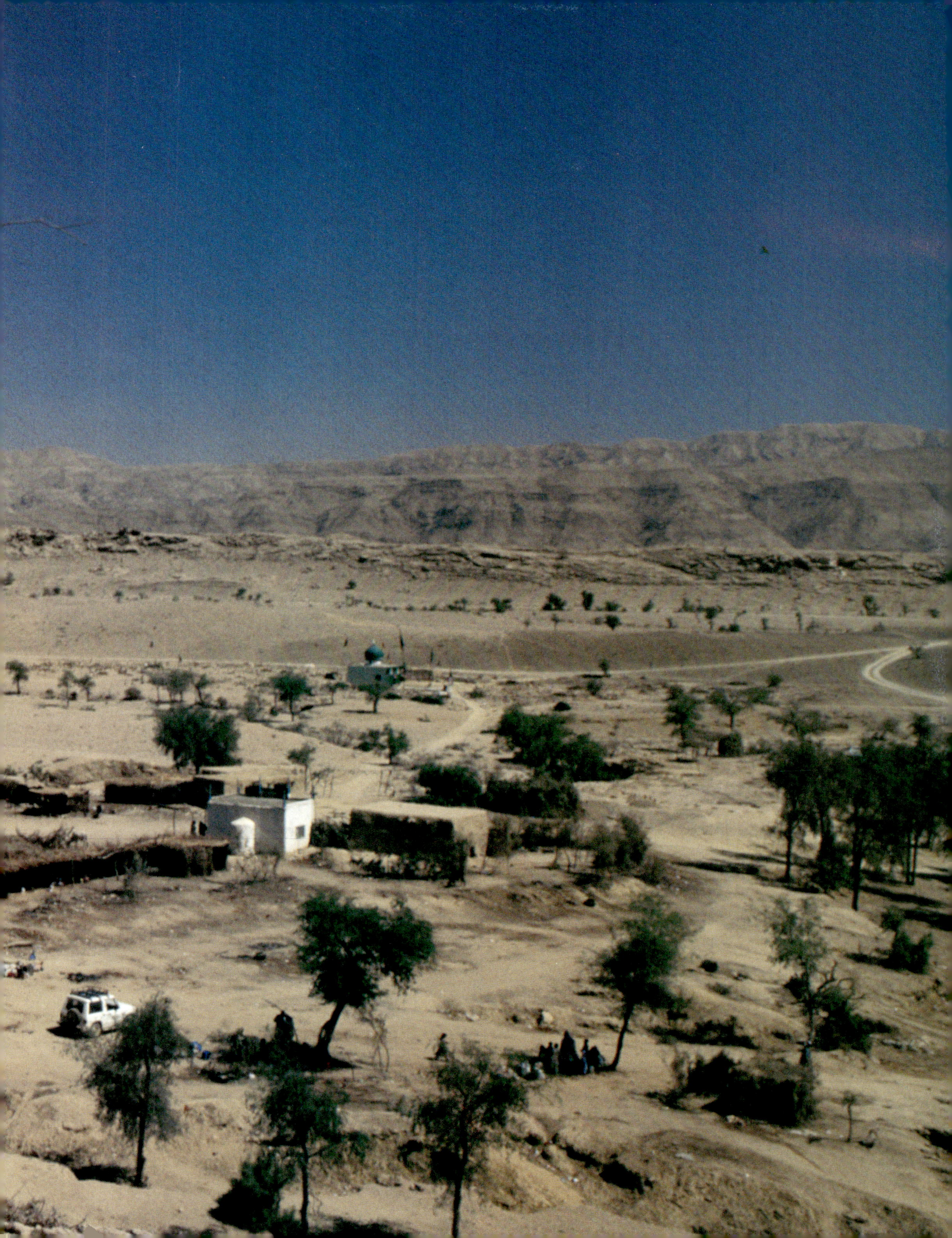

the time that the annual three-day festival picked up. And he also told us a story which Ahmed had overlooked. More likely, it had not yet been invented at that time.

Ari Pir, related the man, a son of Mahmud Ghaznavi, arrived in the Saruna Valley and liking the place sojourned there. Now in those days Saruna was so fertile it yielded a crop each of wheat and paddy annually. And as bad fortune would have it, the good Pir becoming infatuated with the very pretty daughter of the king of Saruna demanded her hand. The king did not take that very nicely, however. Why, holy man or not, damn the cheek of the lice-infested, *bhung*-drinking savage from the Afghan highlands. He ordered the man to be driven out. But this great man of God cursed the king and his kingdom calling down pestilence upon the land. The crops dried up, fertility wasted away, the river ran dry and Saruna became the arid valley it is now. It is not told how Saruna was eventually delivered of the scourge of this holy man or how he met his end here, but the moral of the story, says Marvin, is: don't mess with a man with a hard-on.

I find it singularly uncanny that most of our so-called Pirs are malevolent demons who only turn sweet lakes bitter, fertile valleys barren and gold into worthless sand. It is only about mainstream Sufis that we hear stories of benevolence. And yet vast multitudes of morons all over the country believe in the 'godliness' of those insidious characters. What believer in God, I ask, would be as mean and niggardly as to harm His children, even if for some real or perceived belittling? And what sick mind could even consider such a spiteful and pernicious fiend holy? The creators of these stories, mean-spirited cads, translate the poverty of their own soul into that of their invented heroes and saints.

So far as history is concerned, we find no son of Mahmud so named. But we do know of one famous Ari Pir in Lasbela town and another scarcely known not far from this Ari Pir across the Khirthar mountains in Sindh. The former is none other than Mohammed bin Haroon who was the governor of Makran immediately prior to the Arab conquest of Sindh. On his way east with Mohammed bin Qasim, he contracted malaria and died at Armael, as Lasbela was known to the Arabs. Over the centuries Haroon was corrupted to Ari and his shrine, standing to this day in a quiet corner of Lasbela town, is the site of an annual pilgrimage.

Never having visited the third Ari Pir in Sindh, I know nothing about his shrine. But one thing is clear: that Ari Pir of Saruna lies on the timeless pilgrim route from Sehwan via Sri Mata Hinglaj on the Makran coast to shrines that extended in a coastal chain as far west as Mesopotamia. Long before Sehwan was appropriated by Shahbaz Qalander, it was worshipped by the Hindus as sacred to Raja Bhartari, the 1st century BCE prince of Ujjain turned Sufi. Similarly Ari Pir too would have been sacred to a pre-Islamic saint or a god whose name has now either been lost or appropriately converted to Islam.

I have no doubt in my mind that this pilgrim route was in use when the first great cities of the Sindhu Valley were built; before the melting of the ice sheets (*circa* 7500 BCE) raised sea

The Saruna River breaking out of its confining gorge widens to form the lake at Ari Pir. The view is to the southeast where, hidden behind the trees in the far background, the Saruna meets the bigger Hub.

levels and obliterated the chain of coastal temples. Then our pagan ancestors, the aboriginal Sindhis, would have travelled across the scorching sands, over the Khirthar passes between Sehwan and Saruna en route to Lahut and on to Hinglaj just as the *malangs* do today. In the long and eventful unfolding of history, different religions took precedence in this land but each faithfully incorporating the rites of those that had gone before kept the ceremonial largely unchanged. Sehwan was appropriated by Shahbaz Qalander and Sri Mata Hinglaj (sacred to Kali) by Bibi Nani. Today both are worshipped by Muslims and Hindus alike. And even as that ancient traffic of our ancestors wended across almost five hundred kilometres of harsh country between Sehwan and Hinglaj, so too it does today.

On my first visit thirteen years ago there had been no annual *urs* for Ari Pir. There were only occasional pilgrims who were surely no more than picnickers looking for a diversion from monotonous lives. And Ari Pir with its lovely lake and crocodiles just three hours from Karachi was a good enough place as any. But now that it is a famous site again it has come full circle: we have returned to a time far back in the past when our earliest ancestors resorted here to celebrate a deity whose name we may perhaps never learn.

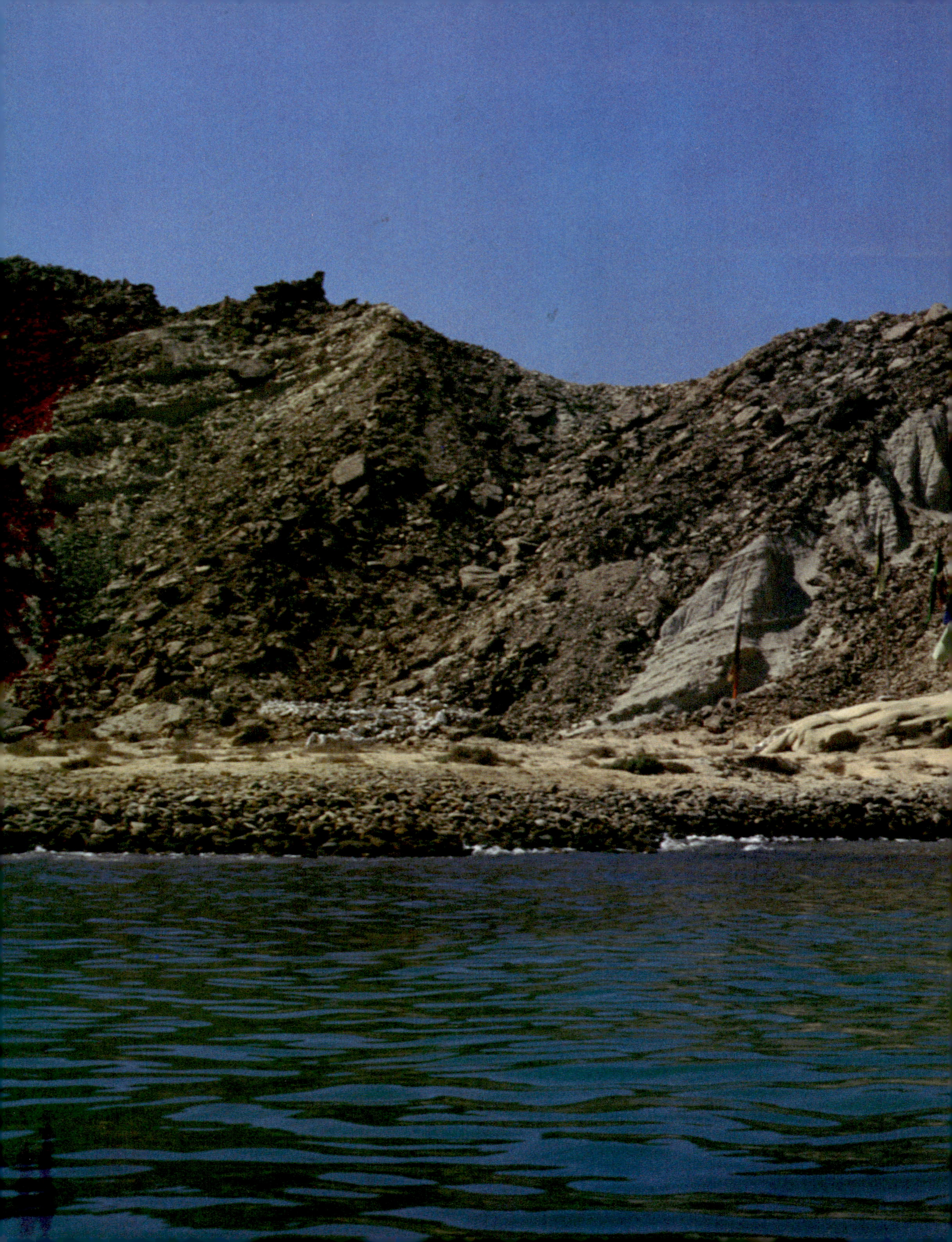

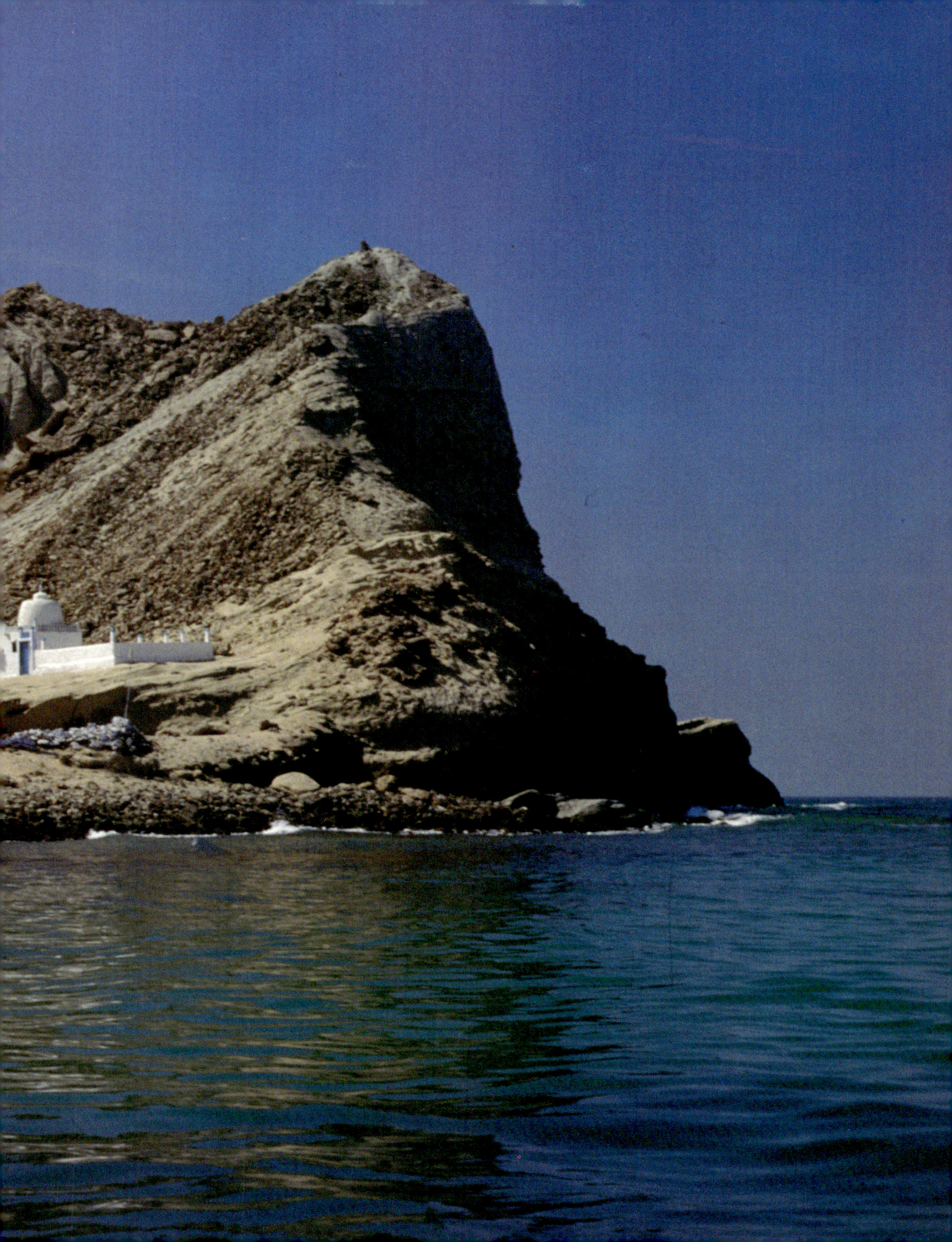

SEA MONSTERS AND THE SUN GOD

Approaching Astola from the northwest. From a distance the island had the outline of a Japanese bullet train.

Sea Monsters and the Sun God

The sea heaved gently as we prepared to set out on the dawn tide. The end of October was a good time for a landlubber like me to be putting out to sea. The last of the monsoon winds had already blown themselves out and the sea was going to be calm until the end of next February. Abdul Majeed, the captain, whose crinkly hair stood erect as if his scalp was electrically charged – just as in the comics, and his coxswain Noor Jan, poled the boat away from the jetty. A couple of smart yanks and the two outboard motors puttered to life easing us out of Pasni fish harbour and into the open sea. The jetty fell away, the rock of Jebel e Zareen loomed to our right wall-like in the darkness and behind us Pasni went dark in another power break. Somewhere in the gloom ahead lay the island of Astola – the object of our voyage. We were following up two thousand three hundred and twenty-four years – almost to the day, after Nearchus, Alexander's admiral of the fleet had set foot on it.

Our ship, scarce bigger than a large rowboat, had no name and the thought that we were to cross twenty-two nautical miles of sea in this dinky little craft petrified me. But Maqsood, the turner, to whom I had been introduced only the day before and who had opted to come out with me appeared unaffected as he calmly pulled on his cigarette. For our captain and helmsman, it was evidently business as usual for no sooner had we cleared the breakwaters that Noor Jan wrapped the ends of the two rudder ropes around his toes and began to nod sleepily.

They have no instruments on board and we might end up in the middle of nowhere, I thought as I took out my compass. Our heading was south by east – the bearing for Astola as I knew from the map. After years of repeated outings to the island the compass, I realised, was no longer necessary for grizzled old Noor Jan. He had charted his course either by the stars, slowly going out overhead, or by Jebel e Zareen, and so true was his reckoning that even when Astola became visible some two hours later, there was need not even to make the slightest adjustment.

The sea was calm, but never having been in the open sea and in such a tiny craft too, I was terrified. I had very nearly backed out just before setting out because Maqsood had been late and I almost took that as an excuse to abort the voyage. Fear had been gnawing at me since the previous evening when I made the deal with the owner of the boat and I had slept fitfully through the night. The moments of wakefulness being filled with the dread of Maqsood failing to show up and us getting lost at sea. When the search and rescue mission would fail to turn up anything, Maqsood would say that since he was to be preserved, Providence had made him oversleep. Strange and inscrutable are Her ways, he would say with a shake and wobble of the head.

Even as I got out of bed at four in the morning to make ready, I wanted something drastic to occur to forestall my voyage. The only emotion greater than the fear of being lost at sea was the thought of humiliation, of being marked a coward afraid of the sea that kept me from aborting it myself. As I offered my excuse, my nervousness would be evident to the captain and even before I could flee Pasni, word of my gutlessness would be out. I would never be able to return to Pasni without disparaging whispers following me about.

Now I sat in the bow with my hands gripping the gunwale until the knuckles went white, and any swell that was only slightly bigger than

The north beach where the fishermen of Pasni and Kalmat anchor to take a break.

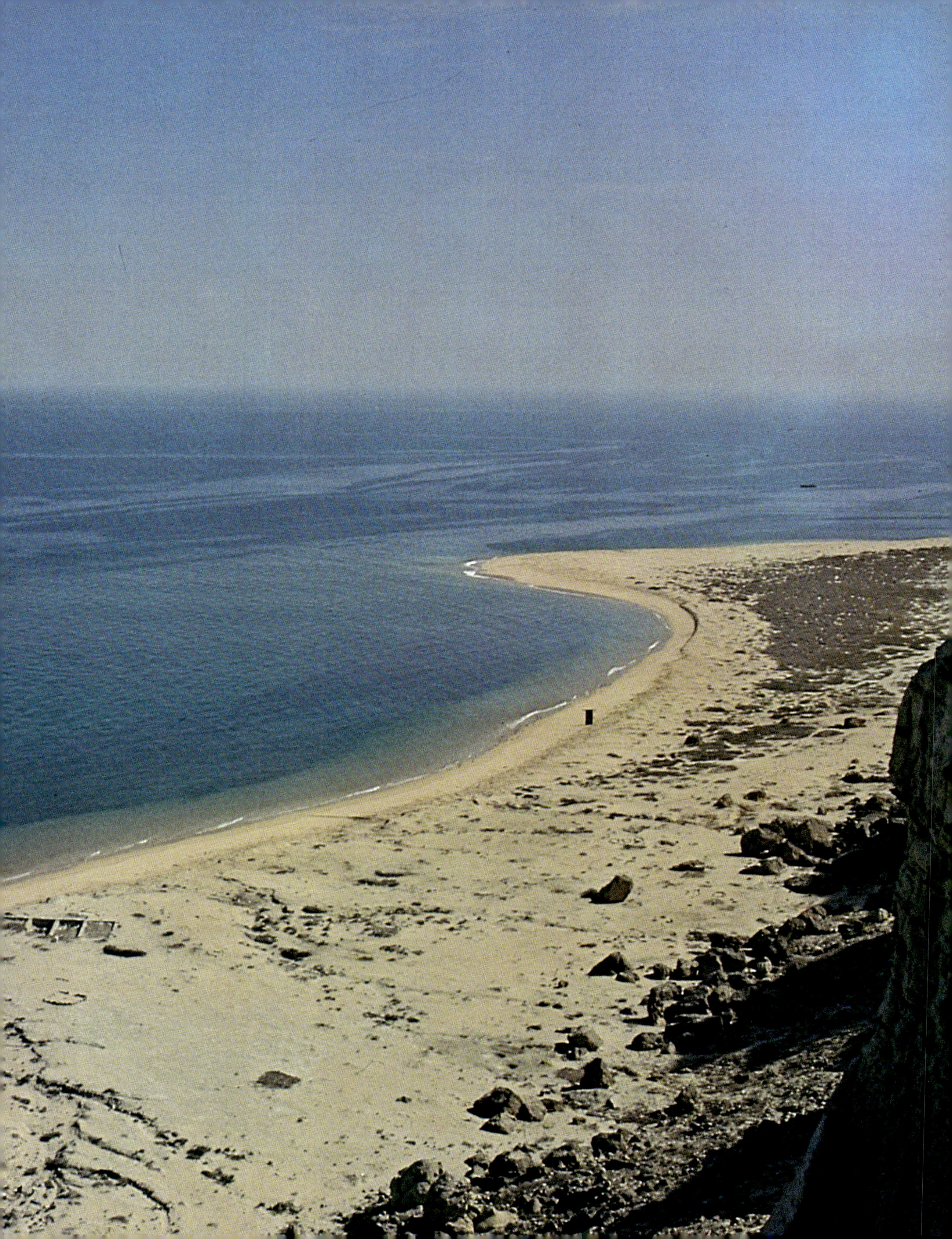

SEA MONSTERS AND THE SUN GOD

Captain Abdul Majeed and his helmsman Noor Jan.

normal sent an electrifying pang of terror through me. I feared giant white sharks (non-existent in our waters) that could chomp our puny craft into half, or monster octopuses (that live only in B-grade films) rising from the deep to grab us in their wet embrace and take us down. My wild imagination gone berserk with fear even conjured up a local version of the Bermuda Triangle. I longed to be off the boat and back on *terra firma* again. But we were out of Pasni, there was no going back now. With the rising of the sun, the sea snakes made for a suitable diversion however. They came in exquisite colours: mauve and gold bands, deep brown, almost black and one that shimmered as liquid silver. They were tightly wound up – the brown one an unmistakable turd; all having come up to warm themselves as the surface warmed in the sunshine.

Astola should normally be visible about an hour out of Pasni. But in the shimmering glare of the rising sun we first saw it only when we were some seven or eight nautical miles from it. The profile it presented us from the northwest was that of a Japanese bullet train. That is not what Nearchus would have seen as he approached from the northeast in November 325 BCE. He would first have seen the towering rock face on the southeast that appears to be a ship under full-blown sail. In an allusion to it, Thomas Holdich (*The Gates of India*) calls this fascinating formation 'sail rock.'

Nearchus mentions the island twice, once when he was anchored at Kalama and then again as he describes his passage further west along the coast of the Ichthyophagi (Fish Eaters, as the people of Makran were known to the Greeks). In the first instance he calls the island Karbinê and tells us that it lay one hundred stadia (ten nautical miles) offshore. Then again he names it Nosala at the same distance off the coast. On both counts Nearchus was grossly under-estimating the distance by several nautical miles. Now, Kalama is Kalamat on modern maps, an inland bay of irregular oblong shape with a narrow mouth leading into its crystal-clear sheltered waters. It lies midway between Ormara and Pasni and cannot be missed as one flies over it en route between the latter and Karachi. Astola lies southwest of here, across a channel twenty nautical miles wide and fifteen fathoms deep.

There is a simple explanation for the two names Nearchus assigns to a single geographical entity. As he approached from the east, he docked at a village where the people called the island Karbinê. A right hospitable lot these villagers were too. They brought the admiral gifts of sheep and fish. The mutton, Nearchus tells us, tasted fishy because there being no grass the animals fed on fish. Then, as he sailed westward for his eventual rendezvous with Alexander in distant Babylon, Nearchus encountered another coastal community on the west side of Kalamat bay that referred to the island as Nosala. It is strange that two communities should call the same geographical entity by different names, but it not entirely unheard of. This second community added to Nearchus's information: the island was uninhabited and sacred to the sun and therefore enchanted.

The admiral noted, 'No one willingly visited this island, and if anyone was carried to it unawares, he was never more seen.' Providence only added to this aspect of the supernatural when a transport ship of the Greek fleet manned by an Egyptian crew, perhaps attempting a landing, disappeared just off the rocky beaches of Astola. Concerned for the well-being of the Egyptians, Nearchus ordered a galley of thirty oars to scout around the island with all hands calling out the names of the lost crew. But the hope that some may have swum to the safety of Astola was soon abandoned for no response came forth. If he had toyed with thoughts of going ashore, it was now decided for him.

In a bid to show that the loss of the transport ship and its crew was merely an unfortunate accident and the 'story about the island [being enchanted] was nothing but an empty fable,' Nearchus had to force the crew of his own ship to go ashore. This they did with much uneasiness and only when the admiral himself accompanied them. Thereafter centuries were to pass before Astola was to receive notice again. This time, in the late Middle Ages. We learn of it being the dreaded haunt of the ruthless pirates of the Balochistan coast. Here they slaughtered their victims after divesting them of all they possessed.

SEA MONSTERS AND THE SUN GOD

Holdich called this feature 'sail rock.' I would sooner term it 'seal rock' for it appears to be a seal rearing up on its front flippers.

Nearchus found the island deserted and without a sign of human habitation, but the fact that he was told of Astola being sacred to the sun shows that at some remote time before the arrival of the Greeks, it had indeed been a site of religious pilgrimage. Though we do not know how long before the Greeks the temple of the sun god (if at all it existed) was abandoned, it is remarkable that the memory of the island's earlier sanctity was yet preserved in 325 BCE.

There is some historical evidence that along the Balochistan and Iranian coast there was a series of temples frequented by the convoys of traders journeying between the great cities of the Sindhu Valley and Mesopotamia. We know that one of these was the famed temple of Hinglaj on the Hingol River. Once it was sacred to the more than five thousand year-old Mesopotamian moon goddess Nania. Today it is holy both for Muslims and Hindus alike. For the former it is the sanctum of Bibi Nani (clearly a derivative of Nania) and for the latter of Durga.* It is also believed that another hallowed spot in this chain was Astola.

Like the thirty-oared Greek galley, we too did a complete circuit of the island. There were no stricken sailors to call out to, only we wanted to see what the island looked like all around. Its southern shore was either shattered rock or vertical sea walls and caves with nary a landing site. Around the bend, the eastern extremity stood tall and proud like a wind-filled sail: the famous sail rock of Holdich. Along the northern shore was a yellow sandy beach about a kilometre and a half in length, then a stretch of rock wall falling vertically to the sea, and yet another smaller sandy beach. Beyond, in the fold of a crescent-shaped hillock was the whitewashed shrine of Khwaja Khizer, patron saint of rivers and seas.

Our captain and helmsman had all along referred to Astola not as an 'island' but as 'mountain of the sea.' And for them the name of this 'mountain' is Haftalar, from where it is easy to derive the modern title Astola. Now '*haft*' is the Persian word for seven, but no amount of quizzing brought forth the meaning of the suffix '*talar*.' Holdich, however, writes that this Balochi word means 'rocky band of cliffs or hills.' Haftalar thus was the Seventh Hill (or mountain, as my captain referred to it) – the seventh in the chain of shrines situated between the valley of the Sindhu and Mesopotamia. The language employed being Persian and its derivative (Balochi) and not Sanskrit (where *haft* would have been *sapt*), I presume the count progressed from the west to the east.

Some eight thousand years ago Astola was indeed a 'rocky band of cliffs or hills', shaped very much like the hammerheads of nearby Ormara and Gwadar and sticking out into the sea. That was when the earth was yet covered with vast ice sheets and the seas were thirty metres lower – today the depth of the channel between Astola and continental Balochistan. Then the Ice Age ended. The ice sheets melted and receded. Water sluiced down the rivers of the world to raise ocean levels destroying innumerable coastal settlements. The Mediterranean broke across the Strait of Bosphorus to turn the sweet water lake that we today call Black Sea bitter. For the ancients it was as if the 'fountains of the deep' had burst open for that is what the Bible tells us.† Shortly thereafter Astola had become an island.

The hill was suddenly an island; but in the collective memory of the aboriginal people of Makran it continued to live as a sacred hill for they and before them their ancestors had worshipped the sun on its wind-scoured flat crest. They did not abandon their god; those who could venture across twenty nautical miles

---

* Nania is believed to be an ancient Mesopotamian deity, but once the script of the Sindhu Valley has been deciphered it should not come as a surprise that she was a goddess of Moen jo Daro and Harappa taken west by traders and travellers. She would have greatly appealed to the Mesopotamian church to be assimilated completely.

† Nomads living around the Bosphorus and the eastern Mediterranean watching the flooding would obviously not have understood the phenomenon. Centuries later the sinking of coastal habitations was still part of the collective memory when raised sea levels altered global climate to bring down increased rainfall. That was when Deluge stories were invented.

SEA MONSTERS AND THE SUN GOD

of open sea in uncertain little craft would surely have taken that voyage of penance to win his favour. At some point in time when coastal travel between the Sindhu Valley and Mesopotamia became commonplace, its route marked by places of worship, the island became part of the chain of temples stretching between the two river valleys. Even though it was an island, they called it Haft Talar – the Seventh Hill, for the ancient collective memory refused to go away. It is a memory that persists to this day prompting my captain to refer to Astola 'mountain of the sea.'

Majeed beached our boat on the larger of the two sandy strands on the north shore and we climbed up through a maze of boulders to the absolutely flat, wind-swept tabletop. Far away to the west was the solar-powered warning beacon. Nearer to us was the temple: a rude low-walled square constructed from badly eroded limestone blocks that could have been cut five hundred or five thousand years ago, and could possibly have come from an earlier building. A swastika and a crude wheel of life, both Vedic signs, adorned the altar smeared with dried blood and vermilion. Above it a frayed flag, bleached a nameless colour by the harsh sun, flapped in the wind. Neither of my two companions knew which god this shrine was dedicated to, but they did know that rich Hindus periodically made the pilgrimage here and sacrificed goats at the altar. Some way off to the east an area was marked out as a mosque.

Perhaps the existing temple was built on the exact site where the aboriginal Makranis had worshipped their sun god. But I had no way of knowing. I only knew that we stood on ground that was sacred to tens of hundreds of generations of those that peopled the cities of Lothal, Kalibangan, Moen jo Daro and Mehrgarh. And to those who lived in Ur and Nineveh. Today the island is a sort of mid-sea headquarters for the fishermen of Kalamat and Pasni who repair here to dry their nets and cook their meals: even as we walked around the island, there were no less than fifteen fishing boats in anchor, and the small sandy beach was crowded with men cooking and mending the nets.

Friends at WWF in Lahore had told me to keep an eye out for the cats of Astola. Fifteen well-fed feral cats, they said, lived on the island. Since this is the largest number that the meagre resources of the island can support, the number is kept steady by the toms cannibalising on the kittens. But I caught only the merest glimpse of one as it fled down a ravine while we were climbing to the top. Once upon a time there were no cats on Astola, however. It was the haunt of rats, sea birds (by the thousands) and briefly, twice annually, of migratory quails coming in from or going out to East Africa. The rats scavenged the leavings of the fishermen who frequented the island and sometimes robbed sea birds' nests. They also did plenty of damage to the nets and other equipment laid out by the sailors to dry.

And so one day a fisherman called Rahim, a native of Kalamat, so it was reported by our captain, brought out a pair of cats and shanghaied them on the island. By and by the cats destroyed the rats and when that was done, they turned upon nesting sea birds. Today Astola that was once a crowded bird colony is deserted. The few that do still resort here are careful to nest only on the detached rock off the southern shore of the island. The cats being unnatural, albeit unwilling, invaders, are believed by naturalists to have upset the eco-system. There are schemes now to exterminate the cats and re-introduce the rats so as to let the sea birds return to their lost nesting colony.

Soon it was time for us to return to the boat for the voyage back to the mainland. Nearchus's sailors had come ashore with great trepidation. But we had kept faith and landed without fear. For me fear set in, as it had early in the morning, when we boarded our tiny craft for the return journey. But Majeed and Noor Jan were both good men who knew how to handle their boat, and three hours and twenty minutes after setting out of Astola we were puttering into the harbour at Pasni. My pilgrimage to the island of the sun had come to pass.

Postscript I: As we were about to set out on the return voyage, there was some commotion in the sea next to us. A pair of marine turtles surfaced and I thought they were struggling to free themselves from a fishing net. I asked my captain to go nearer so we could set them free before they suffocated.

'No, they are not dying,' he said. 'They are making love.' *Yeh to mohabat kur rahe hain.*

The tenderness in his words touched me for it is rare in Pakistan to find a person sympathetic to the natural world. Least of all one like my unlettered captain Abdul Majeed. My mind flew miles to my native Punjab. A Punjabi would have been loud, lewd and profane. It would not have been *mohabat* for him. He would have jeered the reptiles, harrying them by throwing things at them. And such a person may not necessarily have been uneducated.

Postscript II: At exactly 9.45 AM just after my captain had called out, 'Look, sahib! The mountain of the sea,' and when I was mesmerised by the sight of Astola only a few nautical miles ahead, a swell rocked our boat a little too violently for my well-being. I was terrified out of my wits, but it passed. Had I been looking over my right shoulder, to the southwest, I would have seen the dreadful sight of the ill-starred Orion of the Pakistan Navy going down about five or six nautical miles away. None of us saw it crashing, we only heard of the unfortunate accident in the afternoon at Pasni. The evening news bulletin gave out the time of the crash and I realised that the swell had been caused by the Orion as it went under. By the end of the next day we had learned that the crew had all perished.

The island of the sun god, perhaps, is enchanted after all. We who were landing on hallowed ground were spared. In our stead the sun god claimed the lives of the twenty-one good men who flew above his sacred temple.

Past the main entrance, the arched doorway leads into the courtyard that has long been an essential part of vernacular domestic architecture.

LORE OF THE MANSION

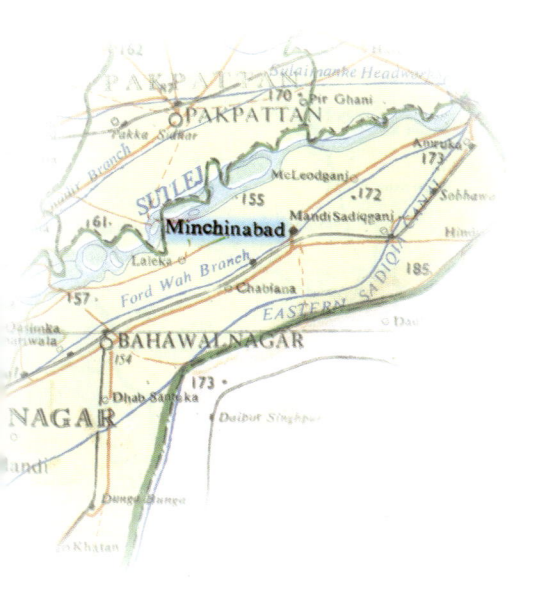

Façade of the main building. The marble arch of the entrance, richly worked in floral designs with figures of a flute-playing Krishna on either flank, is strongly subcontinental. The feature of niche with deity goes as far back as the 2nd or 3rd century BCE. The roofline with its vases and arches is European in contrast.

Lore of the Mansion

Minchinabad, that lies twenty-five kilometres northeast of Bahawalnagar on the highroad that once went on to Fazilka, has no claim to fame. But in the heart of this town of rural Punjab, there is a right lovely *haveli*. Having been built in the 1930s and known as Mahal Nagar Mal, it does not boast of great age, but it does vaunt fine taste and class. Since 1947 when one of the greatest trans-migrations of history took place and the real owners fled east across the new border, this mansion has been the home of a Sukhera family who came from the other side.

Dilshad Hussain Sukhera, the elder, is now

SEA MONSTERS AND THE SUN GOD

Detail of the Krishna figurine.

the keeper of the lore of the mansion. He relates that it was built by two brothers Nagar Mal and Bhajan Lal sometime in the 1930s – the exact year being unknown. Coming from a long line of assiduous merchants of the Agarwal clan that had business interests in distant marts, the brothers came in for a good deal of money when their father passed away. The fortune that became theirs, says Sukhera, was no less than twenty-five million rupees which, in the 1930s, was a royal sum indeed.

Such a fortune could easily have afforded a European architect – or even the best from amongst local experts. Unfortunately there is no information regarding either the builder or outlay for the building. Nor, too, have the Sukheras ever found any architectural plans or other papers related to this beautiful mansion. But they do know that the mansion was once surrounded by vast grounds and agricultural lands that have now been built over. Dilshad Hussain points out that the area where the mosque and row of shops stand across the busy road from the *haveli* was once occupied by the Agarwal family's servants' quarters and generator rooms. It would have been a well-

Notice the faded and barely visible frescoes in the spandrels and in the panels above the arches. The only change wrought in Mahal Nagar Mal since its original owner abandoned it is the wall that now divides the central courtyard of the main house.

Around the first floor rooms and accessible from them, to the outside, runs a narrow gallery. The cast iron filigree at the bottom would have come from foundries in Bombay or Calcutta. Above it ran stained glass windows. The gallery being an extension of the jharoka *afforded* purdah *to the ladies of the house as they looked out into the outer courtyard or even beyond towards the servants' rooms. It also shielded the first floor rooms from direct sunshine to keep them cooler.*

Detail of cast iron grill and woodwork on the first floor gallery.

First floor exterior showing cast iron filigree and stained glass windows. The corbelling of the oriel in the corner is noteworthy as a very typical European feature. Contrasting with it are the stylised cantilever brackets, starkly subcontinental, that support the rest of the overhang.

Doorways such as this leading from the first floor courtyard into the rooms are strongly reminiscent of Italian buildings. With the introduction of European architecture in the subcontinent in the early decades of the 19th century, it became fashionable for the nobility to follow the foreign building style. The nobility, says Kamil Khan Mumtaz, the noted architectural historian, instructed its architects to check out the latest buildings in the cantonments and civil lines and incorporate in their own designs whatever was pleasing to the eye. The niches on either side emphasise vernacular colour.

LORE OF THE MANSION

Above the doorways of the first floor and just below the line where the overhang of the top floor juts out, runs an ornate frieze repeating this theme of winged angels blowing trumpets or wielding spears and bows and arrows. Once again Nagar Mal's penchant for European artistry shows through.

heeled family to have maintained two petrol driven generators to light up the haveli.

While traditionally all such properties that fall into the hands of immigrants of 1947 are allowed to go to seed and disintegrate so that they can sold off and ugly 'plazas' raised in their place, Mahal Nagar Mal has been well looked after by the Sukheras. Nothing has been damaged, not even the tiny sculptures of Krishna playing his flute, or the friezes that run just below the ceiling showing scenes from Hindu mythology. The only change since 1947 has been the cemented wall that now divides the central courtyard – an imperative that arose when the senior Sukhera died and the house passed down to Dilshad Hussain and his brother. It is promising that the Sukheras are aware of the aesthetic value of the building that is their home.

SEA MONSTERS AND THE SUN GOD

Interior of the Chitterwatta post. While the ground floor houses the subordinate staff, the upper floor served as quarters for passing officers. Poor maintenance has led to extensive decay and the building certainly does not have many more years.

Into the heart of the Suleman Mountains

Chitterwatta: what a name for a village, I thought when my friend Raheal Siddiqui visited with tales from the Suleman Mountains. There were stories of men with superhuman strength, school masters possessed of exemplary sense of duty and honour – the kind that would have done Jinnah proud, and men who said what they had to say in poetry that evoked the philosophy of Iqbal. Most of all it was the name that intrigued me.

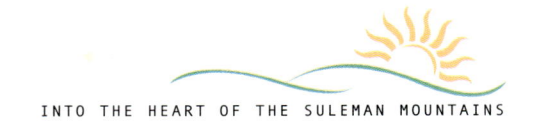

Raheal pronounced it 'Chhitterwatta' and I assumed it had to do something with slippers and rocks – *chhitter* being the Seraiki and Punjabi word for slippers and *watta* being rock or stone.

Now Raheal is a rare breed of civil servant, a man of the old school. He reads (something that so few of us do anymore) and takes genuine interest in his work as an officer of the District Management Group. Within only a few weeks as Political Agent Dera Ghazi Khan, he had already travelled to some of the remotest posts in his jurisdiction and earned the distinction of being the first PA there since the last white officer had packed his bags in 1947. And he had gleaned yarns that he spun in Lahore with such enthusiasm that he left no likelihood of my turning down his invitation to visit. In any case, this was Baloch country, and having travelled very little here, I was not foregoing my chance to do so.

And so it was that we sped northward from Dera Ghazi Khan one day in late March. Raheal and the young Risaldar Khurram Khosa were on tour and Raheal's friend Ibrahim Beg, the telephone engineer from Bahawalpur, and I were the baggage. Past the village of Tibbi Qaisrani (north of Taunsa) on the Indus Highway that is slowly taking on the semblance of an actual highway with its steadily lengthening new surface, we turned west. Not long afterwards we drove through the high gate into the wide enceinte of the Vehowa Border Military Police (BMP) post.

As the PA, Raheal is the BMP Commandant and we stopped to a nicely turned-out guard presenting arms amid much shouting of commands and rattling of rifles. The Inspection Book was brought out for the PA sahib to put down his comments and a lavish tea was laid out. They sent for the man whose father ran a store in Chitterwatta many years ago. We got Om Prakash instead, a grandson of the shopkeeper, who said his father was away in Dera. Om only had a vague recollection of his childhood in Chitterwatta, consequently we learned next to nothing from him.

The Inspection Book had a past PA's comments suggesting that the Vehowa BMP post, being unnecessary, be closed down. On the very next page was a short poem in a beautiful, flowing hand. The poem ridiculed the PA's acumen (or lack thereof) and closed with a word of gratitude for God, and not lowly man, being the Maker of destinies. For had man had supreme power, he would only have brought down infinite suffering on his fellows. The lyric was signed by Risaldar Jehanzeb Jehangir Raz. I knew no visit to Vehowa could be complete without seeing this good man. The poet had since retired from the service, but he was made available.

Smiling a slow smile he told us that the PA had not visited the post at all. Instead he had had the book sent over to Dera, and the record of crime in this jurisdiction being scant had felt the post ought to be abolished.

'Had he visited, his observation would have been different,' said Raz. 'And had I not composed this poem, all succeeding PAs would have mechanically agreed with the remark and

Landscape under stormy skies near Phugla.

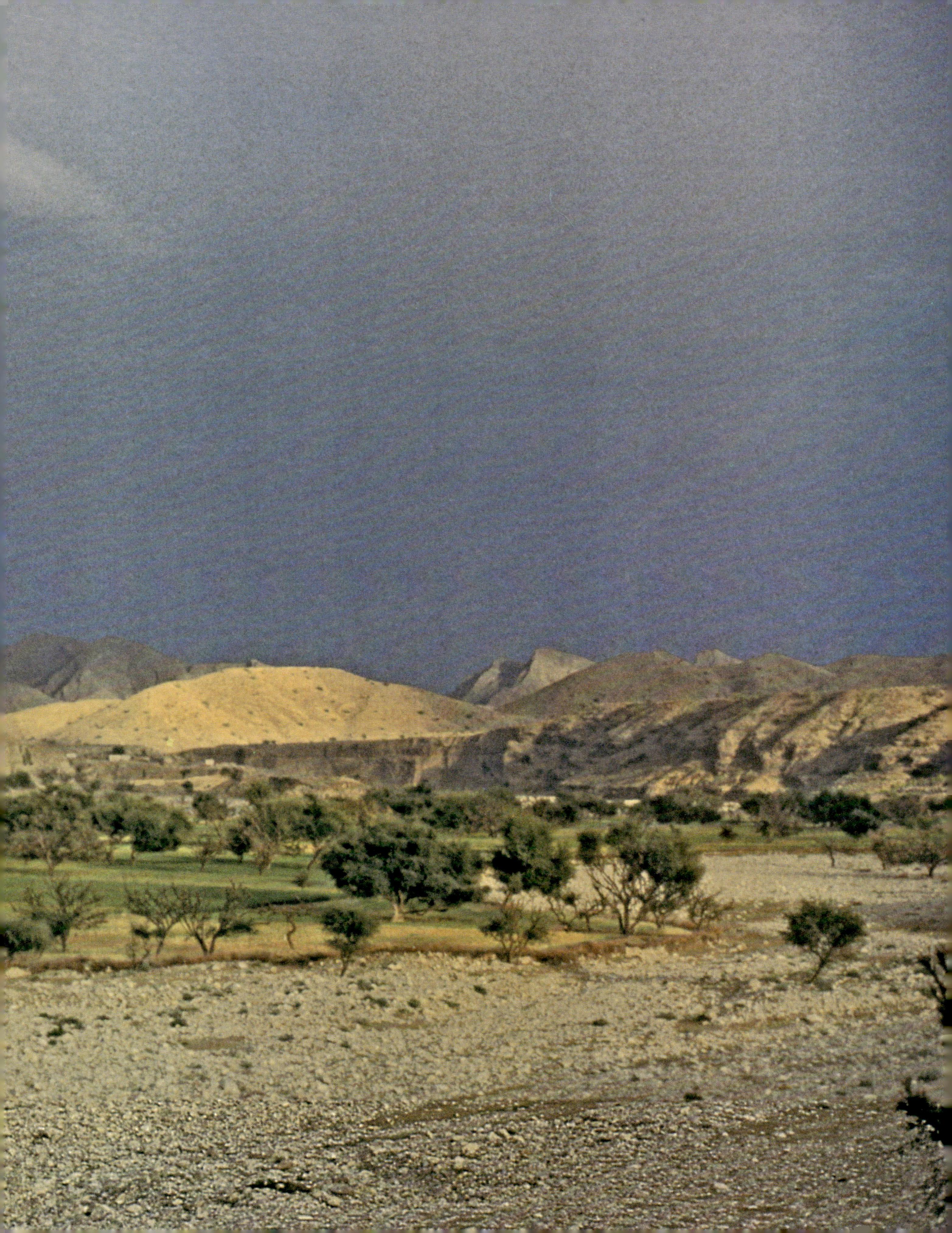

the post would have actually been abolished. Someone had to act, and I did.' The post was saved, but Raz earned the displeasure of his PA. It was just as well that the officer was transferred shortly afterwards.

The Vehowa bazaar called Chhappar Bazaar from the time when the narrow shop-lined alley was covered over with matting, was a fine mix of the old and the new. Here were stores selling film music and gaudy cassette players, digital wristwatches, printed fabric, the kind one sees at weddings in villages, and all sorts of medication. Here too did we find a small, dimly lit hovel with an ageless sort of man poring over some odd bits and pieces. Above his head hung an unlit flyblown bulb and further behind an equally flyblown electric fan that could not have been less than sixty or seventy years old. He said he, the only Pukhtun in this Baloch town, was the local junk dealer. Amid his stacks of dust-laden oddments, the man dusty himself, seemed one of the collection.

Business, he said with an equanimity that comes from a life of few wants, was not too bad. Long ago, too long ago for him to know the number of years, his ancestors had moved south from Dera Ismail Khan to seek their fortune here. He did not know what line of work they pursued. I asked if they had found the fortune they sought and he shrugged his old shoulders, made a wry face but said nothing.

I looked around his shelves and he squinted up from his tinkering to ask what it was I wanted. For some time I had been looking for that old paraffin-burning bicycle lamp that all of us who grew up in the 1950s would remember. I asked if, perchance, he would have one.

'No. Those are not to be had anymore,' he said. 'But I can keep a lookout for one, should you wish to return with your query.' He sounded as if remote old Vehowa was a place you passed by every so often on your way to and from the supermarket.

I suggested he look around his trove for it could not be possible for a man to know every single item tucked away in those crowded stacks of assorted junk. He looked at me sternly and reminded me that he had run his business for close on forty years. There was nothing in his store, he added, that he didn't know of. The interview was closed by him lowering himself visibly onto the gadget he was struggling with.

Item: a sign (in Urdu) in a pharmacy exhorted all believers to donate cash liberally for the 'destruction of Hindustan.' I found myself wondering what warped mind would machinate to destroy a perceived or real enemy, but not urge believers to work their utmost best for the growth and development of Pakistan. I don't understand how our poor and sorry country stands to gain from the destruction of India. How, if that magic occurrence should come to pass, would our shameful state of health care, education and economy improve? Nor too do I understand if such jingoistic Pakistanis have ever paused to consider the fate they wish for the two hundred million Muslims of India in the scheme of that country's overthrow. But then perhaps I am

INTO THE HEART OF THE SULEMAN MOUNTAINS

Chitterwatta village. The rock that gives the place its name can be seen to the lower right of the picture.

no patriot. I fear sometimes that our crazed passion for the destruction of India matched only by the total disregard we have for our own national well-being could indeed, in the end, be the undoing of Pakistan.

We left Vehowa just after midday. An hour and a half later, having followed the Vehowa stream (which becomes a raging torrent after a shower in the hills), we came to a small hut by the roadside. A crowd of men was gathered because word regarding the PA sahib's impending visit had rung through the mountains and this delegation had come to receive him. A formal address was read out and Raheal commended for being the only PA to have made a repeat visit to these remote parts. After braving one visit, no mother's son

SEA MONSTERS AND THE SUN GOD

The Chitterwatta Border Military Police post dominates the landscape from its knoll above the village.

Mysterious signs on the rock, Chitterwatta.

of a PA had ever come back, said the reader of the address. And here was this strange sahib who had returned within six weeks of the first visit.

A vast lunch was ready to be devoured. But the Baloch entertains guests with meat and only meat, and the hapless vegetarian be damned. Besides the two whole lambs there was also a couple of birds, dark and wooden that tasted like nothing in the world. Over the meal, the delegation discussed the various problems among which the road (its absence, actually) featured prominently, some petitions were presented to Raheal and then we took our leave.

We hadn't gone more than twenty minutes when we were ambushed by another similar delegation. There was more meat to be consumed. I balked but Raheal and Ibrahim, brave and good men, sat down to eat. Earlier they had told me of the sure-fire Baloch blackmail employed in the event of a guest declining to accept hospitality: the host declares that his wife stands divorced should the guest not oblige. Since no self-respecting guest would want a hospitable man to be driven into such a dire situation, hospitality at this point is usually accepted. But I had no stomach, or even eyes, for any meat and not wishing to cause a divorce I sauntered off lying that the first meal had left me with a queasy stomach and I needed a secluded rock for a squat.

Under a lowering sky the scenery was still beautiful in a savage sort of way. The broad, pebbly bed of the Vehowa stream was braided with a wide silver-grey ribbon of water. On the far side the gorge rose sharply in a striated wall, on this side gently. In the sparse vegetation on my side, ashy finch-larks trilled and jostled. I stopped to see if they were already nesting in March, but found nothing. From further afield a sonorous double hoot rode the wind to me: the magnificent Indian eagle-owl was very likely watching us from its perch on a crag. Earlier we had surprised a wolf in the rank vegetation along a small stream and one of Raheal's bodyguards had very nearly raised his rifle. Happily for us conservationists the animal fled in good time. I thrilled to the thought that the mountain yet lived.

They had finished when I got back. Ibrahim confirmed that the very real threat of several divorces had been successfully parried. Our hosts seemed relaxed as they sat about slurping their tea and smoking, their conversation punctuated by loud sounds of gastronomic repletion.

Chitterwatta with the BMP post commanding a low hillock and the village sprinkled beneath was made an hour before sunset. *Chitter* meaning 'pocked' in Seraiki (as too in Punjabi); the name comes from a large rock 'pocked' with inscriptions. Here were names of visiting PAs from a hundred years ago to the present. There were some Hindi and Urdu inscriptions together with some sort of hieroglyphic script that I had never seen before. There was also a star; a poor swastika and what seemed to be a crude Wheel of Life – all rather eroded. These and several others were without doubt from a long, long ago time. The

Chitterwatta Post, Raheal tells me, was built by the British to ward off the marauding Pukhtun raiders from Musa Khel Bazaar and from as far away as Waziristan. What attracted these raids was the wealth the traders of Chitterwatta garnered from the passage of a healthy commerce through here, and since all the rich of the village were Hindus, the Pukhtuns legitimised their raids by looking upon their work as holy war.

The post did indeed lessen the intensity of the raids, but even as little as thirty years ago there was sufficient pressure to force the grandfather of Om Prakash (whom we had met in Vehowa) to immigrate. If one were to look at the map, one cannot doubt the tradition regarding Chitterwatta lying on an ancient trade route: it is the shortest connection between Multan and Ghazni. The trade, once lively, now no more than part of the collective memory, is a reminder of the importance of the route. And man has always travelled. Long before man built cities and trade became the purpose, man travelled in search of sustenance. The horse was yet untamed and man unburdened by goods of trade indulged in the most primordial of activities: he walked. This route, like many others, is timeless. Somewhere in that timelessness this rock would have served as a sort of notice board to post news of the comings and goings of the famous and the ordinary. On this rock, friable and susceptible to erosion, the esoteric symbols that intrigued us could not be more than a couple of thousand years old, however. If there had been any earlier artistry, that had either been obliterated by erosion or heavily over written. We ran our fingers over the drawings and I wondered if the fancy of our ancient artists had been excited by the thought that their work was to be admired something like two millenniums later.

The post itself comes straight out of an M. M. Kaye script. But owing to a lack of funds it is falling to pieces. While Raheal attended to yet another delegation (his third that day) Ibrahim and I climbed up the roof with one of the BMP men warning us where not to tread for fear of a roof collapse. We eventually gave up and walked up the hill behind the fort to watch the darkness falling and the stars coming out one by one.

Our departure from Chitterwatta was delayed until midday. All because of Raheal – and not for an entirely useless cause. Being a trained doctor, he had brought along a medicine chest and spent the entire morning ministering to the medical needs of suffering humanity that hadn't seen another doctor in a long, long time. I sent up a silent prayer for all such doctors turned administrators who put their knowledge to good use in such remote places.

There was also the elderly woman called 'Chairman.' All of seventy-five years old, she was a live wire if I have ever seen one. She chattered away with Raheal without waiting for her Balochi to be translated. She smiled, she threw her head back and laughed, she chuckled and slapped one of the BMP men who said something naughty to her. She was as liberated as any woman in Karachi or Lahore. She was the 'Chairman' because, they said, she firmly kept her husband well in line. A very paragon for the women's libbers of Pakistan, if you ask me. Like others of her kind I had seen elsewhere, she earned this status, I felt, because she was past the child-bearing age and was the mother of adult sons. I wished to speak with her, but fearing so much would be lost in the translation, abandoned the idea.

There was also the elderly man with the aging muzzle-loader that he brought out to fire for our benefit. Although it could take down a man, he said, he used it only for partridges. The weapon was loaded: cordite and shreds of old cotton cloth ('to build up pressure') packed hard into the breech. Some lead pellets went in via the muzzle. The fuse was put in place under the cocked hammer. The man aimed at a rock, squeezed the trigger and the hammer fell with a thin, empty click. The crowd jeered and the man looked only slightly fazed. He pulled the hammer back again, aimed and this time a lot of cotton flew with a bang. Up ahead a handful of dirt jumped. We all clapped and the man looked around smugly.

We drove through a landscape of pebbly flood plains twined with thin ribbons of water, caught between stark, brown hills and jagged precipices. Every now and again we passed below escarpments that seemed uncannily like man made fortifications. Phugla was made in time for a late lunch. A great crowd of Baloch men was at hand to receive Raheal. They fired their Kalashnikovs in the air, the guard rattled their service rifles and presented arms, Raheal inspected and then they sat down for the address to be read out. More problems for Raheal to look into: clean drinking water, health, smuggling of wheat and absence of roads. I dozed through the proceedings and never learned how the smugglers were to be tackled.

As we were leaving Phugla storm clouds billowed out from the west and soon sheet lightning went streaking across the darkling sky. Rain was teeming down when we entered Fazla Kuch that, like Vehowa, lives in a time warp broken only by the few ugly concrete buildings that do not belong with the rest of the 19th century village. Here were a couple of shops and an inn that hadn't changed in a hundred years. The ground floor of the mud-plastered hotel was occupied by the cook-house with a large window that had grease-encrusted wire mesh stretched loosely across its frame. It did not only keep the flies out, but light as well. A wooden ladder painted bright green led to the rooms upstairs. The balustrade on the first floor was the same colour as the ladder and the floor of the foyer was thickly laid with fading and dusty carpets. Behind the foyer were three or four rooms for travellers. After years of wandering about this country and looking for traditional inns, this was the first one I saw. And one that was functioning at that.

The building rubbed shoulders with motor workshops where oil-stained mechanics waited for business. Of that there was plenty, one man told me with a smile. Taunsa, rather than the nearer town of Zhob, being of easier access and affording better supplies for the traders of Musa Khel Bazaar, locals routinely travelled up and down this road. Busted road springs

SEA MONSTERS AND THE SUN GOD

The feast at Jhandi post was accompanied by sound effects that were hard to associate with the simple act of feeding.

and shock absorbers on those decrepit, overloaded four wheel drive pick-up trucks are common complaints. Business was good and he had no complaints, the mechanic said pulling lazily on his cigarette.

Ibrahim Beg said farewell to us and rode away. He had wanted very much to be on the expedition to climb the peak of Behu just across the border in Balochistan, but none of us was sure how long it would take to get there and back and he had a job to look after. His inquiries in Vehowa and Phugla revealed that once we left our transport we would have to walk no more than a couple of hours to reach the peak, and if we left early we would be back in time for dinner. Now Behu is 2348 metres above the sea; I estimated Manrka, where we planned to start walking, to be no more than 400 metres. Therefore, we had to be supermen to climb almost 2000 metres in a couple of hours. So far as I reckoned, it wasn't as simple as they made it appear.

But Ibrahim's informants were adamant: so many times they had themselves walked from Manrka to Behu and back in three or four hours and we, softies that we were, would take maybe six hours. Ibrahim was almost enticed. But from years of mountain walking experience I knew otherwise and told him it was just a lot of hot air. None of these heroes had ever

INTO THE HEART OF THE SULEMAN MOUNTAINS

Changing from 4x4 pick-up trucks to horse at Manrka.

been anywhere near Behu. And so as Ibrahim said farewell, I told him we would be very sorry he was no longer to be with us if the climb to Behu turned to be as short as it had been reported.

We left Fazla Kuch in pre-dawn darkness. Horses awaited us at Manrka (the *nr* producing that nasal-palatal sound that only speakers of subcontinental languages can produce). Khurram, the young Risaldar, appeared to have been born in the saddle and Raheal, being just as bad, had brought his riding helmet and crop. I, for my part, have this pathological fear of being dragged behind a demon horse with one foot caught in the stirrup and keep a respectable distance from all horses. But I was forced into the saddle; not only by Raheal, but also by his staff. I did not last there more than fifteen minutes and snapped at the first man who said anything about the walk being long and hard.

We went up a sharp incline to a ridge. Below us spread a cultivated bowl with a single spreading tree in its middle. But Behu was not visible. Our guide said it was behind the khaki ridge in the distance. With a pair of binoculars they showed us the post of Jhandi on that ridge. In a straight line the post was about a thousand metres distant, but going around the ridge instead of descending into the bowl it would be some three kilometres. Again

The peak of Behu in Balochistan as seen from Zain Sar. We would have been supermen to climb it in the time that rumour said was needed.

insistences for me to ride ensued. I snapped at everyone that mentioned 'horse' to me. Following the contours around the bowl we arrived at Jhandi some time after nine.*

Again a delegation was at hand to welcome Raheal with gunfire. Lunch, they said, was ready and I knew it was going to be more roast lamb which at midmorning, with breakfast still sloshing about inside, can be a most revolting sight. And it was. But I politely sat through it picking at a piece of wholesome *kak*, the Baloch bread prepared on a hot stone. If you do not believe that feeding can be an operation of intense activity, you should have witnessed the scene outside where the rest of the delegation ate. On their hunkers this merry lot choffed, chomped, slurped, sniffed and burped as great

---

* As we came over the lip of the bowl there was much shouting between our party and the men at Jhandi Post. Raheal later told me that our escorts were yelling for a charpoy to be kept ready for use as a palanquin because sahib's guest, insisting on walking, would be done in by the time he made Jhandi and would have to be carried to Behu. By the end of the journey I had earned the respect of the Baloch, however.

quantities of meat steadily disappeared into them as stellar matter into a Black Hole until there remained only two rib cages and a few femurs and shoulder blades. Then they sat back to survey this scene of carnage with more burps. Satisfied that the foe had been suitably depleted, they lit their cigarettes and homemade pipes. Then all conversation ceased; only a chorus of belches rose above the soughing wind.

Even at Jhandi there were conflicting reports on the time to be taken to Behu. The range of estimation varied from a couple of hours to half a day. We headed out nevertheless. Beyond the scattered houses of the village we passed a small stone hovel that flew a proud Pakistani flag and it turned out to be the local school – the only one in almost two hundred square kilometres. A bunch of boys and girls squatted in front of the blackboard and the school master, not to miss the opportunity, invited Raheal to inspect. If the diligence he showed was this young teacher's daily routine, he can put innumerable peers of his to shame. In that case he is surely the exemplar to be emulated.

An hour out of Jhandi we heaved ourselves over the lip of the bowl that we had been walking in. This was Zain Sar, 1630 metres above the sea. And a right lovely place it was with its wild olive trees, scattered tiny yellow flowers, superb views and a cool, gusting wind. Far away, in the shadow of dark thunder clouds, Behu loomed. Raheal sent one of his men up a nearby knoll to make radio contact with base. Sure enough they confirmed what we had wished against: that some minister or other was visiting the day after and that Raheal was to return to Dera Ghazi Khan immediately.

As for our mountain, it was yet eight hours away! Since Zain Sar is not connected with Behu, we were to descend about 1200 metres and then begin the long drag up Behu. So much for the estimate of all those who claimed to habitually go up and down that hill. We knew our friend Ibrahim had not missed anything.

We lounged about enjoying the clear mountain air and watched the thunderheads piling up over Behu. It was said that spring is a time of almost daily afternoon storms. The topography of the eastern periphery of the Suleman range is a series of peaks and troughs that begin just below the 30th parallel of latitude at Fort Munro and run up into the main massif of Takht e Suleman northeast of Zhob. The troughs are no more than 400 metres high, while the peaks are nearly all above 2000 metres with Fort Munro being the lowest at 1935 metres and Takht e Suleman the highest at 3379 metres. I suppose it was this unique topography of alternating crests and dips that somehow attracted even weak westerly disturbances and brought down rain as we had seen only the afternoon before.

Our picnic was disturbed by the first drops of rain. We hurried back, brushed aside invitations for more food at Jhandi and went on. As we were coming down the last slope my aging boots simply fell to pieces and I had to get on the horse. It was just as well that we had aborted for I scarcely know what I would have done without boots on the slopes of Behu.

SEA MONSTERS AND THE SUN GOD

Saura Pass: just the place to show school children what a pass ought to be.

Menhirs, Stone Circles and Graves

There is, it was reported, a series of menhirs (free-standing upright stones) and stone circles in the vicinity of Fort Munro, the hill in Dera Ghazi Khan trying so hard – and failing – to hit it off as a summer resort for southern Punjab. And so it was that my friend Khurram Khosa and I drove over the divide between Punjab and Balochistan at Fort Munro. We were on an ancient highway that has carried murderers, ascetics, traders and adventurers back and forth. Beyond the village of Rakni (busy bazaar and a police station with

184

over a dozen brand-new smuggled cars waiting to rust to pieces) we drove on to Bawata.

Outside Bawata, to the south of the road hard by the Balochistan Levies checkpoint, were the menhir and stone circles – entirely unknown outside the area. To my untrained eye the stone circles looked like foundations of corrals and so far as I was concerned could be from two hundred to two thousand years old. The largest of these circles even had a time frame: an angular *mehrab* to the west told us that even if this was a prehistoric circle, something similar to Stonehenge, it had been appropriated at some point and turned into a mosque. Nearby there were several other sets of upright stone slabs that appeared to be the foundations of small rooms. Khurram said so far as he knew the Department of Archaeology had never investigated these puzzling stone relics.

The menhir, standing solitary and upright a little distance away, was remarkable. This was particularly true for I had never before seen one and also because I had no idea such things could be found in Pakistan. Carved out of a single block of blanched limestone it stood about three and a half metres tall. Next to it was a mesquite bush decorated not with coloured rags, the stock in trade of all shrines, but with a largish piece of someone's discarded bed linen. Leaning against the menhir was a slab of rock and on the ground was some rubble in the shape of a rude grave. To this 'grave' the menhir served as a headstone.

Only this was no grave. While the Muslim grave is on the north-south axis this one was out by the perpendicular. Our guide did not know the legend concerning the place. But he did tell us that the slab resting against the menhir was for people afflicted with abdominal pains to climb on and rub their stomach against the menhir. It was, he reported, a foolproof cure. I asked why it was necessary to climb up the single step instead of doing the rub from ground level. There was no answer, but then that is the way all superstitions must necessarily be.

The guide said there were three other similar megaliths. The one by village Tagha outside the town of Barkhan about thirty kilometres to the southwest; the second the same distance south of Bawata by village Checha, and the third some twenty odd kilometres northwest of Bawata outside village Mohma. All three, he said, were of similar material and shape.

If we didn't know a darn thing about our menhir, we were in good company: even megalith experts around the world have thus far been unable to assign any meaning to these mysterious stones. While stone circles like Stonehenge in England and our own all but unknown circle of village Asota (Swabi district in Pukhtunkhwa) may have religious or even astronomical significance because of their alignment with stars or constellations at certain times of year, free-standing menhirs have remained tantalisingly unexplained.

In Europe menhirs (the word, from the language of the ancient Bretons, means *men*, 'stone,' and *hir*, 'long') are sometimes associated with ancestor worship. Mostly, however, nothing can be made of them. Nonetheless, experts agree that they are the manifestation of a great diversity

The mysterious menhir of Bawata.

of beliefs. This stone, then, where men and women afflicted with abdominal cramps rub themselves could well be the seat of the earliest ancestors of the Baloch or of other tribes now long since lost and forgotten. Or of tribes that have migrated away, or indeed of peoples that paused here on their great trek into the Sindhu Valley. Alternatively, could these monuments have been erected by the inhabitants of the great cities of the Sindhu River Valley? This stone could have well been erected by traders, artisans and teachers that we know went west to take their crafts into Mesopotamia six thousand or more years ago.

But we do not know with any certainty. We must wait for the answers.

Done with the menhir, we turned north along a stony trail and were soon driving though one of the most desolate landscapes that I have ever been in. To our east and west ran two parallel ridges separated by the fifteen kilometre-wide valley of the Rakni River. Dry and barren, it afforded meagre pockets of cultivation only in the vicinity of the few hamlets that very likely grew around a spring. In the heat of the March afternoon, there were no people about and we passed only one man, rifle across his shoulders, leading a train of three camels.

Late afternoon found us in the remote village of Hinglun where we were to spend the night at the BMP check post. The village's claim to fame is the nondescript shrine of Muntoor Shah who admonished a passing *lashkar* of brigands for their waywardness. As thieving *lashkars* are, this bunch did not take very nicely to the homily, and one from this party struck off the man's head. Then, as it never fails to happen, Muntoor Shah picked up his severed head, tucked it under his arm and calmly walked into a nearby cleft in the rock. With his head under his arm, he obviously could not see which way he was going or he might not have bashed himself into the rock. The moral of the story, as I see it, is that it doesn't pay to lose one's head over another person's wickedness.

Those who believed in him built his shrine (a rude cubicle), tied some rags to the adjacent tree, a bell to the door jamb and the house was in business. But compared to some other similar

Part of the stone circle with other uprights in its enceinte. Local tradition now turns this prehistoric worship site into a mosque.

business houses, this one does rather poorly for its remoteness prevents a regular and populous pilgrimage. No one was about to unlock the door of the shrine for us, or to explain the significance of the bell that is essentially an adjunct to a Hindu (or Jain) temple. I wondered if there would ever come a time that some shrine attendant would be irreverent and truthful enough to tell visitors that the bell of course was a reminder that the shrine was primarily Hindu (or Jain) converted at an unknown point in time to the true faith.

The village also had three school buildings. The largest one with a high compound wall served as the school master's residence. The others were deserted. The story was that the local politician (who lived in a town nearer the main highway) had machinated during the last democratic government to get these buildings sanctioned and built at official expense. Ostensibly to increase literacy in the area, they were meant only to be used as cattle pens by the politician. Moreover, in order to gratify a needy relative, he had also had that man employed as teacher. This shameless person now tended the big man's cattle, lived in a spacious school building and was home dry with a monthly salary to boot. So much for literacy and so much for the government's much vaunted nab-the-corrupt programme.

But I had come to Hinglun for the tales I had heard of old Khan Mohammed. About thirty-five years ago this man shot and killed another in a gunfight. He was locked up in the BMP post while outside a crowd gathered demanding justice. Then suddenly there rose above the commotion a single gunshot and a cry went up that Sobdar (Mohammed's brother) had been shot. Inside his cell, Mohammed pleaded with the sentry to let him out because outside his brother, very likely in the throes of death, had no assistance. But the man understandably wouldn't oblige. And then, much to the astonishment of all present, they had Khan Mohammed standing beside them outside his cell.

He was restrained by three men and put right back in. Meanwhile, it became known that Sobdar was alive and well and that it was only a rifle gone off accidentally. For people who do not understand the capacity of the human mind, there had to be some quasi-divine explanation and for them Muntoor Shah was at hand. Mohammed, it was said, invoked the saint's help who spirited him through the bars miraculously. But Dafadar Rehmat Khan the post commander showed us the slightly bent bars (an inch thick) and said they are reported to have required straightening after the incident. In a paroxysm of frenzy Khan Mohammed had bent, with his bare hands, the bars of his cell and squeezed himself out. A truly superhuman feat, if there were one – just the right recipe for saintly intervention. But the man would have required no supernatural help; this was only the local version of karate: in that one moment of frenzy he had forced his mind to accomplish what karate experts, having trained their minds, habitually practice by smashing their fists through piles of kiln-fired bricks.

On my request men were sent out to fetch Khan Mohammed. But they all returned to say that he had gone off into the mountains with his sheep. The good Rehmat Khan sent his own brother into the mountains and said that he would be back by dawn with our man. In the event, however, that did not come to pass for the brother returned unaccomplished. Khan Mohammed was elsewhere and we had to leave Hinglun without shaking the hand of this superman. As compensation, on the morrow we were to meet in the village of Barthi with Allah Baksh, the shopkeeper, who swore he was right there in the compound of the BMP post when all that had happened.

'One minute Khan Mohammed was inside his cell, pleading to be let out to assist his brother,' said Allah Baksh. 'The next he was standing right there with us. There was no mistake; I saw it all. He was like a man possessed and I helped restrain him.'

'But what of his invocation to Muntoor Shah that everyone talks of?' I asked.

'Horse feathers! He did nothing of the sort, he only let out an anguished howl like that of a wild animal and sprang out of the cell.' It was so swift that neither Baksh nor the others noticed him struggling with the bars.

Leaving Hinglun we passed northward through scenery of yet more desolation, pausing to examine the ruins on the knoll of Dishtak Sar in the hills of Krimar: stone foundations of an ancient settlement and a graveyard with a view. Below us a stream meandered and all around us looming hills frowned out of the blue midmorning haze. Believing I was an expert Khurram asked how old the ruins could be. I hadn't a clue.

The desolation gave way to the wheat fields of Saura: acre upon acre of swaying gold and scattered trees dwarfed under brown hills. Through the great cleft of the Saura Pass we went. I called for a brief pause for this was where every school child should be taken so that the phrase 'mountain pass' turns from mere phrase into geographical reality, but where, I know for sure, no teacher will ever resort to avail this unique opportunity. To Barthi did we go, yet another one of those straggling villages with school, stores and even a restaurant.

Raheal Siddiqui, who had arrived direct from Dera Ghazi Khan, sat in the sun outside the BMP post at the edge of the escarpment. My first thought upon seeing him: why must he fry his brains in the sun, even if he is wearing his pith helmet? But my friend is like that: entirely impervious to heat and cold. He was looking out on the view he had wanted to show me. And it was indeed a great view with the hills in the distance, glinting water and hutments below. At one end of the escarpment was the abandoned rest house. On the other, another scattering of ruins. Raheal said this was very likely a fortress to protect the route that passed below. Yet another ancient route that is still in use between Taunsa in Punjab and the Pushtun highlands of

The tomb of Muntoor Shah.

Musakhel Bazaar in north-eastern Balochistan. Many years ago Dr Saifur Rahman Dar, the eminent archaeologist, had told me that even in ancient times there was a web of roads criss-crossing this great land of the Sindhu River. Here, in the backwaters of southwest Punjab, we found yet more testimony to his theory.

We had reached the end of our journey. Having set out to walk the high peaks of the district, we had been denied the adventure by circumstances. The peaks would have to wait for another time. That would be another journey. Another story.

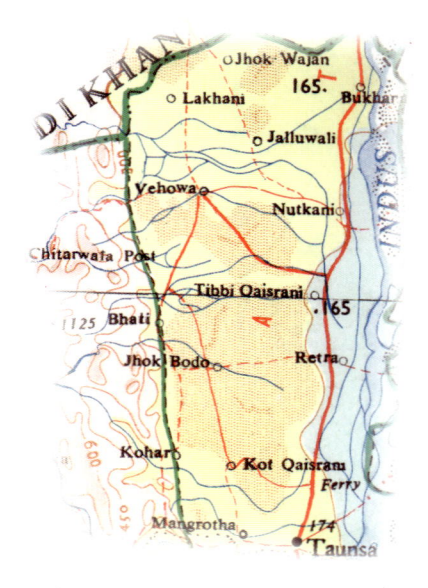

Philosopher Poet of Vehowa

I learned of Jehanzeb Jehangir Raz from his poem in the Inspection Book of the Vehowa BMP Post. Written in response to the PA's observation that the post be abolished, the four couplet poem showed not only the poet's excellent command over the Urdu language, but also a shade of Allama Iqbal.

Born to a Khetran family in the small village of Vehowa in Dera Ghazi Khan district, Jehanzeb Jehangir remembers an easy childhood. The family had a medium-sized land holding managed by his father (himself a poet of Seraiki, Persian, Urdu, Hindi and Punjabi) and life was good. The Land Reforms of Mr Bhutto, however, deprived the family of a great part of their holding and now on the verge of old age Raz faces pecuniary problems.

By his own admission he used to get 'strange notions' in his head from a very early age. He looked up into the sky and contemplated the reality of the blue welkin, the starry night got him thinking about the universe: how would it have started and how it must end, its vastness and man's place in it. Not yet tutored in philosophy, when he was in the 8th grade in school, he one day gathered his classmates and lectured them on the universe. They looked at him as if he had gone barmy for they had never bothered about the things this loony was now talking of. That was the first realisation that not everyone was concerned with the notions that rankled him. That in the village he was alone in his interest in the natural world.

Wrestling with these metaphysical problems, Raz passed his matriculation from Vehowa and moved to Dera Ghazi Khan. But scarce had he finished his FA in 1966 when his father died and he returned home to manage the holding. Jealous relatives soon had him embroiled in tedious litigation over the property. Not certain of the outcome of the litigation and looking for another livelihood he joined the Border Military Police, in 1969 as Dafadar. He was posted at the Vehowa post where he was to spend most of his service.

Even as a schoolboy Jehanzeb Jehangir had given himself the pen name of *Mukhfi* – the Hidden or Unknown. Now he calls himself *Raz* – The Secret. He continued to struggle with the same metaphysical dilemmas that had plagued him as a child. Only years of reading had given a greater depth and substance to his quest. As a young man, the diversity of religious belief caused him sleepless nights and he worried whether he followed the True Faith. The answer evaded Raz and he found himself drawing further and further away from religion. The next many years he was to live without a belief.

Meanwhile, he nurtured his mind with books he found in his late father's collection and with those borrowed from friends. In the intellectual wilderness of Vehowa, however, he could not find one person to engage in any meaningful dialogue. At his post he alone was the reader of books – forever lost in their company. Besides whatever he could get on metaphysics, he read the works of Faiz, Faraz and Iqbal and admits that his own poetry is indeed influenced by these great minds.

Jehanzeb Jehangir Raz

He became known as a bit of a loony: not only was he endlessly reading, but he also had no interest in the goodly sums of money to be made from the uniform of Dafadar that he wore. 'It troubled me that my colleagues were only concerned with the making of money on the side. What made this enterprise doubly criminal was the fact that many of them were also otherwise unjust in their actions,' says Raz. Here then was a man without faith, without a religious belief, but whose character was far superior to those of his peers who wore religion on their sleeves and paraded their godliness.

Presently it came time for the veils to be lifted. And this happened through a series of occult occurrences that Raz hesitates to speak of, but he does mention several dreams that foretold important and not so important events. He says he is a Muslim again, and has been one for several years now. Perhaps it is a measure of his character that he has the courage to mention he is a Muslim without action, that is, he remains irregular in the five times daily prayer. That, he points out, is a habit that has to be developed early on in life, and since he missed out then, he has been unable to follow the prescribed regimen. But he is in no doubt that he has made his peace with his God and thanks him for so blessing him.

There are not many things that he may be proud of, but he feels he did his duty to the nation when he wrote out the long report about gun-running through Vehowa. It was the beginning of the 1980s (he does not remember the exact year), when immense quantities of sophisticated arms and ammunition were being smuggled through the area on the way to various parts of Sindh including Karachi. His report (to the PA) voiced his fear that something truly drastic and unfortunate was due to take place in that sorry province.

His words proved prophetic and Sindh has yet not recovered from its long war within.* But his report was filed away and forgotten for the PA is reported to have said that Raz was merely gratifying his habit of writing petitions and reports. It was said he didn't know what he was talking about. But the fact is that the man knew exactly what he meant and he knew the names of some very influential persons who were actively engaged in that unholy traffic. It was perhaps because of these powerful people that no action was taken on Raz's report. Sindh and Karachi were permitted by the 'patriots' of Pakistan to descend into the dark hell of a long and unjust civil war.

Twenty-eight years of serving cleanly and honestly gave him an unblemished reputation. But in a society that is blatantly hypocritical he received no recognition other than the reputation. After almost three decades he retired from the rank that he had joined the service in. Burdened with pecuniary problems and an ailing heart, he is content that he lived a life unsullied by greed and corruption.

Strangely, there is even equanimity that his poetry has not been published and reached the reading public. He casually mentions that there might be sufficient compositions, disorganised and scattered about in various note books and on scraps of paper, to make two volumes. There is another manuscript as well that deals with the occult experiences that brought him back into the fold of belief. Publishing in Pakistan usually costs a good deal of money and he has none to spare. With his sad, lop-sided smile he says the work might be published and read some day. It will not matter if he is not around to be invited to the book launch.

---

* Now, over a quarter of a century since Raz wrote out his report, Karachi continues to burn and bleed.

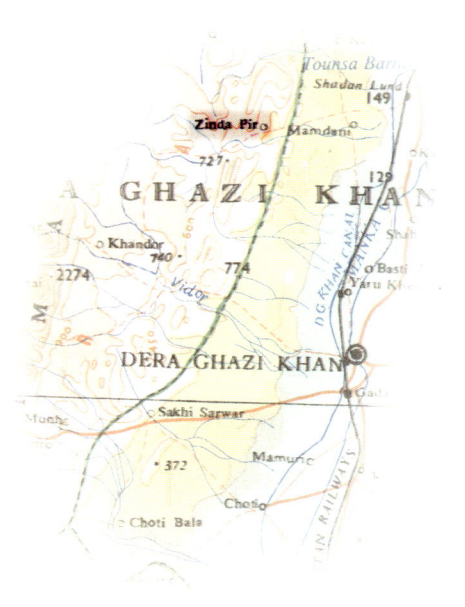

Pouches containing the first shaving of the boy child acquired by the saint's agency adorn the tree. Notice the bell that is sometimes rung by visiting pilgrims. In the background is the cubicle that serves as a sort of shrine.

The Saint who lives

Past Dera Ghazi Khan Cement Factory, we turned westward into the hills and drove the eight kilometres of dusty trail to a sprawling assemblage of clapboard eating and trinket-selling stalls. The shrine of Zinda Pir, the Living Saint, lay a short walk away. We were late. On the way we had passed dozens of tractors going the other way hauling trailers loaded with colourfully dressed people returning from the closing rites of the annual festival of the purported saint.

We took the short walk from the shanty bazaar. The shrine was scarcely impressive: an ill-looking cubicle with a large brass bell hanging on the door jamb. The devotees, mainly women, clanged the bell as one would upon entering a Hindu temple and went in. Inside, since the man had not died only disappeared from the sight of mortals, was a pile of copies of the Koran instead of the usual grave. Outside, by the entrance, was the tree with assorted rags and tiny cloth pouches filled with the first shaving of newborn babies. A child begotten as a result of supplication at this shrine, it was said, had to return here to be shaved and the hair left as an offering. What with most Baloch men having beards and sometimes even long hair, I couldn't help thinking that this shrine may well have been started by some long-forgotten out-of-work barber whose descendents now must

My guide Shams of the Border Military Police prepares to ignite the magic hole.

be right thankful to him.

Further on were the sulphur baths: an open pond where pot-bellied men (as ugly as tadpoles) and some boys splashed about in knee-deep water. Nearby was another hidden behind a rock wall from where we could hear women's voices punctuated by an occasional mischievous squeal. It was the saint's blessing, they said, that warmed the dirty blue-green water and that cured all ills. The curative qualities of sulphur were unknown to the devotees of Zinda Pir.

Shams, my guide, took me up a small slope to a small gash gouged out in the rock. He lit a match and poked it into the hole and a small blue flame appeared, flickered for a while before going out. I stuck my nose into the hole and sensed a faint smell of sulphur. All pilgrims always came up here and performed this little exercise, said Shams. He also said that there was no other rock nearby that burnt. I could not imagine how this little 'miracle' was first discovered, nor the quirky coincidence that would have caused some individual to come up this slope that leads to nowhere, light a match and hold it next to the rock at just the right spot to see the tiny blue flame. But once discovered, the 'miracle' apparently quickly caught on and now it is on the menu of the Zinda Pir pilgrimage.

Our next number was the fifteen-minute hike up the slope across the valley floor. Men, women and children were going up and down. On the top was a row of colourful flags, a few water-pots under a shelter and an elderly green-clad attendant to point us in the direction of the cave where the saint is believed to have disappeared. Hardly a cave, it was more a tear in the limestone wrought by seismic activity and very difficult to enter. After fumbling about a bit, however, I did manage to get in. The twenty thousand-year old cave paintings I had hoped to discover were not there, nor too was the hole as deep as we had been promised. The men at the sulphur pond had said it was connected to Mecca via the tomb of Sakhi Sarwar, but it ended in a jumble of rocks barely three metres from its mouth. I hadn't realised we were this close to Mecca!

Everything about this Houdini of a saint is vague. There are no legends. We only hear of a police inspector who, upon retirement some years ago, repaired to this valley. Forswearing speech the man became a hermit and when he was asked as to who Zinda Pir was, he wrote on a slip of paper that he 'might have been' the prophet

Khizer. They asked if that prophet had visited this lonely river valley. Again the man wrote out that he 'might have.' And so trusting the 'might haves' of some corrupt police officer hoping to atone for all the injustice he had perpetrated in his professional life upon the dispossessed and the powerless, but more likely was on the run from worldly justice, people believe they are supplicating at the shrine of the prophet who had guided none less than Moses himself. The retired inspector apparently followed in the footsteps of his spiritual mentor for it is not known what eventually became of him.

I have no doubt that these 'living saints' were no more then foolish mendicants who, because they were not prudent enough, ended up as dinner for wild beasts. Since no trace was ever found, they became disappearing wizards for superstitious folk. We have no scarcity of such saints that departed into the hungry stomachs of wolves or leopards and one that even met his end in a crevasse on a Karakorum glacier: on a small nameless glacier at the top of Chapursan Valley in Gojal north of Hunza, there is a spot known as Qalander Gum (Lost Saint). That, they tell you, is where the Qalander disappeared from the sight of mortals. In other words the poor soul, uninitiated to mountaineering, fell into a crevasse and died a miserable death. All of them are deified and worshipped as Zinda Pirs.

This site in southwest Punjab, however, has been usurped from Hinduism – and I have no doubt in that. When this conversion took place is not known, however. Not belonging to Muslim shrines, the bell and the way it is clanged as one enters is a manifest *zeitgeist* from our Hindu past. As elements of an earlier faith are incorporated into the new belief system at the shrine of Channan Pir in Bahawalpur or at the hilltop temple of Takht e Suleman in Zhob or on the snowy peak of Musa ka Musalla in Kaghan,* so too has it happened at the Zinda Pir shrine of Dera Ghazi Khan. And as elsewhere, these earlier elements do not disturb the religious sensibilities of the disciples of this Zinda Pir.

For those yearning for sons, a visit to the shrine and the ringing of the bell yields a male child. And then perhaps it also does not. But only the begetting of a boy child is proclaimed to the world: the keeper insisted that *all* seekers did get what they sought and always returned. He seemed incapable of understanding that the sorry parents whose prize for a visit to this shrine was their seventh daughter were forgotten for they never returned to shave the infant's head and leave the offering in a tiny pouch on the tree outside the temple. Only the proud parents of the boy child are registered and so the legend grows fat – and with it the progeny of the enterprising barber.

For many, especially local rural women, the outing is surely no more than an exciting diversion from humdrum lives: here they can let their hair down. Here they can laugh and talk, frolic in the dirty, foul-smelling sulphur pond, shop to their hearts' content (or as much as the purse allows) for cheap and gaudy trinkets, gorge themselves on the goodies the shanty eating-houses offer and, best of all, get away from the drudgery of the hearth and the water hole. It is one hell of a picnic and even if it lasts just a day, it is worth it. On the side, if they can get a son by the saint's blessing, that is a bonus. If not, there is no dearth of other saints to try out.

---

* For these stories see *Prisoner on a Bus.*

SEA MONSTERS AND THE SUN GOD

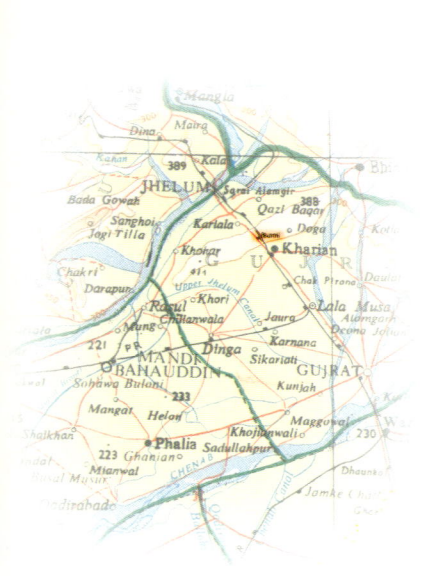

The Mughal water tank, dry after years of drought. The gate posts mark the lower end of the ramp leading into the tank.

A rest house and a memory

The magic of the narrow Grand Trunk Road as it wound through the acacia and *shisham*-covered slopes of the Pabbi Hills between Jhelum and Kharian has been lost to progress. The highway has been widened and straightened and zooming through one hardly notices the clayey vegetation-covered hills.

Lost too is a lovely old rest house that was about eighty years old when I first knew it back in the early 1970s. Bunni Bungla, as it was called, was the property of the Forest Department, if I remember correctly. It was a bulky looking brick building with a pillared veranda on three sides, one large drawing room and two or three other rooms. It sat, unseen from the main road, on a knoll amid tall grass and trees all but forgotten and scarcely visited.

About a hundred metres to the north of the bungalow was the edge of the escarpment. Below it was a wild and desolate sort of gorge where we could surprise foxes if we were quiet enough and hedgehogs even if we weren't. About a couple of hundred yards farther out in this ravine was the main railway line and far away, on the horizon, used to be a crystal line of snow peaks: the Pir Panjal Range of Kashmir. In August, that blessed month of Bhadon, when it used to be what we now only read of in romances and when it meant rain and teeming rain, the landscape used to be magic. Everything would turn a colour so green as to defy definition.

As a young subaltern stationed at Kharian, I and a couple of friends had discovered the rest house by accident on a walk through the Pabbi Hills. Having scrambled up through thickly growing *Phulai* festooned with creepers in a wet August, we were surprised to find ourselves facing the imposing building where we hadn't expected anything. The chowkidar was a right friendly and talkative chap, a chowkidar of the old school. In 1973 they were all veterans of the Raj and this one remembered visiting British officials well. He also told us that at some point General Yahya Khan was placed under house arrest in that rest house and showed us the room used by the General.

There was no electricity and each room had a manual *punkha*. A giant version of those hand-held wicker fans that we still see today. This thing, sometimes with a colourful fringe, hung from hooks in the ceiling. A rope attached to its frilly lower edge went through a hole fitted with a pulley in the upper part of the door jamb and was worked by a professional *punkha*-puller sitting in the veranda. This person, usually a youngster, was on regular payroll in those pre-electricity days and sitting outside the room he would alternately pull and release the rope to swung the fan. It is said that these boys were so adept at their tedious work that they would fall asleep with the rope wrapped around the big toe and even in deep sleep the leg would continue to work back and forth, back and forth. And Bunni Bungla had such a *punkha*-puller too.

Outside, the lawn had its semi-circle of the bitter hedge that we call 'gardenia' with a concentric arc of periwinkles that seemed to be eternally in bloom. Otherwise, it was rather unkempt and used to be rank with tall grass during the monsoon months. But from early October onwards, the grass would begin drying out. That was when the weather turned crisp with a touch of winter and sitting there we could even discern new snow on the distant Pir Panjal – or so we used to imagine. One of our great pleasures then was to go out to Bunni on Sunday afternoons with a few bottles of chilled beer, lie in the dry grass with the sun mellow on our young brown faces and dream great dreams as we watched the shadows lengthen in the ravine below and the light change on the snows of Pir Panjal.

In the few years I spent in Kharian, Bunni was a favourite haunt. Then I left that station and, not long afterwards, the army and went to live in Karachi. In 1985 motorcycling through Punjab I resolved to revisit Bunni, but missed the turn-off. Some years later, having returned

This niché adorns the walls of the ramp leading into the tank.

home to Lahore, I thought of stopping at Bunni the next time I motored to or from Rawalpindi. But that never came to be until recently. The turn-off was not at all difficult to find, but maybe the drought had killed off so much vegetation that it now showed clearly. On the top of the knoll there was a microwave mast but no rest house. The young man minding the microwave station said the rest house was a couple of hundred metres down the road.

But the site was too familiar: the flat-topped knoll, the sharp escarpment, the railway line. Everything was there. Only the rest house and the horizon of crystal snow peaks were missing.

But the latter I knew was lost to us forever because we have ravaged the earth and the air that sustain us. Images from my youth like the sight of Pir Panjal from Bunni or from the peak of Tilla Jogian, are no more. We have pumped so much smoke and filth into the atmosphere that we no longer see the horizon, only a murky greyness. But even if the Pir Panjal was not visible, I knew I was at the right place.

Was there an old water tank around here, I asked. Through rank mesquite I went in the direction the man had pointed. Back in 1973 the old chowkidar had told us that the tank had been built by Babur, the founder of the Moghul empire. The ramp leading into the tank, bone dry in the third year of the drought, was intact, the brickwork still in good fettle. In one or two places some dedicated archaeologist had applied a coat of cement to arrest deterioration. The thickly growing trees resounded (even in May) to the frenzied calls of the Brainfever Bird and the mellifluous whistles of Golden Orioles.

A slightly older man joined me. I asked about the rest house again. The old building, he said, had been pulled down in 1992 (or perhaps the year after) on the orders of the prime minister. That foolish man, brain-dead from a gross excess of fatty foods, had found that old historic building not to his loutish taste and wanted a new-fangled monstrosity to suit his uncultured Gowalmandi mind. Just as Kamran Mirza's *baradari* in the Ravi was 'renovated' on his orders so too did this brainless man want to renovate Bunni Bungla.

I will never know why old, but perfectly

serviceable, buildings must be replaced. Why they cannot be refurbished. Why they must be destroyed even when they have tens of decades of serviceability left. But the grand old bungalow was pulled down and work on the new monstrosity begun. It was perhaps divine justice that the new foundations had scarcely risen from the ground when the unsteady foundations of prime ministership came crumbling down. Work stopped and when the man again got back into the driving seat four years later, it did not resume. Bunni Bungla and the illicit fun that someone was going to have there were forgotten. There were other hare-brained ideas to consider and see that they never came to fruition.

I don't know if young subalterns from Kharian still go walking in the Pabbi hills, but if they do and if they ever scramble up through the thick vegetation they will not find a graceful old rest house on the knoll. They will only find ugly unfinished foundations. Gone is the old house and gone too the unkempt garden and rank grass. No longer can the subalterns of today feel that glow that we as young men had felt with the beer warming our souls and the mellow sun of October our bodies. I wonder if they will even know today what they have missed: the tall grass, birdsong leaping out of the vegetation, the vitreous blue sky, the wild gorge below, the distant glaze of the Pir Panjal and, best of all, the buoyant feeling of growing up in a time of hope and idealism. Their fault is they were born too late.

The only redeeming factor is my friend Khushnood Lashari, a rare breed of bureaucrat, who heads Gujranwala division as the Commissioner. Though even he cannot conjure back the destroyed rest house, he has ordered the overgrown Moghul water tank to be cleaned up and a sign installed to tell passing travellers of the four hundred year-old monument. Perhaps the occasional passer-by interested in our legacy will slow down to take the detour up the knoll. When that happens, something of Bunni will have been salvaged.

For me, however, the recent visit brought on a pang of sadness. The rest house has evaporated like so many of the dreams of our youth a quarter of a century ago. The visit brought back a yearning for the heady days of the 1970s when dreams came easy and when the flush of hope and the verve of youth gave a jaunty lilt to our walk. We were free, almost as free as Jinnah had wanted us to be: free to go to our temples and to our mosques without fear of lurking death. Though we had lost half the country only a couple of years earlier, we yet harboured great visions for what remained. Religion lived in the souls of women and men and not on the tips of forked tongues. The mullah had not yet started his unholy war against Islam, and we were all better folks, surely a bit closer to God for we had not yet fully mastered the vile art of hypocrisy. Honesty was still appreciated and decency was not taken as a sign of weakness. What a great time it was to be growing up in.

The loss of a simple brick building perhaps a hundred years old when mindless politicians destroyed it precipitated a longing for a time that was surely much better. I had never realised how close my association with Bunni Bungla was. The desolation that I felt within at its loss brought that realisation. It felt as if a part of my youth had been stolen away. I knew this time around the past really was another country.

SEA MONSTERS AND THE SUN GOD

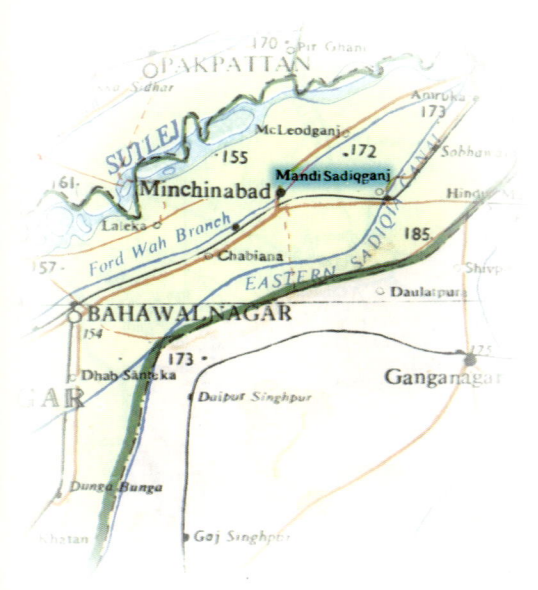

All but erased from memory: Mandi Sadiqganj railway station.

The 'Bumba Mail' called here

Once upon a time, before the new border was drawn and Pakistan came into being, through trains from Karachi to Kolkata via Delhi left what we now call our 'main line' at Bahawalpur, turned northeast to chug through the desert to Bahawalnagar and on to the junction of Mandi Sadiqganj. From here they either carried on through Amruka to Fazilka and onward, or turned due east to Bhatinda, one of the busiest railway junctions in this part of pre-partition India. From Bhatinda travellers could go in any direction on any number of trains.

In undivided India, the Bhatinda loop was also used by some mail trains running between Peshawar and Kolkata. Being a longer, more tedious route in comparison to the direct line through Lahore, Jullundher and on to Delhi, the term 'via Bhatinda' passed into common usage for long-winded verbosity or for a pointless and circuitous journey. The phrase remained in use until the 1970s before transiting unobtrusively into oblivion, perhaps a sign of the thinning of the generation that understood its import.

But then the line was drawn, India was divided and Pakistan came into being as a separate country. Towns and cities that were once nerve centres on ancient travel routes suddenly became places on the unfriendly fringes of the two neighbours. Suddenly they were places that travellers did not pass through on their way anywhere, but border towns where one only went when pressed by business of great importance: from mid-points they became the ends of journeys. Likewise, significant way points on the great trunk railways became terminuses for trains that once chugged haughtily across the vast Punjabi plains.

Time passed and failing to mature as a nation, we became extremely paranoid. As a result it became difficult for ordinary Pakistanis to travel freely to these border towns for fear of being hounded by agents of those dreaded secret agencies who live two hundred years in the past when the camera had not yet been invented and when every traveller was essentially a spy. Not having heard of spy satellites, they still believe that spies must necessarily travel to photograph and map 'vital' installations. Consequently, had it not been for my friend Kashif Noon from Bahawalpur, I might never have gone to the lonely, deserted railway station of Mandi Sadiqganj treading on the Indian border.

Meanwhile, the railway in Pakistan was not doing too well either. Given the lowest priority by successive governments, the once mighty and efficient machinery had ground to creaking sloth and inadequacy by the 1970s. Where even neighbouring India was racing ahead with fast trains and new lines, we were closing down long sections of railway inherited from the Raj. But no railway in the world makes money from hauling passengers; it earns by moving freight. Consequently the last nail in the railway's coffin came with the establishment of National Logistic Cell (NLC) in the 1970s.

The import of vast numbers of lorries and trailers was a fine chance for some powerful persons to nicely line their pockets with hefty commissions. No thought was paid to the fact that a country long and narrow like Pakistan was ideally suited for freight haulage by rail rather than by road. No thought was paid too to the great environmental cost of hundreds of smoke-emitting lorries pounding up and down the country in place of a single locomotive hauling a hundred-plus freight wagons. Nor too to the damage to be done to the already battered roads. The only thought was for the fat bank account in Switzerland. And so the once proud North Western Railway we had inherited at independence came to the sorry pass where we are trying to resuscitate it with all manner of hare-brained ideas.

We left Bahawalpur early, wasted a great deal of time at Bahawalnagar turning ourselves into a self-important and oversized expedition before

SEA MONSTERS AND THE SUN GOD

Once the 'Bumba' Mail called here; now they come here for a moment of peace. The water shed can be seen in the background.

heading out to Sadiqganj. Self-important, for whereas no one would have cared for the two of us pottering aimlessly about deserted railway stations, Kashif's brother who joined us at Bahawalnagar had a couple of friends tagging along. The bonus for travelling with Kashif's brother was an armed escort as well. Through the great throng of country folks crowding the bazaars of Minchinabad, we turned due east toward the border. Presently Sadiqganj rose out of the heat and dust of the plain: stacks of dust-coloured houses surrounded by a thin sprinkling of date palms and other trees.

The railway station was outside the town to the east. A couple of young boys played some childish game in front of the cream-washed building, but seeing our armed guard made

THE 'BUMBA MAIL' CALLED HERE

themselves scarce. The foyer was deserted. On the single platform there were just two men: an older one looking regal, his walking stick leaning against his knee he sat cross-legged on a bench and stared intently into the distance. Near the bench a ruminating goat sat on the floor. The other, younger and bearded, sat on the bench outside the padlocked Station Master's office. Behind him a sign announced that permission was needed before entering the Master's office. Next to it another warned (in red, perhaps for added emphasis), 'Prohibited Area. Photographing is Prohibited.'

Professedly unpatriotic and convinced that India (and perhaps Israel as well) would pay a fortune for a photograph of the padlocked door of the Master's office in the all but disused railway station of Sadiqganj, I committed the illegal act. No sirens were sounded and undercover agents did not materialise from nowhere to take me in. Meanwhile, seeing the crowd of our expedition dawdling about, an elderly railwayman, now retired since three years, came around to investigate. He had known the glory days of Mandi Sadiqganj railway station.

'There were eight trains up and down daily through here until only a few years ago and you should have seen the bustle and splendour of our station,' he said proudly. 'And this was after Partition. Earlier, it was a right glorious station when there were more trains.'

Among those of pre-partition days, he told us, were the passenger trains that commuted between Ferozepur and Bahawalnagar and the ones that returned from Mandi Sadiqganj to Ferozepur after waiting overnight on the outer platform. He pointed out the place where those trains were watered and cleaned overnight for the return. But the greatest of them all was the daily up and down 'Bumba' (Bombay perhaps?) Mail that swept into the station like a storm. It made a short stop, then, with wheels flying sparks, whistle screaming and the booming woof of its boilers reverberating in the quiet of the night, rousing the sleeping Sadiqganj-wallahs, it would go charging out of the station again. Vendors would run alongside, their outstretched hands some time meeting, mostly missing, the outstretched hands of the passengers leaning out of the windows. Then all would be quiet again. Though I could not figure out where the Bombay Mail originated or terminated or which line it ran on to have passed through Sadiqganj, I yet liked the story for its romance.

Somebody was sent off to fetch the key to the Station Master's office and our man showed us in. The office had the usual complement of registers that hang (yes, hang) from the walls. My favourite among this breed of hanging registers is entitled, 'List of Officials in Case of Accident Telegrams.' On the table sat a fat-bellied brass paraffin lamp with a broken glass chimney. The man (whose name I never asked) followed my longing gaze to this antique piece.

'In my time there was electricity and water. Now there is nothing and the Station Master uses this lamp,' he said and added with a chuckle. 'But that is only if he has to work after dark – which is rare.'

He led us outside to the small pitched-roof cubicle that once held large water pots with the sign in Urdu proclaiming 'Drinking Water.' At some point in time the pots were replaced by an electric water cooler. But now even that was gone and the cubicle was empty. The few travellers alighting at Mandi Sadiqganj would have to wait to get home to quench their thirst.

'Its all over for Mandi Sadiqganj. When the steam locomotives were phased out the need for water was reduced drastically. But now with just one train up and one down – and that's diesel, they don't even care for drinking water,' said our man full of complaints. 'In any case, the train is so slow hardly anyone uses it anymore. They take the faster buses now and the station is all but disused.'

On our request the Waiting Room (Gents) was opened. The unswept tile mosaic floor told the tale of a better past. The regulation notices and furniture was all there: the cane settee, the round table and the straight-backed chairs around it and the two chairs that are listed in the inventory as 'Chair, Long Arm.' Great for sleeping in in half-reclining comfort, this chair was nicknamed 'Bombay Fornicator' by some long-forgotten British wit who was apparently also a masochist. Heaven knows how one can justify this title without breaking or at least seriously injuring one's back.

I asked our man if Amruka, now the terminus of this line from Bahawalpur, was any more interesting. The man's emphatic and unequivocal 'No' dissuaded me from asking Kashif to drive me the remaining twenty odd kilometres to the end of the line.

There is no record to show when the last regular service clanked through Mandi Sadiqganj en route to Hindu Malkot (now the terminus on the Indian side) and on to Bhatinda. But from mid-August 1947 for a couple of months it was only refugee trains with their sometimes ghastly manifests of human corpses that called here. Time flew, relations between Pakistan and India worsened and the dream of free travel between the two nations receded. At some point in time, the line between Amruka and Hindu Malkot was also uprooted, perhaps as a precaution against an advancing Indian army. That put an end to the international character of this line.

Shortly after this journey to Mandi Sadiqganj, I read in the papers about the two Koreas, once bitter enemies, making up after fifty years of mindless bellicosity. As surely as night follows day, it will happen likewise one day in our part of the world too. When it does, I wonder if railway engineers would be interested in revitalising the line between obscure Hindu Malkot and Mandi Sadiqganj. But if they do, they will make it possible for railway enthusiasts to embark at Kolkata for Victoria Station in London. What a magnificent dream this is. And what a remarkable journey it will make.

The compound with the Muslim graves. Notice the remaining bits of chevron design contrived by arranging flat stones.

History's uncharted Backwater

A friend working with an international NGO in Lahore showed me some pictures of a 'stone wall with patterns.' It was located, he said, in Nag Valley of Balochistan about a hundred kilometres northeast of the town of Punjgur. I was intrigued. I had never seen anything like these walls with chevron patterns created by an arrangement of shards of stone and large, flat pebbles. And so there I was heading out for the boondocks of Balochistan in the company of two friends from Houbara Foundation International Pakistan.

Some ten kilometres to the east of the little

The treasure hunters' trench.

village of Kirichi (about seventy kilometres east of Punjgur), the walls lie hard by a dirt road.* This is the favoured smugglers' route between Punjgur and Besima (near Kalat in the east) because of an absence of anti-smuggling road blocks. The stone walls make up eight enclosures measuring no more than ten to twelve metres square and all contain Muslim burials. The graves are aligned on the prescription north-south axis and each enclosure has a clearly marked *mehrab* in the west. In all, the graves in the various enclosures and those outside would number about two hundred.

My excitement ebbed away. This site was ordinary, to say the least. It is known that the

---

* For the chance traveller in this area who is, perchance, also equipped with a GPS, the coordinates of the site are: N 27° - 18.373', E 65° - 03.330'.

earliest Arab invaders entered Sindh through Makran (and not by sea as many like to believe). And it is also known that Punjgur was the great city they all passed through. Because the graves appear to be contemporaneous, they perhaps commemorate those who perished by some pestilence or by a thus far unrecorded battle with the sons of Balochistan. As we were pottering about the graves, two passing motorcyclists, the only other people we saw in the two hours we spent there, stopped to chat and, pointing to an adjacent hill, told us of the remains of an ancient castle on top.

Crafted some 5000 years ago and destroyed by 21st century treasure hunters' greed this shard of pottery has stories to tell.

Fossilised Jurassic creatures frozen in their moment of death or desiccated trees serving as superstructure to lower the bucket into the well? Situated to one side of the ancient mound, this well still serves up good water.

We climbed the fifty or so metres and did indeed find a stretch of stone wall and the remains of what was evidently a lookout point. Pottery shards were strewn liberally about. But I, the layman, had no way of judging the antiquity or newness of either the foundations or the pottery. Surveying the flat, tree-less plain below us, however, I was struck by the undulating mound to one side of the grave enclosure. This one, I thought, warranted investigation.

The mound, measuring about forty acres, was covered with broken pottery and dressed stones. As I was quartering the mound I accidentally came upon the treasure hunters' trench. It had been dug perhaps the evening before for the upturned soil was fresh and powdery, and I even imagined that from their secret lookout those men were perhaps watching us with field glasses. The dig had exposed stone walls and foundations of rooms. On top of the fresh soil were the shards of what would have been a large pot or urn. There were just two pieces and both had fine black geometric painting. I knew the treasure hunter(s) would have smashed the vessel in frustration and flung the parts away when it failed to yield the much coveted gold. Consequently, despite all our efforts to recover the rest of the smashed bits, we failed to turn up any more of them.

Back in Lahore I first showed the collection to my friend Tariq Masud of Punjab Archaeology. He said they were ancient, 'perhaps pre-Kot Dijian.' But (shame on me) I did not trust his judgement and resorted to my guru, Dr Saifur Rahman Dar. As I took out the pieces from my bag I could sense the excitement. 'This is an important find,' he said and echoed what Tariq had earlier told me: pre-Kot Dijian.

That is, this pottery was manufactured some time between 3000 to 3500 BCE – that is, it was over five thousand years old! I had also collected several black painted shards. Some of these were parts of ring-based and flat-based platters, others perhaps drinking tumblers or milk jugs. These intrigued Dr Dar. They were, he said, very similar to what is called Northern Black Polished Ware from the Gangetic Valley, dating to mid 1st millennium BCE. This find is significant because this kind of pottery has rarely been found so far in the west. Then there were the coarse terracotta shards that Dr Dar said could be either two thousand or two hundred years old.

So what does all this add to? It adds to a very interesting conclusion: that this site was occupied for no less than four thousand years. From pre-history, through the Achaemenians (the black ware), possibly the Sassanians and into the early Muslim era. That is when some Arab army on its way to the wealth of Sindh encountered the fire-worshipping Baloch defenders of this outpost. It would have been a fierce contest. The invaders fighting for the new faith and their God; the Baloch defending the land of their forefathers.[*] Obviously the invaders prevailed for there are graves. Otherwise their bodies would have rotted in the sun and fattened the vultures and jackals.

To begin with, the Black Ware tells me that sometime in the 1st millennium BCE the traders of this thriving city were doing business as far east as the valley of the Ganga River or northern India. Of course this ware would have been just one item they traded in. Other more esoteric secrets of that ancient city, its culture and commerce, perhaps even its name, await discovery beneath the layers of dust left by the passage of time. That lies beyond the pale of ignorant persons such as us, it is in the domain of the master archaeologist.

As for the graves, several questions rankle: which party of Arabs is buried in the mysterious graves? Who were the defenders? When did it all happen? I have no answers. There will be no answers until the Balochistan Department of Archaeology shakes itself out of its sloth and investigates this priceless site.

---

[*] The belief among the Baloch peoples that they are of Arab stock who arrived in this country with the first wave of Muslim invaders is pure fiction. Modern research shows that they originated on the southeastern shores of the Caspian Sea in ancient Parthia and have lived in this part of the world for a very long time predating the advent of Islam.

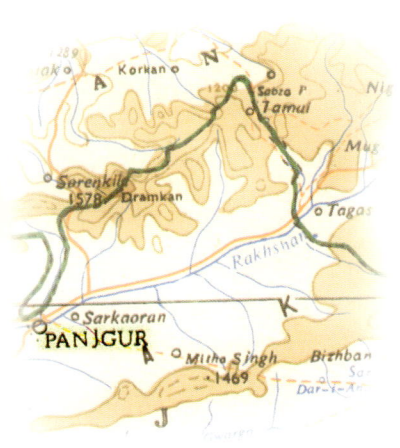

Khudabadan fort. Was it here that the 7th century Raja Chach of Sindh sojourned? History records that he ordered the fort to be strengthening.

Date City

Abu Ishaq Al Istakhri, the Persian from Persepolis (Istakhr), wrote his geography *circa* 950 CE. Among other things, he tells us of Makran being a vast but desert country whose largest city is called Kanazbun. With slight variations resulting either from the alteration of diacritical marks or misreading, other medieval writers and copyists have named this city variously as Kirbun, Kirbuz, Firabuz, Kanazbur (or Kanazbun) and even Kinarbur. By whatever name they called it, they were all referring to that town out in the boondocks of Balochistan, treading on the Iranian frontier, today known to us as Punjgur.

We do not know what the original name

might have been, but there is the possibility that the name was altered owing to the inability of the Arabic to pronounce the *p* and *g* sounds. Again, whatever name they used for it, Arab writers all agreed that Punjgur was no little hick town in the desert, but a goodly and very cultured city. The Arab geographer Idrisi wrote (early 12th century) that the inhabitants of Kanazbun were rich traders and 'men of their word, enemies of fraud .... generous and hospitable.' An accurate portrayal indeed of Baloch traits that holds good even today.

I arrived in Punjgur with my head full of the work of those medieval geographers and a certain image of the place. I imagined a neat little town of mud-plastered two or three storeyed houses lining narrow streets where camels ambled, and a bazaar that could double as a set for the celluloid version of the *Arabian Nights*. It was a bit of a disappointment. The streets were not narrow and had Toyota pick-up trucks and jeeps careening madly up and down and the buildings bordering the roads were all concrete. The mood of sloppy impermanence that marks our buildings today was amply evident in Punjgur.

Only the bazaar was magic. Though the old architecture is all gone, the cover of jute and palm-frond matting above recalls the description of 19th century travellers like Masson and Pottinger. Merchandise has changed considerably since that time, however. Now they sell Iranian products ranging from detergent to cooking oil to shoe polish and groceries. Sarawan, the nearest market town in Iran, is just four hours away with the metalled road beginning (or ending, depending upon one's perspective) on the Iranian side of the border, while Quetta is a full day's dusty, bone-jarring journey and Karachi farther yet.

The bazaar even has a Ghari Chowk – Clock Crossing. But there is no clock tower. The name comes from a time when a couple of watch repairmen kept shop here. With mechanical time pieces phased out by inexpensive electronic watches they went out of business. No one could tell me if they still lived in town; there was only the vague recollection that they were here until the early 1980s. Now folks come here to hock their old tape recorders and radios. A milling crowd of men was trying out each others' machines and engaged in earnest discussion. I saw money and machines change hands and was told that this business continued unabated daily.

In this Chowk also stands one of the oldest and best preserved buildings of Punjgur. The double-storeyed edifice is a business house stocking general merchandise. In the cool, dark interior the youngster manning the till said his grandfather had purchased the property from an Arab trader around 1946. That could well be true, for the *Gazetteer of Makran 1906* does indeed say that a good deal of trade had for long been in the hands of either the Khojas from Gujarat (India) or a few Arabs. Today there were no Arabs to be found, the young man said.

Punjgur lies on the most northerly of the

The spring-fed pond at Ziarat Pir Umar Jan – literally, Mausoleum of the Saint Umar Jan.

three great east-west highways passing through Makran between the lower Sindhu Valley and the Persian empire. The middle route followed the line of the 26th parallel of latitude through the town of Turbat (now reverted to its original name of Kech). Both these routes converged at Awaran at the head of the Kolwa Valley before reaching Lasbela town. The third route, the most treacherous of them all, was the one that followed along the coast. This was, in part, the same route that Alexander took and very nearly paid for the folly with his life.

The *Chachnama*, an original Arab history of the conquest of Sindh that comes down to us in its Persian version translated about 1216

SEA MONSTERS AND THE SUN GOD

(thence translated into Sindhi and later English) tells us of the exploits of Chach, the brilliant usurper king of Sindh (7th century CE). In order to mark out the extent of his kingdom in the west he passed through Armabel (Lasbela town), across the 'declivity and the hills of Makran' to the ancient fortress of Kinarbur. A look at the map will show that the hills lying athwart of the axis used to this day en route from Lasbela via Awaran to Punjgur are the Central Makran Range.

Taking possession of Kinarbur, Raja Chach ordered reconstruction and strengthening of the town's citadel. It is commonly believed that the crumbling mud brick edifice found to this day in the suburb of Khudabadan is the fortress dating back to that medieval time. The king also marked out the border between Makran and the Persian province of Kirman by planting date trees along a river – very likely the Nihing stream some sixty kilometres in the southwest where it even today marks the border between Iran and Pakistan. While this item from the *Chachnama* confirms the extent of the kingdom of Sindh, it also puts paid to the absurd theory propounded by half-baked historians that the date palm was brought to the subcontinent by the Arabs.

In Punjgur I found my old friend Badaruddin Ujan from Sindh in the Deputy Commissioner's

Buyers, sellers and just plain hangers-on mill around in Ghari Chowk.

seat. Very kindly he organised the roof above my head. And so with that and the daily bread assured and young Anwar Ali appointed my guide, I set off to explore.

It is said that the name of Punjgur, meaning Five Tombs, refers to the burial of five early but unknown converts to Islam. Six kilometres south of the airport a dinky little masonry cubicle devoid of any architectural pretensions in the middle of a lovely oasis was supposed to be one of those Unknown Five. Known as Ziarat Pir Umar Jan, it was set by a spring-fed pond in a date grove. In the mausoleum there was only one grave, not five in relation to the

Tea-drinkers in a Punjgur bazaar.

town's name as I had expected. It turned out that those long-dead ones were not buried all together, but were sprinkled around town. According to a friend's report, however, Pir Umar Jan had only recently acquired the name and status of an early convert for, he says, the tomb was unnamed until early 1998.

Watered by the Rakhshan River that rises in the hills of the same name northeast of town and loses itself in the great sandy waste in the west, Punjgur is without doubt the most fertile district in Makran. Though the river is now

A fruit and vegetable market in Punjgur.

severely depleted by the drought, at least one of its underground streams – the ingenious *karez*, continues to flow and water the orchards and cornfields that surround Punjgur.

The earliest reference to the fertility of Punjgur comes from Arrian who wrote a history of Alexander in the 1st century CE. After a long and harrowing passage through the sandy wastes of Upper Makran en route from Lasbela to Turbat, the Macedonians eventually fetched up at a spot where 'provisions were more or less plentiful.' Here Alexander ordered the collection of food grains to be transported to the coast for the fleet. But during transit when his troops, themselves overcome with hunger, looted the sealed grain containers, Alexander sent out a scouting mission for additional food. He asked the natives of the 'inland districts' to turn over as much grain, dates and sheep as they could for the army to purchase. This reference to the rich inland district can only be to Punjgur. So we drove out to an orchard in the suburb of Sordo east of Punjgur. As the keeper laid out bunches grapes and dates for us to sample, he said the produce simply could not suffer the day-long transit to the RCD Highway en route to Quetta or Karachi.

In our ignorance we believe that the best grapes (and other fruit as well) in Pakistan come from Chaman on the Afghan frontier near Quetta. But Chaman, I once wrote, does not have trees enough to turn out a single matchbox! That famous fruit comes from Afghanistan. And Punjgur that bears very fine grapes and the best dates I have ever eaten in Pakistan is not renowned for this produce for a lack of road connection with Quetta and the rest of the country.

Consequently, rather than have it perish on the dirt roads of Balochistan in an attempt to get it out, the growers either sell it only in the local market or fatten their cattle on it. The grapes and the dates were remarkably sweet and succulent and sitting there in the dappled shade of the grove listening to the man expound upon the various qualities of the dozen different kinds of dates and three of grapes, I diligently emulated the cattle until I was very nearly sick. Even so, as we were leaving, the man handed me two large bags of fruit.

Sordo wasn't the only suburb with orchards. All around Punjgur, the valley of the Rakhshan River was choc-a-bloc with verdure. Perhaps it was for this reason and the crisp weather – Punjgur sits on a 1500 metre-high plateau, that British troops stationed here in the 1890s found it a favourable posting. In fact, this was a unique distinction among frontier outposts. In August Punjgur had warm days and pleasant, dry evenings. Since power, which during my visit was still drawn from six aging diesel generators, was shut off at ten every evening, I slept outside. Early in the morning, the chill in the wind would become marked. The only time, they told me, that Punjgur gets unbearable is in late May or June. And in mid-winter the early morning frost is hard and water regularly freezes in the pipes.

As for the name Rakhshan, it is itself of

DATE CITY

Vines and palms: an orchard in Sordo.

singular interest. In Persian it means 'brilliant' or 'resplendent' and such was the name of one of the daughters of Oxyartes, the king of Sogdiana in Central Asia. After defeating him in hard fought contest, Alexander wooed and won over this reportedly gorgeous princess. In the entire Asian continent, so the histories record, she was surpassed in beauty only by the wife of Darius, the Persian king that Alexander had shortly before trounced in battle. The name was rendered Roxane in Greek transliteration and over the years back into Persian and Urdu as Rukhsana. I wonder if this river, hundreds of miles from Sogdiana, was named after another equally comely Persian princess of some unknown age.

In three days I had seen Punjgur and met enough people to begin marvelling at the way Baloch patriotism rises above Baloch nationalism. Except for Pakistani currency and the erratic power supply and telephones, everything else comes from Iran. Friends feting me in a local restaurant pointedly told me that the okra and the chicken served us had come from across the border. This was understandable for these items could not make the long journey out from Quetta, but strangely even non-perishable items like soap and boot polish came from Iran. These imports were preferred for their lower price as compared against similar Pakistan products.

*'Anda Iran ka, Danda Pakistan ka!'** is what they say in Makran. Yet they remain faithful to Pakistan. That, I thought, was marvellous. I have heard talk of 'breaking away' either to be independent or to join the nearest neighbour in some parts of the country. Nothing of the sort here. There was of course bitterness at being treated as a stepchild. There was a questioning as to why the mineral and oil wealth of Makran was not exploited,† why there were no roads and electricity or other amenities. They question the utility of a motorway between distant Lahore and Islamabad that few Baloch will ever use, but which has been paid for in part by money from their province.

There is no love lost between the Baloch of Makran and the army or the rest of our politicians. They have faith neither in the one nor the other. If the great names in Baloch politics had made no change in the lives of the people of Makran, nor too had the army in its one year of power in this latest stint. As for the army, it is the 'Punjabi army' – a chilling reminder of the Bengalis' reference to this great monolith of the State that holds the Baloch people is some disdain, as indeed it did the Bengalis.

The least popular are those moronic 'secret agents' of the army that prowl the street in their Ray-Ban aviator glasses and starched white *shalwar-kameez* suits advertising their identity from miles away. One such was Shafiq of Lahore who had forty kilograms of prime dates that he wanted shipped home and was looking for someone to ferry them free of charge. He boasted of not having had to pay for them. The insinuation was clear: no one dare ask for compensation for what he desires for himself. Yesterday it was a few crates of dates; tomorrow it will be something of greater value. Misuse of office begins at the lowest level. That is also where disenchantment begins among those that suffer.

One afternoon Badaruddin Ujan drove me out to Gharibabad in the precinct of Chitkan. Chitkan, incidentally, is a name used as an alternate for Punjgur and some local intellectuals believe it to be an ancient name of the district. There, Badar had earlier told me, was an ancient tomb believed to be the burial of one of the five holy men that give the district its name.

From afar the tomb of Shaho Qalander looks like a large stub of clay sitting atop a low rise by the Gharibabad graveyard. Closer up the

---
* Literally, 'Eggs from Iran, chastising rod from Pakistan.'
† I am not aware of any known reserves in Makran.

Tomb of Shaho Qalandar.

ruined clay and burnt brick structure, with the brick veneer of the dome gone, reminded me of similar buildings I have seen in the neighbouring district of Kharan. All of them mystify because of their multiple burials. Like those buildings, its outside walls too bear decorative thirty centimetre square terracotta tiles. Here can be seen images of horses with riders in conical helmets, peacocks, ducks winging across a chequerboard background and inexplicable geometric designs. Most of these tiles, however, have been plundered. Inside, the burial chamber has a single simple grave draped with the mandatory green sheet of a Muslim saint.

Lawyer Mohammed Hayat Rakhshani, the Keeper of the Tale, was at hand to recount. Shaho is clearly not an Arabic name, he said. It is Balochi rising from the Persian word Shah for king. The theory, therefore, that Shaho was an Arab is balderdash and he was very likely a Persian or Baloch chieftain. But the tale of interest concerns the fakir who came from somewhere in Iran and took up residence in this graveyard when Hayat was yet a child and a student of the local mosque school. Now, in those days, this shrine was much frequented by local women and the mullah thought it improper for an outsider to be resident in its vicinity.

Gathering together his two dozen odd students, the mullah visited the fakir and forced him to move to the mosque where all his needs were looked after. After about a month of there residing, the fakir one day disappeared. But the day before the cut and run act, he called together some village elders and told them that he was no fakir who sought the ultimate riches of nirvana, but a seeker of treasures mundane. And having heard of this shrine being a receptacle of a vast treasure had dug up the interior only to find a subterranean vault teeming with human skeletons. It was useless, he is supposed to have said, to remain in this place therefore.

Hayat relates that after the phoney fakir's departure, his brother and some other friends reopened the subterranean vault and did indeed see the skeletons. From the neck part of one, these adventurers recovered a brass amulet. When they opened it they found only some ash in it. It was therefore concluded that the grave must date back to the time of the Fire Worshippers.

I seriously doubt the story of this building's antiquity for two reasons. For one, Zoroastrians expose their dead to the elements and for them a ceremonial burial is nothing short of sacrilege because the human body defiles the pure earth. Secondly, one of the buildings in the group of eight tombs in Mashkel sub-division, in the westernmost reach of neighbouring Kharan district, once had a fascinating dating element in its decoration. The tile in question, now plundered, pictured a man with a long-barrelled gun in pursuit of three ibex. I photographed it in 1987, but when I returned to Mashkel in 1996, the tile, together with many more, was missing.

There is reason to believe that a Pakistani architect now living in England is guilty of this plundering. But there is no proof, only hearsay concerning her departure from the site with the tiles packed in crates. The sad fact is that the building has been deprived of a definite dating element. Since these buildings in Kharan have never been investigated by an expert the disadvantage caused by this plundering is heightened. Consequently, it has been postulated that these tombs are indeed ancient, perhaps from the Sassanian dynasty that came to an end with the Arab conquest of Persia. But as I have pointed out Fire Worshippers do not bury their dead. Consequently, though we may never learn the whole truth about these tombs, it might be that they date to some time in the 16th century when firearms were introduced to this area.

Meanwhile, Punjgur in far away and unfrequented Balochistan lives out its days in virtual oblivion. No one celebrates its grapes and dates.

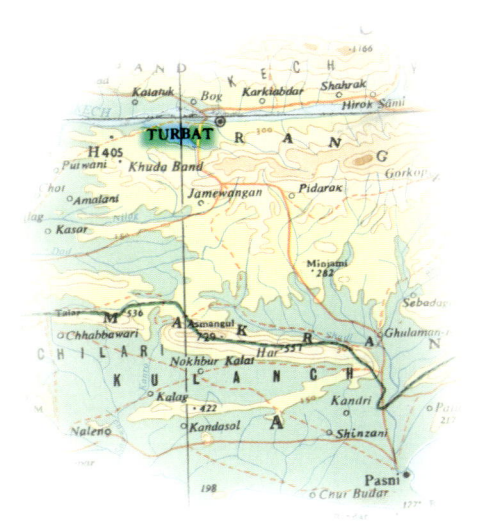

The ruins of the ancient castle and settlement outside Turbat town. Surely this is the site of the old town of Kech.

A Town called 'Tomb'

Turbat is 'grave' or 'tomb' in Persian. But it is the name of that far off town in southwest Balochistan, the seat of the Commissioner of Makran division. Far from being a dead or even moribund place, Turbat is very much a living, vibrant town where one can stop at street corners and discuss the future of the country with great names in Baloch politics. Turbat of dusty streets and tasteless concrete architecture, whose only monument is a hundred and fifty year-old mud brick fort and one picturesque bazaar where they sell fruit and grains. This latter alone makes a visit to Turbat worthwhile. But as place names go, the name is bizarre, to say the least. And the mystery concerning this morbid name lies in its adoption: it is difficult to pinpoint when this strange name first came into common usage.

Arab geographers of the early Middle Ages

tell us of a town called Kej on the great highroad into Sindh. This was the road that followed the 26th parallel of Latitude from Kirman (Persia) to the village of Hoshab, ninety kilometres east of Turbat, and thence to Awaran en route to Lasbela and the opulent marts of Sindh. Because of the Arab inability to pronounce the *ch* sound, Kej (sometimes also Kez) was simply a mispronunciation of Kech which we hear of from other authorities.

Early 18th century European maps place a town called variously Kidge or Kedge and eventually Kech by an ambiguous river that flows from the north to the south through Makran. This error concerning the river's course continues on down to 1867 when the British explorer Colonel Goldsmid prepared his 'Sketch Map of Beluchistan and Eastern Persia' and showed the river flowing past 'Kedge' from the north to the south. In the following thirty years Makran topography seems to have become better known. The 1896 map by T. H. Holdich shows the 'Kej River' in its proper perspective. Although this map shows two minor villages, Kalatuk and Sami, in the vicinity of modern Turbat, it nevertheless omits Turbat itself.

Whatever they called it in days bygone; we know that ancient Kech lay on or very near the site of modern Turbat in the fertile Kech Valley on the banks of the river of the same name, once perennial but now bone dry for many years. The Kech River here flows from east to west for over a hundred kilometres and not from north to south as the early maps denote. It only deviates to the southwest about forty kilometres west of Turbat, undergoes a name change to Dasht and falls into the Arabian Sea seventy kilometres due west of Gwadar. Early explorers, having been acquainted only with its southernmost reach either by physical examination or from hearsay, presumed it to flow on the same alignment in its entire course. Thereby resulted the mapping error to show it flowing from the top to bottom of the sheet all the way. As for the name, so far as I have been able to determine, it was only in 1906 when British administrators wrote out the *District Gazetteer* of Makran, that the accompanying map for the first time carried the name of Turbat.

In the esoteric pages of history, there is one reference to this strange label for a town. The year 943 CE saw a man called Muhammad Abul Qasim, better known then and now as Ibn Haukal, set out on a long journey from his native Baghdad. For twenty-five years he wandered about the Muslim world. When he returned home in 968, he tarried just a year before setting off to explore Africa. There he remained for the next eight years. When he eventually returned home for good he set about to write his compendium of geography entitled like an earlier work, *Book of Roads and Kingdoms*.

In this work Ibn Haukal mentions a town by the name of Kabar (sepulchre in Arabic) in Makran. In their translation of this work, Henry Elliot and John Dowson insert in parentheses the word Kiz as clarification. Now, as a native of Baghdad, Ibn Haukal's mother tongue would have been Arabic, while it is right likely that he also spoke Persian. In Makran he might, therefore, have heard the name Turbat and realising it meant 'grave' in Persian appropriately

A TOWN CALLED 'TOMB'

Long ago, when the Arabs first arrived in Turbat the markets in town would have looked quite like this. But now this is the last remaining vestige. Everything else has turned to ugly concrete.

translated it into his native Arabic. If this hypothesis is correct, Turbat would have been known as Kech to its native population while the Persians and the Arabs, for some obscure reason, would have likened it to a burial ground.

The name becomes ever more intriguing because when the Arabs first arrived here the local population was largely Zoroastrian. Now, adherents of this ancient religion believe that the human body sullies the good earth and therefore do not bury their dead but expose them to the elements for scavenging birds to pick the bones clean. Consequently, there would have been no tombs in this area. But the name stuck so the question is what was the origin of the tomb (or tombs), if they ever existed here? We know that Alexander led his Macedonians through Turbat; I am therefore inclined to believe that in the early Middle Ages, some graves from Alexander's time were still extant. They were perhaps a good few in number and certainly would have been lavish for the Arabs to name the locality after them.

Alexander passed through Turbat twelve hundred years before Ibn Haukal wrote his geography. Though his historians do not mention a place name, there does appear to be a reference to Turbat or Kech in the annals of Alexander.

221

In recording his march westward from Lasbela, the historian Arrian tells us how after many travails Alexander and his army eventually fetched up at a more fertile place 'where provisions were more or less plentiful.' So plentiful, in fact, that the king organised a baggage train to take supplies to the coast for his fleet. On their journey to the coast, however, the men in charge of the train, terribly overcome by hunger, helped themselves to the supplies.

When the matter was reported to him, Alexander, in recognition of the urgency of their need, did not punish these officers. Instead, he ordered another foraging raid to 'inland districts.' We know that leaving Lasbela, the Macedonians followed the road due west through Awaran to Turbat and suffered greatly in the intervening barren and waterless desert. Across this frightful waste, the first region that could afford plentiful supplies was Turbat, watered as it was by the Kech River. The 'inland district' that Alexander's men raided for additional supplies was without a doubt Punjgur, less than two hundred kilometres to the northeast. Unfortunately none of Alexander's historians assign names to these two places and we do not know what the Greeks would have called Turbat or Punjgur.

No investigations have ever been carried out to determine the location of Kech, and locating it near modern Turbat is scarcely more than a vague guess. And a fairly good one at that.

Ask anyone for the ruined castle of Ari Jam and they will point you in the direction of the hulking clay mound a few kilometres outside Turbat town. The highest part of the badly eroded mound is indeed the remains of a brick-lined castle from whose ruined battlements the verdant line of mimosa and tamarisk trees lining the Kech River can be seen beyond the surrounding date groves. And they'll also tell you that Ari Jam, the King of Kech, was the father of Punnu. This hapless prince, it is narrated, travelled to distant Bhambore in Sindh for he had heard of the devastating beauty of Sassi, the washerman's daughter.

Besotted hopelessly upon seeing her, he resolved to go into her father's service and remain the rest of his life in Sassi's presence. But his brothers, not quite agreeable to a prince reducing himself to a lowly station, drugged the two lovers. And when they were in a swoon, tied Punnu to his camel and made off for Kech. Upon waking Sassi set out in search of her loved one and at one point was forced to call down divine intervention in order that her honour may be saved. Not long after, Punnu having escaped his brothers clutches, came upon her fresh tomb and beseeched the Lord to let him be interred with his beloved. The earth opened up a second time and the two were reunited in death. The celebrated tomb of the lovers lies about forty kilometres due north of Karachi off the highroad to Hub Dam and the story is immortalised by the great Shah Latif.

Now if Ari Jam and his love-sick son had ever lived, it must have been around the latter half of the 16th century. Indeed a cursory study of the castle of Ari Jam on the topmost layer of the mound shows that it was occupied at that time and for about two or three hundred years

No dearth of supplies in Turbat.

afterwards. Recently a team of archaeologists (my informant wasn't sure if it was French or Italian) had been looking at the mound again and had concluded that it had been in continuous use for over three thousand years.

I suspect that the mound of Ari Jam's castle is the keeper of the secret of that ancient town that its inhabitants called Kech and which to outsiders was a tomb. It keeps the secret of Alexander's sojourn and that of Ibn Haukal's. Surely in those layers of ruined and forgotten habitation lies the record of a thriving town that was 'nearly as large as Multan' in the Middle Ages. One day, I am sure, when experts put the spade to the clayey mound in earnest, they will unravel the mysteries of Kech that so tantalise the inquiring mind.

SEA MONSTERS AND THE SUN GOD

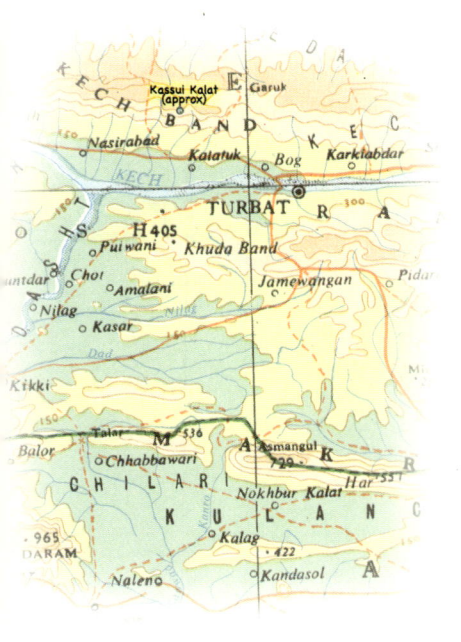

The ruins of Kussui Kalat – the Castle of Kusso, a Baloch shepherd. My guide Rahim leads the two hangers-on who had joined us at the bottom of the hill. The bricks in the picture were used as building material together with dressed stone quarried locally. There was little vegetation in these hills when this fortress was built and the bricks would have been carted to the site from a distant kiln.

Riddle in the Kech Hills

The *Chachnama*, an early history of the Arab conquest of Sindh is a great repository of knowledge concerning the Arab invasion of Sindh. Among other things (like revealing the base character of some early Muslim heroes) it recounts how Hajjaj bin Yusuf, the governor of Iraq, famous for having sent his nephew and son in law Mohammed bin Qasim on the successful expedition against Sindh, earlier deputed a man called Saeed Kilabi to Makran.

On the borders of Makran, Kilabi met one Safahwi Hammami of the tribe of Alafi (we are not told who this man was) and asked him to join whatever expedition Kilabi was hastening to. It comes out of the words of the *Chachnama* that Hammami had some sort of gripe against Hajjaj and took offence at Kilabi's presumption that he would join the man's enterprise. There also appears to have been an altercation between the two when Hammami refused to join up. This cost him not only his head but his skin as well: Kilabi cut off the poor man's top, and dispatched it to bin Yusuf. The *Chachnama* tells us that he also flayed the body, but does not say what the cruel man did with the skin. The book goes on to tell us that having then installed himself in Makran, Kilabi 'succeeded in securing more wealth from Hindustan (than was ever secured before).'

Now it came to pass that as he one day went travelling through his domain Saeed Kilabi came upon a group of Alafis. As kinsmen of Hammami they took it upon themselves to avenge what they thought was a needless and unjust murder. In the ensuing fight Kilabi was killed and his army routed. The Alafis took control of Makran and Kilabi's force was obligated to retire to Iraq. Upon hearing of the death of his favoured administrator, an incensed Hajjaj bin Yusuf ordered the retaliatory killing of one of the local Alafi elders. But even that not sufficiently cooling his wrath, he commanded his representative in Makran* to persecute the Alafis wherever and whenever he came across them. The injunction according to the *Chachnama* was, 'Find out the Alafis, and try your best to secure them, and exact the vengeance due to Saeed [Kilabi] from them.'

So great was the pressure on these people that by the year CE 703 growing Arab influence in Makran had forced many of the Alafis to seek asylum with Dahar, the king of Sindh. They were still in Dahar's service when bin Qasim arrived at the gates of the country in 711 and they joined the Sindhis to fight gallantly against the invading Arabs. However, even so, the following year (704) Mohammed bin Haroon, the new governor of Makran, found an Alafi straggler in his domain and having murdered him wrote a gloating letter to Hajjaj bin Yusuf in Iraq. The *Chachnama* records that bin Haroon continued in his victorious career in Makran for the next six years when he accompanied Mohammed bin Qasim to Sindh. On the way died of a severe attack of the ague at Lasbela. His tomb stands in that town to this day.

Five years is a long and trying time for a persecuted people. If Baghdad, their home country, tormented them, Makran offered little solace. For those in such a situation, it would only be natural to seek a safe haven, a place difficult to assault where they could retire in the event of an attack by a larger force. Ever since I had first read the *Chachnama* many years ago, I had wondered about the location of this secret asylum – if at all it existed. If it did, I knew it would be the earliest Arab garrison in the subcontinent.

Recently in Turbat, friend Dr Taj Baloch told me of the little known site of Kussui Kalat – Castle of Kussu, up in Kech Bund (hills) northwest of town. Perched high up on a remote hilltop, the ruins were difficult to reach, he said, access being only from one side through a narrow and desolate gorge. A team of French

---

* A new administrator to fill Saeed Kilabi's seat had evidently been dispatched in the meanwhile.

The water channel that trained rain water to a tank, now lost, and also perhaps the mosque; is lined with flagstones to prevent seepage.

archaeologists had recently spent some time there and from the surface collection of artefacts had deduced that the site was early Muslim. From what Taj described, it was clearly a safe haven – the citadel of the last stand. It could not have been a residential fortress so inaccessible and inhospitable it seemed to be

from the description.

Taj had scarcely stopped speaking when the words of the *Chachnama* concerning the persecution and flight of the Alafis filled my mind. And so it was that another friend, Bijjar Baloch, borrowed a pick-up truck and drove me west on the highroad to Mand on the Iranian frontier. At the village of Shaikan he handed me over to his cousin Mohammed Rahim, the Levies Jemadar. A quick cup of tea and we were motorcycling north in the dry bed of the Shorma stream. Ten kilometres on, the hills closed in around us. Another six and we had to abandon Rahim's motorcycle. Since leaving Shaikan we had not seen a soul, save the man and his family who sat about a tent in a small tree-less open place between low hills. Rahim stopped to chat, but we declined the offer of tea and bread and drove on.

The gorge where we left Rahim's bike was narrow and wild. As we walked away I glanced back and said I hoped it would be safe. With a little laugh Rahim pointed to the sandy river bed and said there were no human footprints: no one had been there for many days. And no one could be expected any time soon. Wending our way upward, we passed occasional heaps of dressed

This best preserved portion of walls is adjacent to what I perceive was the Chief of Security's residence.

stones. Taj had warned me to keep an eye out for them, for these, he had said, were the remnants of lookout posts.

An hour after leaving the bike we heaved ourselves onto the bowl-shaped crest. It was littered with cut stone and bricks. Scattered about the top were the remains of no less than fifteen buildings. The mosque was easily discernible because of the *mehrab*; the chief's house from its large size. The house that overlooked the sheer fall into the valley below had perhaps belonged to the Chief of Security who would have kept a lookout at odd hours. Sadly, one of the rooms in this house had been dug up: the treasure hunters' spade has reached even this remote site.

Here too was a stone-lined water channel bordered with fired bricks that had me marvelling at the Arabs' facility to transport them to this remote and inaccessible place for even in the early Middle Ages there were no trees in the Kech Hills to fire brick kilns. The impetus of rain water running down the slope was broken by two stone piers before the water was trained into the channel. Though only a small length of it now remains, it once must have run on to the mosque or perhaps to a brick or stone-lined tank that may be smothered beneath the debris of ruined buildings. But Makran was a dry country in the 8th century, and this channel and the tank could scarcely have relieved periodic water shortages and the everlasting dread of a water famine. When they were holed up here, the Alafis would surely have sent out regular water-collecting convoys to the nearest stream – perhaps the same Shorma that we had travelled along.

Among the debris we collected several pieces of blue pottery with dark foliate designs, but our haphazard fossicking failed to turn up any coins or arrowheads. We climbed to the vantage of the house of the Chief of Security. Below us was a spreading panorama of fold upon fold of clay hills and narrow valleys. I could almost see it happening: alerted by the cloud of dust in the bed of the Shorma, the Alafi lookout spots bin Haroon's troops an hour before they begin the long climb up the gorge. Warnings are rushed to the outlying pickets whose remains we had passed on our way up. When the unsuspecting imperial vanguard enters the tight gorge leading up to this castle it is cut to pieces by the Alafis in their turrets. Realising quickly what they are up against, the governor's men reorganise to make a concerted assault but in the restrictive confines of the chasm only the infantry can advance and then just two abreast. It is hard work to clear the turrets of the defenders but despite the casualties, the invaders keep at it. The clatter of running fights in the gorge prepares the defenders in the citadel for what lies ahead. They fight hard; their very survival depends on their valour and they rout their assailants. Bin Haroon's troops retire in discomfiture only to return again another day.

Though the *Chachnama* simplifies the story, the end for the Alafis would not have come in a single action. Surely bin Haroon and his army had to fight long and hard to overcome the rebels. But I have no doubt in my mind that it was here in the ruins of Kussui Kalat that the Alafis' last struggles were fought out against the imperial Arabs. When the end came and they fled to Sindh, the Alafis' safe haven fell into disuse and its name – if it had one, was forgotten. Decades, perhaps even a few centuries, were to pass, the houses were to be reduced to mere foundations, the water tank choked with debris and articles of daily life all but turned to dust when a Baloch, Kussu by name, having chanced upon them would have given the sad and ghostly ruins his own name.

No one could tell me who this man may have been. He could just as well have been an ordinary shepherd or a tribal chief. He may have passed through here or sojourned in this wild gorge for a period of time. For the locals he is as unknown as the hapless Alafis who made their last stand in these hills.

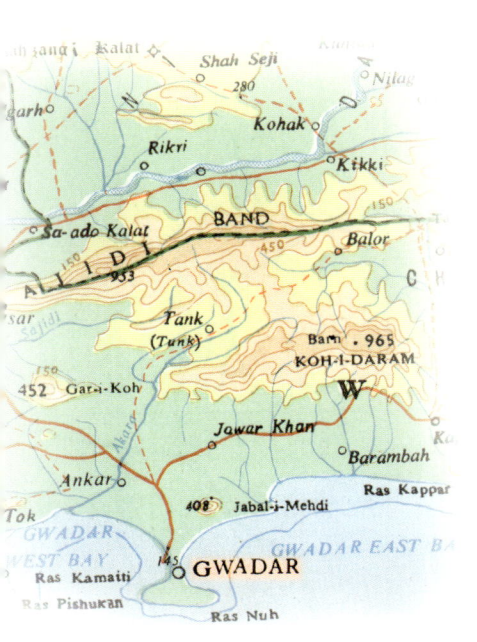

All that remains of the 16th century Portuguese water tanks on Koh e Batil, the Gwadar hammerhead, is a dry depression and a few trees. Now as Gwadar races towards becoming another Karachi, this will be built over and soon forgotten.

Gateway of the Breeze

The taxi drove me the winding road up Koh e Batil, the massive sheer-sided hammerhead of Gwadar to see the 16th century Portuguese water tanks. The tanks turned out to be a disappointment being no more than a largish clay-choked, bone dry depression fringed by a few date trees. But the views from the vantage of the peak were priceless: the shimmering blue-grey Arabian Sea to the south, the town of Gwadar sprinkled far below on the narrow isthmus to the north with the graceful arcs of the east and west bays of Gwadar on either side of the habitation. Both bays were dotted with dozens of fishermen's boats. Far away, beyond west bay, the curiously shaped hills of Pishukan scraped the welkin just like the skyline of some modern city. From my vantage, the idyll spread out below seemed part of a Mediterranean resort.

Here on the Makran seaboard, they have always been fishermen. Alexander's chroniclers

SEA MONSTERS AND THE SUN GOD

In the old quarter of Gwadar this street overlooking the east bay once had cantilevered balconies and eaves. In August 2000, its inhabitants could scarcely have believed their poor lives were about to be turned around. Now in 2006, they are being offered alternate property farther north.

tell us of the Ichthyophagi – the Fish Eaters. The Greeks lament the absence of any other food but fish and tell us that even the Fish Eaters' cattle ate only fish which gave its flesh a fishy taste. This tradition of a fishing culture giving its name to the land evidently goes farther back into history. The *Shahnama* of Firdausi, the great Persian poet, relates that Makran was part of the Persian empire during the Heroic Age (about 600 BCE) when Kai Kaus and Kai Khusro ruled that country. Even to the classical Persians this was the land of the Mahi Khoran (Fish Eaters again). No surprise then that the Makranis' pronunciation of the name of their land 'Mukkoran,' is a clear throwback on the ancient Persian name.

While the seaboard was understandably the Land of the Ichthyophagi for the Greeks, inland Makran was Gedrosia. Thomas Holdich, a 19th century British author believes that the name actually was Gadroz. '*Gad*' in Avestan (ancient Persian), he says, was the same as '*bud*' (bad) and '*roz*,' as it is today, was day. The significance, therefore, of the ancient Avestan name was of a singularly unpleasant place, something that we know Alexander discovered much to his unhappiness as he made his way back to Persia at the end of his Indian Campaign. Here, in the sandy wastes of Gedrosia, he lost nearly thirty thousand soldiers and followers besides much of his treasures.

The chronicle of Nearchus, Alexander's admiral of the fleet, gives a fairly recognisable account from Karachi as far as Pasni. Thence on, it gets somewhat muddled. Yet we can just make out that Barna where 'grew many palm trees, and [w]here was a garden wherein were myrtles and flowers' was possibly Gwadar. I cannot comment on how the name would have changed from Barna to Gwadar, but I heard a quaint and pleasing reason for the present name. It came from the Punjabi (a Kharral from Okara!) *moharrar* of the town police station. According to Alam Sher it was a compound of '*gwat*' meaning breeze in Balochi and '*dar*' for gateway. It was, he explained, because of the steady breeze that sweeps Gwadar through the year.

What transpired between the visit of Nearchus to Barna and the arrival around 1550 of the Portuguese at 'Guadel' is not known. The reason simply being that the ancient coastal road was not the favoured route any longer. The major roads connecting the Sindhu Valley and Mesopotamia in the early Middle Ages ran through Punjgur or Turbat in the north. Portuguese power waned shortly afterwards and Gwadar reverted to the Baloch. In the 18th century it was held by the Buledis, a Baloch tribe, who relinquished it to the bane come down from Afghanistan under Nadir Shah. In time, the Gichkis, a Rajput clan believed to have migrated from Rajasthan, displaced the Pukhtuns and took control of Gwadar. By 1780 the Khan of Kalat, the supreme power in Balochistan who had shortly before annexed it, had ceded Gwadar to the Sultan of Muscat. There it remained until it was returned to Pakistan in 1958. It is in consequence of this annexation by Muscat that many Makranis still hold dual Pakistan-Muscat nationality and innumerable work in that gulf kingdom to bring home petro-dollars.

Friends in Turbat had organised that I stay with the chief of the Communication and Works Department at Gwadar. When I arrived at Noor Ahmad's waterfront bungalow on the west bay, he was preparing to go away for a couple of days on business. But he instructed his cook and helper to see that I didn't starve to death and went away leaving the house to me. That, then, is Baloch hospitality.

If the Portuguese left behind that all but ruined water tank on the hammerhead, the Arabs of Muscat gave Gwadar its fort and police station. The former, a totally dilapidated hulk locked away and inaccessible, lies at the south end of the Shahi Bazaar overlooking the east bay. It awaits the day when some excessive fall of rain or a seismic disturbance will bring it tumbling down. But the stone-built partially whitewashed police station at the other end of town looked prim.

Alam Sher Kharral who told me the story of Gwadar's name took me around. Underneath one of the first floor rooms he said was the oubliette. Pounding with his feet he produced the hollow drumming which he said was proof of the sealed off room below. In the floor, set evenly with flagstones, a different group of tiles was the spot where the opening had been sealed. Prisoners were lowered through this opening and thereafter nothing ever came out – not even their bones when they died. Rumour had it, said Kharral, that the oubliette was littered with the remains of those who had been imprisoned by successive Arab governors and forgotten. It must have been the almighty stench of rotting flesh that prompted a somewhat more faint-hearted governor to close off the gruesome dungeon.

If the police station smacked of peninsular Arabian architecture, the bazaar reminded me of pictures of African east coast port towns. Shahi Bazaar, my favourite market, was named rather pompously: narrow, unpaved street, lined with decrepit and fading buildings nearly all of which flaunt rotting timber cantilevers that once supported ornate balconies with verandas running under them. The name of the bazaar was a hangover of the better times that Gwadar has seen. As little as a hundred years ago it was galvanised by the commercial activity of merchants from as far away as Aden, Basra, Bahrain in the west and Gujarat and the Malabar coast in the east.

The view north from Koh e Batil shows the narrow isthmus with the east (right) and west bays. Those who dream great dreams for Gwadar see this strip of land bristling with skyscrapers.

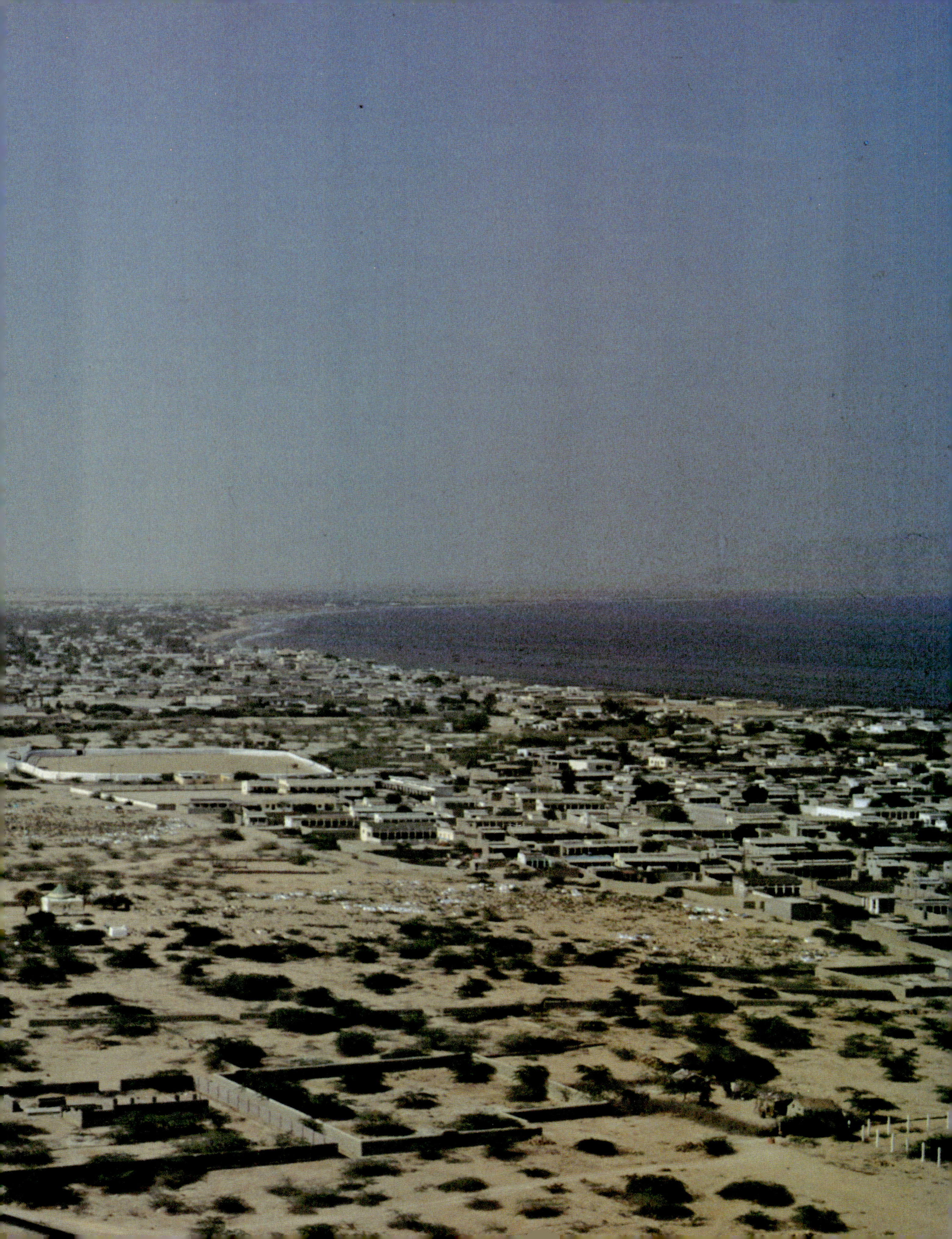

SEA MONSTERS AND THE SUN GOD

All that remains now was a betel leaf seller whose legend read, 'Malabar Pan House.' I asked the young man minding the kiosk if there were many Malabaris in Gwadar. The restaurant next door, he said, belonged to the man who also owned the kiosk and he was the one to know. But the man was visiting Karachi for business and I never got a chance to speak to him. Of the Gujaratis few remain, the rest have all made for the more amenable commercial climes of Karachi and, even better, Muscat.

Sadruddin was one who remained, making a living as a government contractor. Introducing me to him, my host Noor Ahmad had said he was great fun. But the dour, sixty plus giant hardly seemed to fit the description. In the evening as I sat on the roof of Ahmad's home watching the sun set, Sadru arrived with a packet under his arm. It was the spirit of good cheer. As we worked our way through it Sadru opened up and told me of his exploits under the influence of Viagra. Needless to say that his boasts could set any non-user green with envy. He also spoke of a great infatuation with Benazir Bhutto and his longing to one day be able to walk up to her and confess.

Sadru also told me of the gold-panners in east bay. I went out there at low tide the following morning and found dozens of men of various ages busily scrabbling away in the gooey sand. For their labours nearly all of them had tiny balls of gold to show. They did it whenever they had time, said one man, and it appeared a not so tedious diversion from the hard work of minding

The Omani fort that now serves as the police station.

the fishing boats out in open sea. Even as little as fifteen minutes of working the sand never went unrewarded and paid for incidental expenses.

Miles from any river system that could possibly wash down the metal, its presence was odd. I suspect it was a reminder of a time forgotten when east bay, or more likely, Shahi Bazaar behind the waterfront, was lined by goldsmiths' workshops. A reminder of an affluence that has long since deserted Gwadar.

From the time I had first arrived, I was convinced that Gwadar held great promise for being the playground of the rich and the famous of tomorrow. I could imagine both bays lined with pleasure houses and the hammerhead with hotels, restaurants and watering holes. So I went to the only restaurant on the hill. Hamid Qaisrani, who runs it, is a Dera Ghazi Khan Baloch and he came down on my high hopes for Gwadar like a wet blanket.

There was nothing for the tourist in Gwadar, he said. I pointed out the vast, empty and unlittered beaches. He didn't approve. There was, moreover, no infra-structure, not enough water for the present population, leave alone visitors. His list was long. But he had made his hotel at a prime spot, I said. He had, but it was scarcely earning its keep.

Whatever Qaisrani may have to say, I am still convinced that Gwadar will one day be a great place to visit. My Baloch friends agree, but they also point out that Punjabi and Pukhtun mullahs will have to be kept out of the place. Indeed, the only religious unrest in recent years was stirred up not by local mullahs, but by bearded miscreants imported from Leiah and Bhakkar in Punjab.

Postscript: Upon leaving Turbat some days earlier a friend had given me a name and said this person would meet me off the bus in Gwadar. As our bus was approaching the town, I saw a car preceding us. Every time the bus stopped, a young man would leave the car to look at all disembarking passengers, once even sticking his head in the door to peek inside our bus. He never even so much as glanced in my direction, even though I was clearly the odd man out. But when we hit the town, he disappeared.

Two days later as I was walking past the ruined fort, I saw the same car again. I hailed it and asked the man if he was my Turbat friend's acquaintance. Abdul Jalil wasn't the one, but he knew this acquaintance just as well and said he could drive me to the man's store. I told him it didn't really matter anymore and we chatted a while. Then, as he was leaving, Jalil asked if I needed to get on a plane.

'How do you know that?' I asked totally taken by surprise.

'Just asking, since I work for PIA and the bus ride out of Gwadar is so damned tedious,' said Jalil.*

This was too good to be true. He took down my name and instructed me to collect my ticket the following morning! Where else could such a thing happen?

---

* Two years after publication of this piece I was again in Gwadar where I sought out my benefector. Rather pleased, Jalil reported that the Deputy Comissioner having read the piece had told him about it. My friendship with this good man continues to this day.

Approaching the summit of Been Gah.

Upon the 20,000-Foot Mountain

The mullah who ran the mosque school in the village of Patra looked me over, head cocked to one side, eyes loaded with scepticism and an almost waggish, incredulous half-smile on his lips.

'This man cannot get up the mountain,' he said with finality. 'He is too old.'

Fully aware of my bald pate and silver temples, I never try to defend such pejorative proclamations regarding my abilities, but this time, like a fool, I took offence.

'I've been on mountains higher than your piddling little hill,' I said fighting hard the urge to end my challenge with an appropriately vicious 'You stupid, ignorant and uncivil fool.'

UPON THE 20,000-FOOT MOUNTAIN

Khurram Khosa, my friend and companion on this outing, sensing my umbrage advised me to hold it for the mullah was to be our host. Offending him could jeopardise our chances of a meal and overnight facility on returning. I shut up, but the man was relentless.

'Have you ever climbed a hill before?' he wanted to know.

'A few.' I said.

'How high have you been?'

'Nineteen thousand feet.' I replied smugly.

'Been Gah is a full thousand feet higher than that!' he retorted. For good measure he added, 'And you're too old.'

Twenty thousand feet! That shut me up. That and an empty stomach.

We had driven out of Dera Ghazi Khan on the road to Loralai. A dozen kilometres short of the village of Rakni we left the tarmac and took the north-bound dirt road. Four hours out of Dera we stopped at the village of Burg for lunch which in true Baloch fashion was a vegetarian's nightmare. The meal being a drawn-out affair, we ended up staying for the night. In pre-dawn darkness the next morning we drove out to Patra for my little tryst with the mullah.

Khurram had organised a horse for himself and a camel to carry the gear up to the summit of Been Gah for we planned to spend the night on the top. But the animals and their handlers were nowhere to be seen. Shumbay Khan, a man from the village, said the mullah, had gone out hours ago to collect the animals and should be returning any minute now. Having heard this refrain one time too many, I knew we were in for a long wait.

The mocking mullah of Patra. He may not have known any geography, but he fed us well and put us up for the night.

Presently Shumbay Khan arrived and our party of four adults and a young camel handler set out. The tiny settlement of Zurgut clinging to the hillside was made in an hour. We paused to collect a couple of items of crockery from one of Shambay's relatives before attacking the slope ahead. It was a pleasant dander in the shade of the western contours and in another hour we had crossed a saddle, the last bit of which was so steep Khurram had to relinquish his horse. This last drag brought us onto the contours of the main massif with the peak lying just ahead.

We ran into a Baloch shepherd and within no time there was a mob of no less than twenty of various sizes shouting and laughing with our party. My dream of being on a quiet hillside was rather shot to pieces.

Normally Been Gah would have been under a thin veneer of snow in December, but the drought had completely altered that. Moreover, it was a rather mild winter and so the shepherds had remained around the top allowing their sheep to mop up the last blades of grass. They said they would descend only if the next few weeks would bring some snow and kill the grasses. I knew there would be no peace and privacy that I had so looked forward to and secretly resolved to return to Patra after a couple of hours on the top.

We stopped for tea before clambering up the last few metres to the flat top of Been Gah. And what a vantage point it was. At 2138 metres (7013 feet) above the sea, it wasn't yet the highest Punjabi peak that, being another two hundred metres higher, lies twenty kilometres to the southwest. The views all round were as fantastic as the name promised. Saura Pass that we had crossed on a journey back in March was visible in the east. To the north stood the bare, brown peak of Behu that we had almost climbed during that last trip, and in the west ridge after folded ridge stretched far into Balochistan: we were treading the border between that province and Punjab.

With no comment from any quarter concerning the name, Been Gah in my mind came from the Persian – from which Balochi derives. From here, I could imagine some early Baloch patriarch surveying the surrounding country and satisfied with the extent of the outlook, named the hill Been Gah – Prospect Point.

The imagination of ancient Baloch peoples in naming the hill was not to be faulted. Disappointingly, however, there were no legends of dragons and treasures or of *angrez* officials or stories of djinns connected with Been Gah. Intellectually, it was singularly barren. This was odd. Being an up-thrust in an elongated ridge, the upward movement of the rocky outcrop has riven the peak of Been Gah with deep chasms particularly around the periphery. In our superstitious society mysterious caves and chasms are always the spawning ground of supernatural stories. But surprisingly not here. The mechanism that gave the hill its evocative name had strangely failed to create fantastic stories to go with it.

But of course there was the Cave of the Bear just below the crest: a dank cleft in the shale measuring about five metres wide and about twice as long. It wasn't completely dark and perhaps that was the reason there were no stories of the supernatural connected with it. There were signs of the cave having been used by the shepherds, but there were no bears anywhere near it. And given the veritable bazaar of shepherd habitations near the top, their absence was quite understandable.

The shepherd elders approached Khurram with a request for us to stay overnight. I bluntly said there was too much shouting and I would hate to be in the middle of all this carrying on.

Khurram Khosa looks out to the east. The cleft in the hill to the left of the photo is Saura Pass that we had crossed some months before this trip.

The elders commuted the request to tarry just long enough for a meal. But that meant roast lamb and Khurram knew I was vegetarian, so he wheedled and submitted rather lame excuses until our sentence was fully remitted and we were granted leave to begin our return journey.

By six thirty in the evening we were back in Patra where the mullah was awaiting us with a pot of vegetable stew: after we decided to return, Khurram had sent the young camel handler ahead with a special request for a vegetarian dinner. Directly upon seeing him, I pulled a long face and told the mullah how he had been right about the height of the hill and how I had foundered only a couple of hours out of the village. He launched himself on a gloating I-told-you-so routine. I rubbed it in, telling him that he had, in fact, made a mistake about Been Gah being only 20,000 feet. It was, in reality, a full 70,000 feet high!

Even for a retarded mullah this was too much. He looked at me askance.

'No!' he said suspiciously. 'It cannot be as high as that.'

'Sorry, my mistake. It's 70,000 feet from the sea. From your village it is only 20,000.' I corrected myself secure in the knowledge that religious studies in the Muslim world have never

Prayer time on the top.

yet made a geographer, or, if truth be told, anything but a mullah of anyone.

Yes, said the mullah with visible satisfaction, yes indeed. From Patra the summit of Been Gah was certainly no less than 20,000 feet high. It was the highest mountain in the world, he gloated. Meanwhile, the others arrived and deflated the man by telling him that I had made it to the top swimmingly. Not the one to be discomfited he looked me over a second time and said I seemed too old for my age, I must have been a sickly child to have lost my hair and gone grey so early on in life. Since I wasn't even a Baloch and had made it to the top of Been Gah and back in the course of a single day, I could not be any older than twenty-two, he concluded.

I let that pass for I took cruel pleasure in the picture of the mullah being embarrassed boasting about his hill being the highest in the world to someone who knew his geography. Moreover, the mullah's household had served up a great little pot of stewed vegetable marrow. If for nothing else, the man could be forgiven for the hospitality.